HUMAN SUBJECTIVITY 'IN CHRIST' IN DIETRICH BONHOEFFER'S THEOLOGY

T&T Clark Studies in Systematic Theology

Edited by
Ivor Davidson
Ian McFarland
Philip G. Ziegler

Volume 31

HUMAN SUBJECTIVITY 'IN CHRIST' IN DIETRICH BONHOEFFER'S THEOLOGY

Integrating Simplicity and Wisdom

Jacob Phillips

LONDON • NEW YORK • OXFORD • NEW DELHI • SYDNEY

T&T CLARK
Bloomsbury Publishing Plc
50 Bedford Square, London, WC1B 3DP, UK
1385 Broadway, New York, NY 10018, USA
29 Earlsfort Terrace, Dublin 2, Ireland

BLOOMSBURY, T&T CLARK and the T&T Clark logo
are trademarks of Bloomsbury Publishing Plc

First published in Great Britain 2020
This paperback edition published in 2021

Copyright © Jacob Phillips, 2020

Jacob Phillips has asserted his right under the Copyright,
Designs and Patents Act, 1988, to be identified as Author of this work.

All rights reserved. No part of this publication may be reproduced or
transmitted in any form or by any means, electronic or mechanical,
including photocopying, recording, or any information storage or retrieval
system, without prior permission in writing from the publishers.

Bloomsbury Publishing Plc does not have any control over, or responsibility for,
any third-party websites referred to or in this book. All internet addresses given
in this book were correct at the time of going to press. The author and publisher
regret any inconvenience caused if addresses have changed or sites have
ceased to exist, but can accept no responsibility for any such changes.

A catalogue record for this book is available from the British Library.

Library of Congress Cataloging-in-Publication Data

Names: Phillips, Jacob, author.
Title: Human subjectivity 'in Christ' in Dietrich Bonhoeffer's theology:
intergrating simplicity and wisdom / by Jacob Phillips.
Description: 1 [edition]. | New York: T&T Clark, 2019. |
Series: T&T Clark studies in systematic theology; 36 |
Includes bibliographical references and index.
Identifiers: LCCN 2019009775 (print) | ISBN 9780567688606 (hardback: alk.paper)
Subjects: LCSH: Subjectivity–Religious aspects–Christianity. |
Theological anthropology. | Identity (Psychology)–Religious
aspects–Christianity. | Bonhoeffer, Dietrich, 1906-1945.
Classification: LCC BT702.P53 2019 (print) | LCC BT702 (ebook) | DDC 233–dc23
LC record available at https://lccn.loc.gov/2019009775
LC ebook record available at https://lccn.loc.gov/2019980369

ISBN: HB: 978-0-5676-8860-6
PB: 978-0-5676-9827-8
ePDF: 978-0-5676-8861-3
eBook: 978-0-5676-8862-0

Series: T&T Clark Studies in Systematic Theology, volume 31

Typeset by Deanta Global Publishing Services, Chennai, India

To find out more about our authors and books visit
www.bloomsbury.com and sign up for our newsletters.

CONTENTS

List of abbreviations   x

Chapter 1
SIMPLICITY AND WISDOM   1
1.1   The problem   2
    1.1.1   The 'dangers' of *Discipleship*   2
    1.1.2   The challenge of the unreflective   5
    1.1.3   'Standing by' *Discipleship*   9
1.2   Main lineaments in seeking integration   12
1.3   Integrating simplicity and wisdom   17

Chapter 2
THE SIMPLICITY OF *DISCIPLESHIP*   23
2.1   *Discipleship*: Overview and simplicity as singularity   23
    2.1.1   *Discipleship* in overview   23
    2.1.2   Simplicity and singularity in *Discipleship*   25
2.2   The simplicity of *Discipleship*: Four loci   27
    2.2.1   'Seeing only Christ'   27
    2.2.2   The 'hiddenness of the disciple'   29
    2.2.3   'Simple obedience'   31
    2.2.4   'Purity of heart'   33
2.3   Summing up   34

Chapter 3
INTERPRETING THE SIMPLICITY OF *DISCIPLESHIP*   37
3.1   The reception of *Discipleship* as detour or reiteration   37
3.2   The trajectory of interpreting the simplicity of *Discipleship*   39
    3.2.1   Eberhard Bethge: 'The Challenge of Dietrich Bonhoeffer's Theology' (1967)   39
       3.2.1.1   Background and overview   39
       3.2.1.2   'The child' in *Act and Being*   40
       3.2.1.3   Reflection as 'bedevilled' in *Creation and Fall*   41
    3.2.2   Clifford J. Green: *The Theology of Sociality* (First Edition 1972)   42
       3.2.2.1   Overview   42
       3.2.2.2   'Simple obedience' and the abrogation of the will   44

	3.2.3	Ernst Feil: *The Theology of Dietrich Bonhoeffer* (1985)		45
		3.2.3.1	Overview	45
		3.2.3.2	Omitting the theological subtext to *Discipleship*	46
		3.2.3.3	Omitting the philosophical subtext to *Discipleship*	47
	3.2.4	Michael DeJonge's *Bonhoeffer's Theological Formation* (2012)		48
3.3	Summing up			51

Chapter 4
SIMPLICITY AND THE TRANSCENDENTAL ATTEMPT — 53

4.1	*Act and Being*: Philosophy in relation to theology		54
	4.1.1	Aims of *Act and Being*	54
	4.1.2	Philosophy and theology in *Act and Being*	55
4.2	The transcendental attempt		59
	4.2.1	'Genuine transcendentalism'	59
	4.2.2	'Post-Kantian transcendentalism'	61
4.3	Transcendentalism and the simplicity of *Discipleship*		62
	4.3.1	Subject–'object' singularity	62
	4.3.2	The hiddenness of the 'I'	63
4.4	Summing up		65

Chapter 5
THE *ACTUS REFLECTUS* AS WISDOM: RECONCILING THE UNREFLECTIVE AND REFLECTIVE IN *ACT AND BEING* — 67

5.1	Bonhoeffer's presentation of Barth in *Act and Being*		68
	5.1.1	Holy Spirit as subject and the 'believing I'	69
	5.1.2	Barth's theology as transcendentalism	71
	5.1.3	Bonhoeffer's critique of Barth	72
	5.1.4	Bonhoeffer's critique of Barth based on the *actus* distinction	74
5.2	'Self-understanding-in-remembrance' and the 'Christian conscience'		76
	5.2.1	'Self-understanding-in-remembrance'	76
	5.2.2	The 'Christian conscience'	79
5.3	Towards the *actus reflectus* as 'wisdom'		80
	5.3.1	'Self-understanding-in-remembrance' as wisdom	81
	5.3.2	The 'Christian conscience' as wisdom	82
5.4	Summing up		84

Chapter 6
TOWARDS PRACTICAL DISCERNMENT AS WISDOM: UNREFLECTIVE AND REFLECTIVE AGENCY IN *ETHICS* — 85

6.1	*Gestaltung* and the reflective		85
	6.1.1	*Ethics* and *Discipleship*	85
	6.1.2	'Unreflective doing' and 'simple obedience' as *Gestaltung*	86
	6.1.3	*Gestaltung* and *Gestalt*	88
	6.1.4	Commensurability with the reflective	91

6.2	\'Not knowing good and evil\' and the reflective		92
	6.2.1 Reflection and the \'content\' of conscience		92
	6.2.2 Reflection on the basis of Christ\'s reconciliation		96
	6.2.3 Critical issue with \'reflective discernment\' in *Ethics*		97
6.4	Summing up		99

Chapter 7
THE 'TRANSCENDENTAL UNITY OF APPERCEPTION' AND THE 'CATEGORICAL IMPERATIVE' IN THE 'FLOW OF LIFE' — 101

7.1 The transcendental unity of apperception — 102
    7.1.1 A basic aim of the first *Critique* — 102
    7.1.2 The transcendental unity of apperception — 103
    7.1.3 'Original' and 'pure' apperception — 106
    7.1.4 'Pure' apperception interrupting 'the flow of life' — 108
7.2 The categorical imperative — 109
    7.2.1 Aims of the *Groundwork of a Metaphysic of Morals* and the *Critique of Practical Reason* — 109
    7.2.2 The categorical imperative — 110
    7.2.3 'Pure practical reason' and the imperative '*in concreto*' — 113
    7.2.4 'Pure practical reason' interrupting 'the flow of life' — 115
7.3 Summing up — 115

Chapter 8
ARTICULATING THE 'ORIGINAL TOGETHERNESS' OF LIFE: WILHELM DILTHEY IN RELATION TO DIETRICH BONHOEFFER — 117

8.1 Wilhelm Dilthey in overview — 117
    8.1.1 Dilthey's life and intellectual milieu — 117
    8.1.2 Basic terminology of Dilthey's philosophy — 120
        8.1.2.1 *Erlebnis* — 120
        8.1.2.2 A 'descriptive' method — 122
        8.1.2.3 *Verstehen* — 123
    8.1.3 Dilthey and neo-Kantianism — 126
8.2 Scholarship on Dilthey's relation to Bonhoeffer — 128
    8.2.1 References to Dilthey in Bonhoeffer's work — 128
    8.2.2 Interpretations of Dilthey's influence on Bonhoeffer — 129
8.3 Summing up — 133

Chapter 9
THE UNREFLECTIVE 'I' AND REFLECTIVE SELF-UNDERSTANDING IN DILTHEY — 135

9.1 Dilthey's unreflective 'I' — 135
    9.1.1 'Reflexive awareness' and *Erlebnis* — 135
    9.1.2 A concrete and temporal apperception — 140

	9.2	Reflective self-understanding in Dilthey	144
		9.2.1 From 'reflex to reflection'	144
		9.2.2 Reflective self-understanding	146
	9.3	Coordinating the unreflective and reflective	148
		9.3.1 An explicative continuity	148
		9.3.2 An implicative continuity	150
	9.4	Summing up	152

Chapter 10
UNREFLECTIVE AND REFLECTIVE AGENCY IN DILTHEY 155

- 10.1 Unreflective and reflective consciousness in feeling and willing 155
  - 10.1.1 The Kantian background 155
  - 10.1.2 Brentano on feeling and willing 158
  - 10.1.3 Dilthey on feeling and willing 159
- 10.2 Unreflective agency in Dilthey 161
  - 10.2.1 Act–content unity in *Gefühle* 161
  - 10.2.2 An act–content unity involving both *Gefühle* and *Wollen* 162
  - 10.2.3 Act–content unity in *Wollen* 163
    - 10.2.3.1 'Pure volition' in obligation to an 'other' 163
    - 10.2.3.2 'Pure volition' as obligation to an 'ought' 164
- 10.3 Reflective agency in Dilthey 166
- 10.4 Summing up 169

Chapter 11
GESTALT: AESTHETICS AND AGENCY IN WILHELM DILTHEY 171

- 11.1 Reflection and aesthetics 171
  - 11.1.1 From agency to aesthetics 171
  - 11.1.2 Poetics as reflection in *Gefühle* 174
- 11.2 *Gestalt*: Aesthetics and agency 176
  - 11.2.1 Dilthey on *Gestalt* 176
  - 11.2.2 Aesthetic reflection and *Gestalt* 178
    - 11.2.2.1 Aesthetics as involving reflection on *Gestalt* 178
    - 11.2.2.2 *Gestalt* and 'having-to-be-thus' 180
- 11.3 *Gestalt* as locus of continuity 181
- 11.4 Summing up 182

Chapter 12
INTEGRATING SIMPLICITY AND WISDOM 183

- 12.1 Integrating the unreflective and reflective in the cognitive 183
  - 12.1.1 Explicative continuity 183
  - 12.1.2 Implicative continuity 187
- 12.2 Integrating the unreflective and reflective in the practical 189
  - 12.2.1 Continuity between Dilthey's aesthetic reflection and unreflective agency as obligation to another 189

12.3	Integrating simplicity and wisdom	194
	12.3.1 Explicative continuity as integrating simplicity and wisdom	195
	12.3.2 Implicative continuity as integrating simplicity and wisdom	197
	12.3.3 Practical explicative continuity as integrating simplicity and wisdom	199
12.4	Broader implications of integrating simplicity and wisdom	200

Bibliography	204
Index	211

ABBREVIATIONS

CpJ	Immanuel Kant, *Critique of the Power of Judgment*, ed. Paul Guyer, trans. Paul Guyer and Eric Matthews, Cambridge: Cambridge University Press, 2000.
CpR	Immanuel Kant, *The Critique of Pure Reason*, trans. and ed. Paul Guyer and Allen W. Wood, Cambridge: Cambridge University Press, 1999.
CprR	Immanuel Kant, 'Critique of Practical Reason', in *Practical Philosophy*, trans. and ed. Mary J. Gregor, Cambridge: Cambridge University Press, 1999.
DBW2	Dietrich Bonhoeffer, Dietrich Bonhoeffer Werke 2 Band: *Akt und Sein: Transzendentalphilosophie und Ontologie in der systematischen Theologie*, herausgegeben von Hans-Richard Reuter, München: Chr. Kaiser, 1988.
DBW3	Dietrich Bonhoeffer, Dietrich Bonhoeffer Werke 3 Band: *Schöpfung und Fall*, herausgegeben von Martin Rüter und Ilse Tödt, München: Chr. Kaiser, 1989.
DBW4	Dietrich Bonhoeffer, Dietrich Bonhoeffer Werke 4 Band: *Nachfolge*, herausgegeben von Martin Kuske und Ilse Tödt, München: Chr. Kaiser, 1989.
DBW5	Dietrich Bonhoeffer, Dietrich Bonhoeffer Werke 5 Band: *Gemeinsames Leben und Das Gebetbuch der Bibel*, herausgegeben von Gerhard Ludwig Müller und Albrecht Schönherr, München: Chr. Kaiser, 1987.
DBW6	Dietrich Bonhoeffer, Dietrich Bonhoeffer Werke 6 Band: *Ethik*, herausgegeben von Ilse Tödt, Heinz Eduard Tödt, Ernst Feil und Clifford Green, München: Chr. Kaiser, 1992.
DBW8	Dietrich Bonhoeffer, Dietrich Bonhoeffer Werke 8 Band: *Widerstand und Ergebung: Briefe und Aufzeichnungen aus der Haft*, herausgegeben von Christian Gremmels, Eberhard Bethge und Renate Bethge, in Zusammenarbeit mit Ilse Tödt.
DBW12	Dietrich Bonhoeffer, Dietrich Bonhoeffer Werke 12 Band: *Berlin, 1932–1933*, herausgegeben von Carsten Nicolaisen und Ernst-Albert Scharffenorth, München: Chr. Kaiser, 1997.
DBWE1	Dietrich Bonhoeffer, Dietrich Bonhoeffer Works in English Volume 1: *Sanctorum Communio: A Theological Study of the Sociology of the Church*, ed. Clifford J. Green; trans. Reinhard Krauss and Nancy Lukens, Minneapolis: Fortress, 1998.
DBWE2	Dietrich Bonhoeffer, Dietrich Bonhoeffer Works in English Volume 2: *Act and Being: Transcendental Philosophy and Ontology in Systematic Theology*, ed. Wayne Whitson Floyd, Jr, trans. H. Martin Rumscheidt, Minneapolis: Fortress, 1996.

DBWE3	Dietrich Bonhoeffer, *Dietrich Bonhoeffer Works in English* Volume 3: *Creation and Fall: A Theological Exposition of Genesis 1–3*, ed. John W. de Gruchy; trans. Douglas Stephen Bax, Minneapolis: Fortress, 2004.
DBWE4	Dietrich Bonhoeffer, *Dietrich Bonhoeffer Works in English* Volume 4: *Discipleship*, trans. from the German edition ed. Martin Kuske and Ilse Tödt; English edition ed. Geffrey B. Kelly and John D. Godsey; trans. Barbara Green and Reinhard Krauss. Minneapolis: Fortress, 2003.
DBWE5	Dietrich Bonhoeffer, *Dietrich Bonhoeffer Works in English* Volume 5: *Life Together; Prayerbook of the Bible*; ed. Geffrey B. Kelly; trans. Daniel W. Bloesch and James H. Burtness, Minneapolis: Fortress, 2005.
DBWE6	Dietrich Bonhoeffer, *Dietrich Bonhoeffer Works in English* Volume 6: *Ethics*, ed. Clifford J. Green; trans. Reinhard Krauss, Charles C. West, and Douglas W. Stott, Minneapolis: Fortress, 2005.
DBWE8	Dietrich Bonhoeffer, *Dietrich Bonhoeffer Works in English* Volume 8: *Letters and Papers from Prison*, ed. John W. de Gruchy, trans. Isabel Best [et al.], Minneapolis: Fortress, 2010.
DBWE9	Dietrich Bonhoeffer, *Dietrich Bonhoeffer Works in English* Volume 9: *The Young Bonhoeffer: 1918–1927*, ed. Paul Duane Matheny, Clifford J. Green, and Marshall D. Johnson, trans. Mary C. Nebelsick with the assistance of Douglas W. Scott, Minneapolis: Fortress, 2001.
DBWE10	Dietrich Bonhoeffer, *Dietrich Bonhoeffer Works in English* Volume 10: *Barcelona, Berlin, New York: 1928–1931*, ed. Clifford J. Green; trans. Douglas W. Stott, Minneapolis: Fortress, 2008.
DBWE11	Dietrich Bonhoeffer, *Dietrich Bonhoeffer Works in English* Volume 11: *Ecumenical, Academic, and Pastoral Work: 1931–1932*, ed. Victoria J. Barnett, Mark S. Brocker and Michael B. Lukens; trans. Anne Schmidt-Lange [et al.], Minneapolis: Fortress, 2012.
DBWE12	Dietrich Bonhoeffer, *Dietrich Bonhoeffer Works in English* Volume 12, *Berlin: 1932–1933*, ed. Larry R. Rasmussen; trans. Isabel Best and David Higgins, Minneapolis: Fortress, 2009.
DBWE13	Dietrich Bonhoeffer, *Dietrich Bonhoeffer Works in English* Volume 13, *London: 1933–1935* ed. Keith Clements, trans. Isabel Best, supplementary material trans. Douglas W. Stott, Minneapolis: Fortress Press, 2007.
DBWE14	Dietrich Bonhoeffer, *Dietrich Bonhoeffer Works in English* Volume 14: *Theological Education at Finkenwalde: 1935–1937*, ed. H. Gaylon Barker and Mark S. Brocker, trans. Douglas W. Stott, Minneapolis: Fortress Press, 2013.
DBWE15	Dietrich Bonhoeffer, *Dietrich Bonhoeffer Works in English* Volume 15: *Theological Education Underground: 1937–1940* ed. Victoria J. Barnett; trans. Victoria J. Barnett [et al.], supplementary material trans. Douglas W. Stott, Minneapolis: Fortress, 2012.
DBWE16	Dietrich Bonhoeffer, *Dietrich Bonhoeffer Works in English* Volume 16: *Conspiracy and Imprisonment: 1940–1945*, ed. Mark S. Brocker, trans. Lisa E. Dahill; supplementary material trans. Douglas W. Stott, Minneapolis: Fortress, 2006.

GMMa	Immanuel Kant, *Groundwork of The Metaphysics of Morals*, in *Practical Philosophy*, trans. and ed. Mary J. Gregor, Cambridge: Cambridge University Press, 1999.
GMMb	*The Moral Law: Kant's Groundwork of the Metaphysics of Morals*, trans. and analysed by H. J. Paton, London: Hutchinson University Press, 1948.
GSI	Wilhelm Dilthey, *Gesammelte Schriften. Bd. 1, Einleitung in die Geisteswissenschaften: Versuch einer Grundlegung für das Studium der Gesellschaft und der Geschichte*, Göttingen: Vandenhoeck & Ruprecht, 1959.
GSII	Wilhelm Dilthey, *Gesammelte Schriften. Bd. 2, Weltanschauung und Analyse des Menschen seit Renaissance und Reformation*, Göttingen: Vandenhoeck & Ruprecht, 1957.
GSIII	Wilhelm Dilthey, *Gesammelte Schriften. Bd. 3, Studien zur Geschichte des deutschen Geistes: Leibniz und sein Zeitalter; Friedrich der Grosse und die deutsche Aufklärung; Das achtzehnte Jahrhundert und die geschichtliche Welt*, Göttingen: Vandenhoeck & Ruprecht, 1959.
GSV	Wilhelm Dilthey, *Gesammelte Schriften. Bd. 5, Die geistige Welt: Einleitung in die Philosophie des Lebens. 1. Hälfte, Abhandlungen zur Grundlegung der Geisteswissenschaften*, Göttingen: Vandenhoeck & Ruprecht, 1957.
GSVI	Wilhelm Dilthey, *Gesammelte Schriften. Bd. 6, Die geistige Welt: Einleitung in die Philosophie des Lebens. 2. Hälfte, Abhandlungen zur Poetik, Ethik und Pädagogik*, Göttingen: Vandenhoeck & Ruprecht, 1958.
GS XIX	Wilhelm Dilthey, *Gesammelte Schriften. Bd. 19, Grundlegung der Wissenschaften vom Menschen, der Gesellschaft und der Geschichte: Ausarbeitungen und Entwürfe zum zweiten Band der Einleitung in die Geisteswissenschaften (ca.1870–1895)*, Göttingen: Vandenhoeck & Ruprecht, 1982.
SWI	Wilhelm Dilthey, Selected Works Volume 1: *Introduction to the Human Sciences*, edited, with an introduction, by Rudolf A. Makkreel and Frithjof Rodi, Princeton, NJ: Princeton University Press, 1989.
SWII	Wilhelm Dilthey, Selected Works Volume 2: *Understanding the Human World*, ed. Rudolf A. Makkreel and Frithjof Rodi, Princeton, NJ: Princeton University Press, 2010.
SWIII	Wilhelm Dilthey, Selected Works Volume 3: *The Formation of the Historical World in the Human Sciences*, edited, with an introduction, by Rudolf A. Makkreel and Frithjof Rodi, Princeton, NJ: Princeton University Press, 2002.
SWIV	Wilhelm Dilthey, Selected Works Volume 4: *Hermeneutics and the Study of History*, edited, with an introduction, by Rudolf A. Makkreel and Frithjof Rodi, Princeton, NJ: Princeton University Press, 1996.
SWV	Wilhelm Dilthey, Selected Works Volume 5: *Poetry and Experience*, ed. Rudolf A. Makkreel and Frithjof Rodi, Princeton, NJ: Princeton University Press, 1985.

Chapter 1

SIMPLICITY AND WISDOM

In the book *Discipleship*, Dietrich Bonhoeffer presents encountering Christ as something disciples cannot reflect on without 'tearing themselves away' from Jesus.[1] He approaches discipleship as something belonging only to 'direct' or momentary consciousness, something that is broken if the disciple enters into self-reflection. This extends into the practical domain, for Bonhoeffer presents following Christ as simply unreflective obedience to Jesus's commands. He claims that if one reflectively evaluates one's practical options about how to follow Jesus, one is torn away: 'the only required reflection for disciples is to be completely unreflective in obedience'.[2] This articulation of human subjectivity 'in Christ' is challenging, precisely because it presents the human response to the call of Christ as entirely unreflective; as involving a direct communication or disclosure to the hearer which is absent of any human reflective or interpretive mediation whatsoever. Bonhoeffer characterizes this unreflective human subjectivity in assent to Christ's call as the stance of 'simplicity'.

There are obvious anthropological and epistemological problems with this stance per se, and also critical tensions within Bonhoeffer's other works, where quite different and perhaps even contradictory stances on human subjectivity and human agency in Christ are set out. Perhaps the most decisive among these is found in Bonhoeffer's *Ethics*, where the unreflective or uninterpretative disposition of 'simplicity' is no longer presented with uncompromising exclusivity as it is in *Discipleship*, but now as continuous or harmonious with 'wisdom' (which Bonhoeffer considers intrinsically reflective). Moreover, he presents the unreflective and reflective not only as commensurable but as integrated, so they are inalienably bound up with each other, and neither is authentic without an integral link to the other. But Bonhoeffer's exploration of simplicity and wisdom lacks the means or the full development to address the problems involved in resolving or harmonizing unreflective and reflective facets to human subjectivity in Christ. This is the task undertaken by this book: integrating the unreflective and reflective as 'simplicity and wisdom'.

---

1. DBWE4, 71.
2. Ibid., 154.

In undertaking this task, this book draws extensively on the work of the philosopher Wilhelm Dilthey, whose intellectual convergence with Bonhoeffer is considerable, although hitherto underappreciated. Both Bonhoeffer and Dilthey seek to articulate a view of human subjectivity as integrated and harmonious, while involving centrally unreflective facets. Outlining how we can understand human subjectivity as integrated, without undermining the uncompromising demands of the unreflective in *Discipleship*, will among other things demonstrate – against much secondary interpretation – that *Discipleship* retains an important and indeed central place in the development of Bonhoeffer's theological programme and trajectory. Indeed, we shall see that the difficult or 'radical' statements with which this enquiry begins, rather than being sidelined on account of their challenging or seemingly divergent nature, can and in fact should be understood as a centrally important pivot or key point of orientation for much of Bonhoeffer's subsequent work, and more broadly, for effectively describing human subjectivity in Christ. This book thus presents important constructive outcomes by arriving at a theological framework for interpreting Bonhoeffer's statement that 'only the one who combines simplicity and wisdom can endure'.[3]

1.1 The problem

1.1.1 The 'dangers' of Discipleship

Dietrich Bonhoeffer (1906–45) is widely recognized for the 'rhetorical force' and 'power' of his articulation of Christian discipleship,[4] expressed most fully in the book *Discipleship* (*Nachfolge*). This work gained him the most attention during his own lifetime, and remains enduringly popular long after its 1937 publication.[5] However, its reception in the academy has been considerably more problematic, having famously been classed as the product of an unfruitful 'detour'[6] in Bonhoeffer's theological development in 1961 by Hanfried Müller, with reservations still voiced today – albeit more subtly – notwithstanding the general move towards a more homogeneous interpretation of the corpus in recent decades. For example, Stephen Plant comments that *Discipleship* has 'a disturbing style' which is 'its strength and its weakness', giving the impression 'there can be no other way of understanding

---

3. DBWE6, 81.
4. Stephen Plant, *Bonhoeffer: Outstanding Christian Thinkers*, London: Continuum, 2004, 98.
5. DBWE4, 1.
6. Eberhard Bethge, 'The Challenge of Dietrich Bonhoeffer's Life and Theology', in Ronald Gregor Smith (ed.), *The World Comes of Age: A Symposium on Dietrich Bonhoeffer*, London: Collins, 1967, 44, 64–5. The term originates with Müller, who uses it only with *Life Together*, while Bethge extends to include the period 1933–39 generally; cf. Hanfried Müller, *Von der Kirche zur Welt*, Hamburg-Bergstedt: Reich, 1961.

Christian faith';[7] Clifford Green claims it presents Christ 'as a mighty *power*' who negates healthy ego strengths 'as well as self-serving power';[8] and Christiane Tietz states that *Discipleship*'s 'simple obedience' is 'a difficult conceptuality' for the contemporary reader.[9]

Contributing to many of the concerns surrounding *Discipleship* is the ambiguity in Bonhoeffer's own comment from Tegel prison that 'today I clearly see the dangers of that book, though I still stand by it'.[10] It seems that the 'rhetorical … force' of the work,[11] or what Tietz calls its 'radical and strong tone', contributes to its being seen as critically challenging and therefore exhibiting certain 'dangers'.

The aspects of the book which appear 'dangerous' include the aforementioned presentation of the human response to Christ as entirely unreflective. *Discipleship* features numerous statements that demonstrate the intensity of Bonhoeffer's prose, yet when we examine his statements and subject them to critical analysis, we are faced with considerable difficulties. The difficult or radical statements pertaining to the unreflective can be gathered into four groups, each of which articulates a particular aspect to Bonhoefferian simplicity respectively.

The first group is based on Bonhoeffer's description of discipleship as foundationally centred on 'seeing *only* Christ'.[12] He claims those who follow Jesus are 'fully absorbed in seeing God',[13] and he outlines a view of discipleship which involves a complete focus of the disciples' attention on Christ, to the degree that there is no self-reflection whatsoever. He states, 'the only thing left for us is to look away from ourselves' and 'to look to' Jesus Christ, whose 'image' (*Bild*) is '*always* before the disciple's eyes', for 'I no longer cast even a single glance on my own life'.[14] To look at oneself in thinking (to self-reflect) breaks this exclusively 'simple' vision of the disciple, most basically because in reflecting on oneself one cannot 'always' and 'only' be seeing Christ, as directing attention to oneself turns one away from the direct apprehension of Christ.

Before considering why this is challenging, there are three further groups of *Discipleship*'s 'radical' statements to be outlined. As well as claiming we must 'see only Christ', Bonhoeffer intensifies his already uncompromising position by claiming self-reflection itself is inherently suspect. To reflect on oneself, he

---

7. Plant, *Bonhoeffer*, 98.

8. Clifford J. Green, *The Sociality of Christ and Humanity: Dietrich Bonhoeffer's Early Theology, 1927–1933*, Missoula, MT: Scholars Press for the American Academy of Religion, 1972, 195.

9. Christiane Tietz, *Dietrich Bonhoeffer: Theologe im Widerstand*, Munich: C.H. Beck Wissen, 2013, 72 (my translation).

10. DBWE8, 486.

11. Plant, *Bonhoeffer*, 106.

12. DBWE4, 86, 161, 288 (my italics).

13. Ibid., 108.

14. Ibid., 280, 281, 287.

implies, is to see oneself 'out of' one's 'own power' and 'out of the flesh',[15] alluding to the spirit–flesh conflict of Pauline literature and thus implying self-reflection is in some way intrinsically dubious. This leads Bonhoeffer to ask: 'How can I protect myself from myself' from 'my own reflection?'[16] He concludes that one's life as a disciple must be *hidden* from oneself, intimating that the drive to behold oneself precludes or negates following Christ as something unavoidably precarious. Bonhoeffer implies that self-reflection undermines following Christ because it is intrinsically linked with a desire for self-possession, a desire to behold and grasp oneself ('out of the flesh'), which inherently precludes simply belonging to 'Christ alone'. This view is perhaps brought to its sharpest expression in *Discipleship* when Bonhoeffer states that 'knowing only Christ' means therefore 'no longer knowing oneself' and admonishes his readers to turn Peter's denial ('I do not know the man') onto themselves, thus always remaining 'hidden' from self-reflection.[17]

These uncompromising assertions are not restricted to self-reflection in the sense of beholding oneself as 'object'. *Discipleship* also involves equally challenging formulations focused on more practically orientated facets of human subjectivity. Here, Bonhoeffer extends his criticisms of reflection beyond *self*-reflection and into the realm of practical reflection or discernment, in the sense of reflecting on the best course of action through evaluating ends and discerning how to proceed. The third and fourth groups of difficult statements are centred on the practical domain, where we encounter some of the best-known passages of the book, involving what Bonhoeffer terms 'simple obedience' (*einfältiger Gehorsam*).[18] To be a disciple is, for Bonhoeffer, to stand under the command 'simply go and obey', and to practise 'simple, literal obedience' to the commands of Christ.[19] Simple obedience issues in deeds following immediately from Christ's commands, leading Bonhoeffer to state that 'the call goes out, and without any further ado the obedient deed of the one called follows'.[20] Simple obedience is unreflective, for its deeds are not arrived at through reflectively 'beholding' or mirroring different desired ends to oneself in deciding what to do. Bonhoeffer thus considers Christ himself to ground deeds of simple obedience, not the reflective considerations of the disciple as agent; or more precisely, these deeds issue directly from the command itself. There is only one grounding (*Begründung*) for the 'correspondence' of call and deed in simple obedience he claims, and this is Jesus himself, whose authority is described as 'inscrutable' (*unbegründbar*).[21]

---

15. Ibid., 150.
16. DBW4, 159 (my translation).
17. DBWE4, 86.
18. Ibid., 77f.
19. Ibid., 181.
20. Ibid., 57.
21. DBW4, 45 (my translation).

This move into the practical domain will present us with further difficulties, and before outlining these there is a final set of closely related examples to consider. This fourth group denotes reflection in the practical sphere as inherently dubious in that evaluating how to proceed derives from inauspicious grounds. Bonhoeffer implies that grounding one's deeds on reflective decision-making is innately linked with a desire to establish transparent warrants for action, which provide a self-legitimizing and autonomously validating sense of ethical security. Again, to follow Christ, for Bonhoeffer, means belonging to 'Christ alone' and therefore not being reliant on any self-legitimization of one's deeds. To act unreflectively in obediently belonging to 'Christ alone', he claims, means not 'knowing good and evil'.[22] This is a development of Bonhoeffer's interpretation of Genesis, where he connects ethical decision-making with the consequences of the Fall, involving primarily a fallen desire for self-validation.[23] In Bonhoeffer's interpretation of Lk. 18.18-23, he claims that just as the serpent challenges Eve to question the command of God, or find grounds for interpreting it a certain way, the rich young man seeks grounds to rearrange the commandments of God according to his own criteria. This causes him to be 'torn away' from 'from simple (*einfältig*) childlike obedience' and into 'ethical doubt'.[24] Reflecting on how best to proceed then not only leads to actions grounded on the disciple as agent, but the very desire to measure one's actions is itself presented as obviating authentic discipleship through its innate proclivity towards establishing apparently secure warrants for acting. This is why Bonhoeffer states that 'the only required reflection for disciples is to be completely unreflective in obedience', claiming that 'my own will … must die, must be killed', and 'the word "kill" must be spoken' in articulating the 'simple obedience' of following Christ.[25]

1.1.2 *The challenge of the unreflective*

Each of the four sets of examples above aptly demonstrates Bonhoeffer's concern to preserve the 'immediate and inscrutable authority'[26] of Jesus by centrally emphasizing the place of the unreflective for human subjectivity in Christ. To be 'seeing only Christ' and remaining 'hidden' from oneself means not beholding oneself as 'object' (a reflection). To reflect on oneself as a disciple is seen as undercutting the very disposition which qualifies oneself as such, for it mediates Christ's authority through one's own subjectivity by recognizing oneself as Christ's, while that act of recognition is seen by Bonhoeffer as belonging to 'Christ alone'. To act in 'simple obedience' and not 'know good and evil' means one does not undergo a reflective 'split' between oneself as agent and one's desired ends; one does not

---

22. DBWE4, 62.
23. Cf. DBWE3, 103f. and DBWE6, 300f.
24. DBWE4, 71.
25. Ibid., 154.
26. DBW4, 45 (my translation).

'reflect' one's options to oneself in deciding how to proceed. Reflectively discerning how to respond to Christ's call is to focus on one's own interpretation of Christ's authority, to mediate it and render it explicable as transparent and legitimizing. To stand under Christ's 'immediate and inscrutable authority' is thus for Bonhoeffer a sine qua non of authentic discipleship itself. So, as he puts it, 'if I look at the path instead of at him who is walking ahead of me, then my foot is already slipping.'[27]

However, under critical analysis, this articulation of discipleship arguably yields several significant problems. On the most basic level, we are faced with straightforward anthropological and epistemological issues. In the first place, we must ask how sustainable or realistic it is to 'always' and 'only' see Christ; to maintain a complete focus of attention on Jesus so one 'no longer cast[s] even a single glance on [one's] own life'. This seems jarring because self-reflection is a natural, unavoidable and intrinsic aspect of human life. Similar problems apply with respect to the practical examples above, for 'simple obedience' assumes that the disciple can respond to the call of Christ without interpretation or mediation, yet establishing the contours of an entirely *im*-mediate realm of human understanding is deeply challenging, and something unlikely to gain a broad scholarly consensus. This problem is further intensified because decision-making is another unavoidable and necessary facet of being human, and if we cannot reflect on our options, it is impossible to see how the resulting deeds have full human integrity, as rational and free.

These basic problems converge to point to the key issue at stake: if reflection is unavoidable and necessary, yet Bonhoeffer considers the centre of discipleship to be unreflective, there seems to be a fundamental problem in this depiction of following Christ. If the disciple cannot reflect on the essential nexus of his or her being a disciple, then the point of acknowledging Christ's authority threatens to become separate or even ruptured from the 'I' who reflects, for the reflecting 'I' seems unable to bring itself *as a disciple* into reflection, without rendering Christ's authority mediate and explicable, thus intrinsically undermining the central qualification of obedient discipleship. We therefore see that there are some specific 'dangers' of *Discipleship* which arise from the challenge of the unreflective: how to retain the essentially unreflective core of the human response to Christ, without rendering our understanding of human subjectivity in Christ as fragmented, dislocated or ruptured with the reflective.

Moreover, the challenge of the unreflective is rendered significantly more acute by Bonhoeffer's own concerns elsewhere in the corpus to integrate reflective and unreflective aspects of human subjectivity. These seem, prima facie, to contradict the uncompromising exclusivity of always 'seeing only Christ', remaining 'hidden' from oneself, acting in 'simple obedience' and 'not knowing good and evil'. Among his earlier writings, this concern is exhibited most extensively in *Act and Being* (1927). Here, Bonhoeffer uses a duality given considerable attention in this book (see Chapters 4 and 5), the *actus directus*

---

27. DBWE4, 176.

and *actus reflectus*.²⁸ In the most basic terms, the *actus directus* refers to an unreflective act of apprehension, in which the 'I' beholds an 'object' in what Bonhoeffer calls 'intentionality pure and simple' (*Intentionalität schlechthin*),²⁹ without any reflective self-awareness, whereas the *actus reflectus* refers to a process whereby the 'I' 'mirrors itself to itself'³⁰ in reflection. Bonhoeffer's concern with integrating these two is apparent in his attempts to articulate two instances (which he calls 'self-understanding-in-remembrance' and the 'Christian conscience') of an *actus reflectus* which, he claims, does not 'break' [*zerbrechen*] the 'intentionality to Christ of the *actus directus*'.³¹ As will be demonstrated in Chapter 5, these attempts at integration are not altogether successful, but the point for present purposes is that Bonhoeffer wants to avoid making the unreflective (as *actus directus*) completely insurmountable to all human reflective activity tout court, and crucially, his motivation here is to avoid presenting a dislocated or ruptured understanding of human subjectivity in Christ. This is clear in his oft-repeated criticism of Karl Barth, where he asks if Barth's refusal to permit of any proper reflective grasp of the 'believing I' threatens to present the unreflective subjectivity of the *actus directus* as insurmountably aloof to self-reflection, rendering the 'I' that believes a 'heavenly double' (*himmlischer Doppelgänger*) to the 'I' that reflects.³² Bonhoeffer is thus explicitly aware of the danger of dislocation in an exclusive emphasis on the unreflective.

This concern for integration endures in the later writings and is arguably presented most extensively in *Ethics* (1943–44). In these manuscripts, there are numerous points which appear to contradict assertions in *Discipleship*. For example, in *Ethics* he claims we must 'seriously consider the consequences of our actions', and that 'responsible action must not want to be blind',³³ and yet in *Discipleship* he states that there is 'literally no time' to question what the will of God might be, and we must simply act 'like a blind man' in obedience.³⁴ In addition to moments of apparent contradiction, the manuscript 'Ethics as Formation' features an attempt to integrate the unreflective and reflective, suggesting again that Bonhoeffer wishes to respond to a danger of fragmentation or dislocation. Here, the unreflective 'simplicity' of *Discipleship* is seen as integrally and inalienably bound

---

28. This book translates what Bonhoeffer calls *actus reflexus* as *actus reflectus* (as does Michael DeJonge, *Bonhoeffer's Theological Formation*, Oxford: Oxford University Press, 2012; see 79–80). By doing so, we wish to avoid confusion in the later chapters, where we shall see Wilhelm Dilthey speaks of direct/unreflective conscious as 'reflexive', in the sense of a 'reflex action' (spontaneous and non-deliberative mode of conscious activity).
29. DBWE2, 43; DBW2, 36.
30. DBWE12, 305.
31. DBWE2, 156–7; DBW2, 156.
32. DBWE2, 99.
33. DBWE6, 225, 268.
34. DBWE4, 76, 91.

up with human reflective activity as 'wisdom', to the degree that neither simplicity nor wisdom can be authentic without an integral link to the other. He asserts that 'a person is simple' who unreflectively 'keeps in sight only the single truth of God', like those who 'see only Christ' in *Discipleship*. But, he goes on, 'Only the one who combines simplicity and wisdom can endure.' A wise person is identified as one who 'sees reality in God', sees 'reality as it is', and looks 'into the depth of things'. This is unavoidably rather cryptic at this point, but in this description of wisdom Bonhoeffer points to a reflective disposition which intertwines with simplicity. Here, 'wisdom', or discerning how to proceed by seeing 'reality as it is' and looking 'into the depth of things', not only seems a long way indeed from the 'simplicity' of *Discipleship* (being 'completely unreflective in obedience'), but is presented as a necessary counterpoint to it.

The statement that 'only the person who combines simplicity with wisdom can endure', specifies that it is the *combination* of simplicity and wisdom which is necessary for ethical endurance.[35] In this passage, we are presented with a conceptual duality which promises to offer a hermeneutical key for answering the challenge of the unreflective. For this reason, this book follows Bonhoeffer by grouping together the unreflective elements of his presentation of human subjectivity in Christ under the theme of 'simplicity', with the reflective being treated under the theme of 'wisdom', seeking thereby to extend his own attempts to reconcile the two and render them integrally interrelated.[36]

The 'simplicity and wisdom' passage therefore provides an invaluable hermeneutical key, but the manuscript containing it is unfinished, and, as shall be seen in Chapter 6, Bonhoeffer's *Ethics* does not convincingly achieve the harmonization of simplicity and wisdom he is looking for. The challenge of the unreflective in Bonhoeffer's theology therefore remains unresolved. Insofar as the difficult statements of the simplicity of *Discipleship* still carry a critically jarring

---

35. Bonhoeffer contrasts the combination of 'simplicity and wisdom' with six dispositions of ethical conduct, each of which is focused on either unreflective *or* reflective approaches to moral dilemmas. On the unreflective side, an unthinking 'ethical fanaticism', an uncritical preoccupation with 'the way of duty', or a straightforward maintaining of 'private virtuousness'. On the reflective side, he describes 'reasonable people', 'men of conscience', or those who act 'in their ownmost freedom'. DBWE6, 78–9.

36. The thematization of 'simplicity and wisdom' in this book differs from a recent study of Bonhoeffer, *Becoming Simple and Wise* by Joshua A. Kaiser, Eugene, OR: Pickwick Publications, 2015. The main differences stem from the fact that Kaiser's focus is theological ethics, whereas this project is focused on systematic and philosophical theology. Kaiser focuses on certain practical issues presented by 'simplicity and wisdom' (see 18; 77ff.), but does not analyse the philosophical–theological detail of these issues in the way undertaken in this book. Moreover, Kaiser's base text is the *Ethics* manuscript 'God's Love and the Disintegration of the World', whereas ours is *Discipleship*, which in turn entails the *centrality* of simplicity (or 'becoming simple') which is not his concern (181). Nonetheless, we will refer to certain aspects of Kaiser's work in this study.

force, we are left with the significant question of how, once again, to preserve the difficult statements of *Discipleship*, without presenting a view of human subjectivity in Christ which is dislocated, fragmented or ruptured. In other words, how to establish a critically robust framework for integrating simplicity and wisdom, so that one's being 'in Christ' is not so reflectively ungraspable that the 'I' who believes and is obedient becomes a 'heavenly double'.

1.1.3 'Standing by' Discipleship

The foregoing discussion makes clear that the centrality of unreflective obedience in Bonhoeffer's articulation of Christian discipleship threatens to appear unsustainable insofar as being in Christ must be reflected on to some extent, and Bonhoeffer himself sees it as necessary to incorporate reflection into his account of human subjectivity in Christ elsewhere in the corpus. The task of integrating simplicity and wisdom, then, is to maintain Bonhoeffer's articulation of discipleship as centred on a fundamental nexus of simplicity, while incorporating the unavoidable need for reflective wisdom. This task can be understood as 'standing by' the simplicity of *Discipleship*, while acknowledging the 'dangers' therein. It is clear that reconciling the reflective with the uncompromising demands of *Discipleship* will not be achieved through conceiving of any straightforward unity or synthesis. To preserve or 'stand by' the difficult statements of *Discipleship* will simply not permit of any easy resolution with the reflective. We need to find a way to 'stand by' the view that to be a disciple is 'always' to be 'seeing only Christ', to remain 'hidden' from oneself, and to act in 'simple obedience' without 'knowing good and evil', without undermining the fact that these elements of *Discipleship* are intrinsically distinct from self-reflection and practical discernment. The task is therefore to avoid fragmentation or dislocation between 'simplicity and wisdom', and yet to integrate the two without positing a straightforward unity or synthesis. Approaching simplicity and wisdom with these two conditions of avoiding both diastasis and synthesis in mind, presents a further dimension to this conceptual duality, which will prove important in working towards the integration sought.

The avoidance of both diastasis and synthesis while integrating 'simplicity and wisdom' calls to mind discussions in Bonhoeffer scholarship surrounding his frequent use of oppositional terms and the various ways secondary commentators understand their interrelation.[37] That Bonhoeffer's thinking is characterized by 'oppositional pairs'[38] has long been acknowledged in the literature, and there are grounds to suggest that understanding the interrelationship of oppositional pairs has been a significant strand of Bonhoeffer interpretation for some decades. In the early period of Bonhoeffer's critical reception, the defining opposition was between

---

37. See Ernst Feil who describes the *actus* distinction as a basic 'commitment [*Ansatz*]' which Bonhoeffer 'pursued throughout his life', *The Theology of Dietrich Bonhoeffer*, Philadelphia: Fortress Press, 1985, 52.

38. Clifford J. Green, in DeJonge, *Formation*, xi.

the church and the world. This opposition was considered important because of the reception of the prison literature, where his challenging assertions involving 'religionless Christianity' and the 'world come of age', required much unpacking and led to high-profile misappropriations, most famously by John Robinson.[39] These discussions centred around three loci: Bonhoeffer's early preoccupation with ecclesiology in *Sanctorum Communio* and *Act and Being*, his alleged offsetting of church and world as antagonistically opposed while at Finkenwalde and the deeply world-affirming tenor of his final writings, *Ethics* and *Letters and Papers*.

The church and world opposition is worthy of mention here because in Bethge's 1961 discussion of it, he adopts a turn of phrase which suggests a move towards seeing the relationship as more than simply a question of two discrete theological items of concern (church and world), but as undergirded by something more fundamental, namely, an underlying thought-form or pattern of thinking in which oppositional pairs are juxtaposed with a unity which is conceived Christologically. This is seen in Bethge's statement that 'the oneness of the reality established' by Christ 'is not a synthesis and not a diastasis'.[40] Here, Bethge not only challenges Müller's presentation of the Finkenwalde period as representing a point of rupture (diastasis) between church and world, but also challenges Robinson's injudicious downplaying of the revelational reality of the church as unwarrantedly synthesizing the two. In pointing to Christ as a centre of 'oneness' in Bonhoeffer's thinking which is neither a 'diastasis' nor a 'synthesis', Bethge uncovers something which promises to offer a framework for understanding the interplay of oppositional pairs in Bonhoeffer's work, which could helpfully elucidate their interrelation more broadly. Indeed, to present reflective wisdom as in diastasis with unreflective simplicity would lead to the fragmentation and rupture of the self we wish to avoid. Yet, insofar as 'standing by' the difficult statements of *Discipleship* will not permit any straightforward unity or synthesis, we are faced also with the necessity of retaining the inherent *distinctness* of simplicity and of wisdom. If we are to take Bonhoeffer seriously and 'stand by' his stance that being a disciple means 'seeing only Christ' in 'simple obedience', any integration of this with 'seeing reality as it is'[41] in wisdom will need to involve a mode of reconciliation or 'oneness' in which the unavoidable differentiation between the two is preserved. For this reason, let us follow Bethge and seek a mode of oneness which is 'neither diastasis nor synthesis'.

Focusing here on the interrelation of oppositional pairs in Bonhoeffer's writing provides an opportunity to situate this book in relation to the work of Michael DeJonge, whose approach to Bonhoeffer's reconciliation of oppositional pairs is importantly distinct from the way 'simplicity and wisdom' is integrated into this project. Green comments that DeJonge's achievement works 'by laying bare an enduring feature of Bonhoeffer's mode of theological reasoning', namely, 'the

---

39. John Robinson, *Honest to God*, London: SCM Press, 1963, 75f.
40. Bethge, 'Challenge', 74.
41. DBWE6, 81.

1. Simplicity and Wisdom

reconciliation of oppositional pairs by his understanding of Jesus Christ'.[42] The key duality of DeJonge's analysis is act and being, the focus of the *Habilitationsschrift*, for he argues that act and being concepts of revelation (discussed in Chapter 5) are combined Christologically, through what he considers *the* decisive breakthrough of Bonhoeffer's theology, 'his distinctive concept of person'.[43] The poses the question of whether the simplicity and wisdom duality can also be seen as reconciled, 'solved' or 'annulled' by Bonhoeffer's understanding of Jesus Christ.

If we connect DeJonge's work to Bethge's comment about avoiding diastasis and synthesis, the former seems to veer towards synthesis, as demonstrated by Green's statement that for DeJonge, all oppositional pairs are 'annulled' by Christ. Nonetheless, if we were to take DeJonge's lead and apply his person-centred reconciliation of oppositional pairs to the unreflective–reflective problematic, there is good reason to proceed in this direction. In 'Ethics as Formation', Bonhoeffer presents a Christological mode of oneness between the two, seeming perhaps to resonate with DeJonge's Christological 'solving' of the oppositional pairs in Bonhoeffer's theology through Christ's 'person'. Bonhoeffer states that 'as an ideal, the unity of simplicity and wisdom' is 'doomed to failure', being 'highly contradictory'. However, he goes on to state that this is 'grounded' in 'the reality of the world reconciled with God in Jesus Christ'.[44] With this, he interprets the unity of simplicity and wisdom as grounded in Christ, drawing on Mt. 10:16, in terms of the world and God being reconciled in Jesus. He thus implies human beings can look on themselves (self-reflect) and engage in considered decision-making (reflective discernment), while in unreflective apprehension and obedience. The reasoning is that, insofar as we and our actions belong to the world, and the world is reconciled with God in Christ, somehow by looking at Christ we can maintain a point of unreflective simplicity (keeping 'in sight only the single truth of God'), while simultaneously reflecting on ourselves and our deeds (seeing 'reality in God'). He thus states, 'No one can look at God [simplicity] and at the reality of the world [wisdom] with undivided gaze as long as God and the world are torn apart', but 'because there is one place' where God and world are reconciled, it is 'possible there and there alone to fix one's eyes on God and the world together at the same time'.[45] This might well affirm a reading of the simplicity and wisdom duality in a way similar to DeJonge's.

However, 'standing by' the uncompromising exclusivity of the 'dangerous' statements of *Discipleship* must make us question any such move towards synthesis. To say that one can 'fix one's eyes on God and the world together at the same time', because oneself and one's deeds (the worldly) are reconciled with God in Christ, cannot directly be reconciled with other statements of Bonhoeffer's, such as the assertion that disciples must 'protect' themselves from reflecting on themselves in

---

42. Green, in DeJonge, *Formation*, xi.
43. DeJonge, *Formation*, 71.
44. DBWE6, 82.
45. Ibid.

Christ, for 'in the same moment [they] would desire to see it, [they] would lose it'.[46] For this reason, 'standing by' what Bonhoeffer writes in *Discipleship* is advanced more convincingly through seeking an integration of simplicity and wisdom which is – following Bethge – understood as 'neither diastasis nor synthesis'. Bearing this in mind presents a different interpretation of the Christological oneness to DeJonge's, in that Bonhoeffer's invocation of Mt. 10:16 meets us, not as a Christological synthesis, but precisely as a deepening of the problem itself. That is, Bonhoeffer's claim that combining these two is necessary for ethical endurance, and that Christ himself is the basis of this combination, by no means precludes the inherent differentiation of simplicity and wisdom, nor the unavoidable 'dangers' of the book *Discipleship*. Rather, Christology defines the fundamental problematic of this book itself; for Bonhoeffer considers Christ's domain to include all reality (unreflective and reflective) in oneness, yet it is clear from the positions taken in *Discipleship* that these two cannot be straightforwardly synthesized, solved or annulled from the human perspective. In the next subsection, the main lineaments of this book will be set out, applying the hermeneutical key of simplicity and wisdom in seeking an integration which is neither a diastasis (fragmentation/rupture/'heavenly double') nor a synthesis (Christological annulment/solving of the problem).

1.2 Main lineaments in seeking integration

Chapter 2 will commence this inquiry by giving more attention to the four sets of difficult statements set out above. It centres on the observation that the terminology of *Discipleship* tends to involve words denoting 'oneness' for the unreflective (e.g. *einfältig, einfach* and *Einfalt*) and 'twoness' for the reflective (e.g. *Zweifel, Zweideutigkeit* and *Zwiespalt*). This semantic juxtaposition shows how reflection seems at first glance to be presented by Bonhoeffer as innately problematic in and of itself per se. This is, of course, an immediate obstacle for answering to the fundamental challenge at stake, so *Discipleship* is brought into dialogue with the aforementioned points in the corpus where Bonhoeffer is not so critical of reflection. This demonstrates that considering reflection to be innately negative is not the most accurate rendering of his position.

This argument is conducted on two fronts, cognitive and practical. Cognitively, reflection refers to self-reflection, beholding oneself in thought, apparently precluded by 'seeing only Christ' and the 'hiddenness of the disciple'. Practically, we are dealing with the reflective evaluation of options, apparently precluded by 'simple obedience' and 'not knowing good and evil'. On both fronts however, each of the four aspects of simplicity need not preclude all self-reflection per se, but should rather be seen as presenting *requirements* for self-reflecting in Christian life which it is necessary to meet, in order to avoid undermining or negating the

---

46. DBWE4, 287–8.

unreflective core of that life in discipleship. Indeed, the groundwork for this is provided by Bonhoeffer himself. On the cognitive side, *Act and Being*'s discussion of transcendental philosophy describes self-reflection in relatively neutral terms, in relation to transcendental philosophy, in which 'I reflect on myself; I and myself move apart'.[47] Yet, Bonhoeffer also highlights specific problems with self-reflection in what he calls 'post-Kantian transcendentalism' (i.e. German idealism). This suggests that self-reflection can be relatively ambivalent if approached correctly and is not inherently problematic. On the practical side, Bonhoeffer claims in *Ethics* that we must 'seriously consider the consequences of our actions', and 'after responsibly weighing all circumstances' the resulting deed 'is completely surrendered [*ausgeliefert*] to God the moment it is carried out'.[48] Again, Bonhoeffer suggests that the reflective need not always preclude following Christ, in this case, insofar as it remains grounded on Christ and not on any self-validating criteria, and therefore does not undermine 'simple obedience' and 'not knowing good and evil'.

Before exploring how reflection might be conducted within the conditions alluded to by the above-mentioned moments of the corpus, it will be necessary to evaluate scholarly discussion of the point where the apparent rupture between the unreflective and the reflective in Bonhoeffer's approach to human subjectivity is most sharply put in relief: the critical reception of *Discipleship*. Doing so discloses three aspects to the literature which provide important foci for achieving this book's aims.

The first focus involves an omission on the part of some scholars to bring the philosophical sections of *Act and Being* on transcendentalism into sustained dialogue with the detail of *Discipleship*. The second involves the tendency to connect unreflective elements of *Discipleship* exclusively with the *theological* discussions from *Act and Being*. The third involves the suggestion given by the literature, that *Ethics* could helpfully inform problems with 'simple obedience' of *Discipleship*. Taking the insights gleaned from this survey of Bonhoeffer scholarship, Chapter 4 will explore the salient moments of the philosophical section of *Act and Being*, Chapter 5, *Act and Being*'s theological sections, and then pertinent points in the *Ethics* manuscripts in Chapter 6.

In Chapter 4, two outcomes are presented. First, it is shown that Bonhoeffer defines the *actus directus* precisely in terms of direct intentionality.[49] This resonates strongly with the 'seeing only Christ' of *Discipleship*; a fact often omitted by secondary commentators. Secondly, Bonhoeffer's discussion of Kant's transcendental philosophy provides us with a promising way to understand how we might engage in self-reflection while retaining a certain 'hiddenness' from ourselves, based on what Kant calls the 'transcendental unity of apperception'.

47. DBWE2, 33.
48. DBWE6, 225.
49. DBW2, 36.

Chapter 5 investigates the theological sections of *Act and Being*, focusing on Bonhoeffer's responses to problems he detects in Barth, which show how deeply Bonhoeffer is orientated by the aspects to the transcendental attempt disclosed in Chapter 4. Bonhoeffer understands Barth's own critique of self-reflection to lose sight of the key aspect of the *actus directus*, which is its intentionality. In this theological context, he is speaking of the intentionality towards Christ. He goes on to propose two modes of self-reflection to maintain the intentionality of a theological *actus directus*, focused on Jesus: 'self-understanding-in-remembrance' and the 'Christian conscience'.[50] Nonetheless, in these attempts, Bonhoeffer seems to lose sight of the 'hiddenness' of the self-reflecting subject, which was importantly established with Kant's 'transcendental unity of apperception' in his philosophical discussion, and which resonates strongly with the 'hiddenness of the disciple' in *Discipleship*. Chapter 5 therefore concludes that we need to examine Kant's 'transcendental unity of apperception' more closely, to ascertain how it might inform an integration of simplicity and wisdom.

Before doing so, it is necessary in Chapter 6 to give some attention to *Ethics* in relation to the practical side of this enquiry. On this front, Bonhoeffer brings us closer to fulfilling our goals. First, by approaching obedient action as Christ's 'formation [*Gestaltung*] of the world',[51] we gain some commensurability with the reflective, insofar as we can envisage reflecting on how best to enact Christ's *Gestaltung,* and arrive thereby at deeds grounded on Christ alone, and which resonate thereby with 'simple obedience'. Secondly, Bonhoeffer considers we can engage in practical reflection to discover 'God's will' while not knowing good and evil, a stance we can term 'purity of heart'. 'Purity of heart' is differentiated by Bonhoeffer from bearing an 'absolute criterion of what is good'.[52] But, it remains unclear how a reflectively discerned knowledge of God's will is critically distinguishable from knowing an absolute good; how this does not present another self-legitimizing point of ethical security. Bonhoeffer contrasts knowledge of God's will with the understanding of an absolute good found in Kant's practical philosophy, so we are presented with the task of investigating certain pertinent aspects of Kant's approach to practical reasoning in Chapter 7.

Chapters 5 and 6 present us with two main concerns rooted in Bonhoeffer's Kantian inheritance, and the discussion of these in Chapter 7 provides vital background for bringing the potential depth of Dilthey's contribution into view. First, it will be seen that Kant describes the 'transcendental unity of apperception' as an aspect to human subjectivity which is experienced in 'the flow of life',[53] but which also functions as a conceptual boundary to self-reflection. As approached conceptually, it must by definition be represented only as abstract and non-temporal. Bonhoeffer explicitly wants to avoid approaching human subjectivity

---

50. Ibid., 129f., 155f.
51. DBWE6, 98.
52. Ibid., 247f.
53. Bonhoeffer's term (DBWE6, 384), discussed in Chapter 2.

as abstract and non-temporal,[54] so the task which then emerges is to enquire into how we might articulate this 'transcendental unity of apperception' as it pertains to consciousness, while preserving its 'hiddenness' without recourse to pure conceptuality.

Chapter 7 then turns to Kant's presentation of an 'absolute good', or rather, his 'categorical imperative'. First, it will be seen that, for Kant, this imperative arises in concrete human experience, but is also 'distilled' from this originary experience to be articulated conceptually, and grounded as universal and abstractly necessary through its relation to 'pure practical reason'. The fact the imperative actually arises in concrete experience is shown by one of the best-known of Kant's statements, in which he says, 'the moral law within me' is something he need not 'seek', for he claims, 'I see [it] before me and connect [it] immediately with my existence'.[55] Bonhoeffer's suspicion of an 'absolute good' arises from its conceptual articulation; the abstract and universal nature of the Kantian imperative given by its basis in pure practical reason, for this means it is by definition self-legitimizing or self-validating. Therefore, the task emerges of articulating the demands that arise in concrete experience, without grounding them abstractly and universally. Doing so promises to show how the imperatives that arise in life itself might offer material to reflective discernment without being grounded in a self-legitimizing way.

With both the cognitive and practical concerns of the discussion of Kant in Chapter 7, the tasks set before us share a fundamental characteristic: seeking to describe or articulate facets of life, without 'distilling' or 'splitting off' abstract structures or conditions from concrete lived-experience. Chapter 8 therefore begins a constructive exploration of a philosopher who explicitly and consistently attempts to articulate human experience precisely in what he considers its 'original togetherness',[56] with an approach that seeks to avoid what he terms a 'truncating'[57] of the richness of concrete life by analytically breaking down, and uncovering abstract conditions for, 'lived-experience': Wilhelm Dilthey. Dilthey directly tackles the problems with 'abstraction' in Kant's 'transcendental unity of apperception' and the 'categorical imperative', and in doing so his philosophy proposes what have been called 'quasi-transcendental features',[58] meaning structural conditions and generalities which are intended to offer analogous points of reference to those Kantian facets, but as embedded 'in' concrete lived-experience.

Chapter 9 commences a detailed study of Dilthey's work by examining his understanding of unreflective and reflective facets of human subjectivity in the cognitive sphere. Here, something highly promising for this enquiry comes to light, insofar as Dilthey is seen to present a hidden, unreflective nexus to lived-experience which he approaches in a way which ensures it remains concrete and

---

54. As witnessed in his critique of Barth's 'heavenly double'.
55. CprR, 269.
56. Rudolf A. Makkreël and Fritjof Rodi, in SWIII, 2.
57. SWI, 49, 79.
58. Makkreel and Rodi, in SWI, 34.

temporal. Moreover, Dilthey also arrives at understandings of the continuity between the reflective facets of life with this unreflective centre. The first of these I call an 'explicative continuity', for Dilthey builds on the observation that reflection explicates moments of unreflective, lived-experience. That is, experiences are undergone in direct consciousness, but the meaning of those experiences is arrived at subsequently through self-reflection. Importantly, however, Dilthey holds that momentary experiences continue to unfold interpretive meanings – self-reflective meaning is never fixed or final – and this entails that oneself remains, in a sense, 'hidden' to the full grasp of reflective self-possession. Insofar as we continually discern new interpretations of what certain experiences mean through self-reflection, the unreflective centre of the original experience is a source of meaning always (at least in part) hidden from the reflective gaze. The second mode of continuity Dilthey offers, I call 'implicative'. Here, he builds on the observation that self-reflection changes self-understanding, and the resulting changes in turn effect the way we live unreflectively. That is, having acknowledged attributes about oneself through self-reflection, such acknowledgements can simply be borne by us in the 'flow of life', and thus become (or are 'implicated in') unreflective consciousness. Yet, in such circumstances we are not directly (or reflectively) aware of the attributes in question, they simply condition our lived-experience. For this reason, the reflective and unreflective are continuous for Dilthey, but the unreflective remains 'hidden' in lived-experience itself.

These two continuities provide important advances with respect to the cognitive side to integrating simplicity and wisdom, so the immediate task for Chapter 10 is to analyse Dilthey's practical philosophy; his approach to unreflective and reflective agency. Two outcomes arise from this analysis. In the first place, one of Dilthey's discussions of unreflective agency involves acting in service to the will of another person. In this case, a person can bear a commitment or obligation towards another which is not continually subject to being reflected on at every moment where it directs behaviour and action; it is just carried through life. But while this commitment to another is simply a 'given' in momentary lived-experience, reflective decision-making still occurs in terms of discerning how best to serve the needs or wants of that other. In this way, there is a certain commensurability between unreflective and reflective agency in Dilthey. It then becomes necessary to examine Dilthey's understanding of reflective agency itself. This leads to the finding that Dilthey considers reflective agency to involve the evaluation of criteria for action that are autonomously centred on the deliberations of the agent. It therefore runs counter to Bonhoeffer's critique of self-legitimizing criteria, leaving us with only modest gains attained from Dilthey's practical philosophy.

Chapter 11 therefore turns to certain points in Dilthey's philosophy where he describes modes of reflection which are not centred on the reflecting agent. These are to be found in his literary aesthetics or 'poetics', particularly, where he understands that reflection occurs in a way which is 'disinterested', meaning the desires or inclinations (interests) of the reflecting subject are withdrawn. Dilthey holds that aesthetic 'objects' (such as poetic images) are evaluated by a reflecting subject (such as a reader of poetry) in terms of how appropriately they express the sense one has of the subjectivity of another (the poet). This mode of reflection involves Dilthey's notion of *Gestalt*, his concept for articulating the fullness of human personhood. Dilthey maintains that, in aesthetic (disinterested) reflection, the subject evaluates aesthetic 'objects' in terms of their appropriateness in relation to the *Gestalt* of another. By bringing this mode of reflection into relationship with Dilthey's unreflective agency as service to another, considerable progress is made. This finding allows us to envisage that, in reflecting on how to fulfil the needs or wants of another, an agent evaluates appropriateness in relation to the *Gestalt* of this other, and therefore reflects without autonomously centred criteria.

1.3 Integrating simplicity and wisdom

The continuities between the unreflective and reflective in Dilthey's philosophy just outlined, are put to work in the final chapter to address this book's motivating problem or quandary: integrating simplicity and wisdom. There are three ways in which this is achieved. First and secondly, by applying Dilthey's explicative and implicative continues to the cognitive side to the problem, and thirdly, by applying his practical and aesthetic continuity to its practical side.

Calling to mind the requirements of simplicity as outlined in Chapter 2, 'seeing only Christ' and the 'hiddenness of the disciple', integrating simplicity and wisdom in the cognitive sphere will involve articulating modes of reflection which neither break the intentionality to Christ of the former nor surrender oneself entirely to the reflective gaze and thus trespass the latter; an approach to reflection in which one is still 'seeing only Christ' and remains to some extent 'hidden' from oneself.

In the first place, Dilthey's explicative continuity between unreflective and reflective consciousness works from the supposition that we discern what moments of life mean through reflecting on them, and insofar as these moments continue to unfold new meanings, the unreflective centre of consciousness is not exhaustively self-possessed by reflective activity. To transpose this discussion into a theological register; the first step is to envisage Dilthey's 'moments of lived-experience' as moments of discipleship: occurrences in life which align with Bonhoeffer's understanding of unreflective apprehension of Christ, where 'I no longer cast even a single glance at my own life'. Examples of such moments which come to mind could involve instances of prayerful or liturgical intensity, hearing a rousing sermon or being overwhelmed by some item of beauty. In such moments one is, as described by Gerald Manly Hopkins, 'In a flash, at a trumpet crash, ... all at once what Christ is'.[59] Let us then envisage, secondly, the reflecting subject seeking to understand what such a moment of life might mean. This will inevitably involve turning to other discrete aspects of his or her life: particular relationships, events, challenges, realizations, personal developments, and so forth. The third step, then,

---

59. From the poem *That Nature is a Heraclitean Fire and of the Comfort of the Resurrection* by Gerald Manley Hopkins.

is to picture how such discrete elements of life might be given meaning through self-reflection, precisely by being approached as the unfolding or explication of a momentary unreflective apprehension of being 'all at once what Christ is'. That is, while many aspects of life are mysterious, perplexing and unfathomable, they can be given meaning through being understood as the unfolding of what traditional Christian language might call a moment of grace, a 'call', a 'commission', or even, an 'anointing'.

For Bonhoeffer, the disciple must 'see only Christ' and remain 'hidden' from him or herself, and transposing Dilthey's 'explicative continuity' into a theological register promises to ensure these requirements are met. While considering moments of an unreflective, direct apprehension of Christ in relation to other aspects of life certainly involves self-reflection, the discernment of meaning itself only takes place in a way centred on the unreflective apprehension of being 'all at once what Christ is'. We might consider someone discerning that a particular set of testing professional duties are outworkings of one such moment. But even when reflecting on those professional duties in this way, Christ remains in the centre, for Christ is at the very centre of the original moment which orientates the discernment of meaning. In this case, complex self-reflection can be considered still to be 'directed at' Christ, insofar as that which is gleaned about oneself is entirely centred on Jesus himself. This approach to self-reflection can thereby be considered as one in which a person 'sees only Christ' precisely while considering his or her own life reflectively. Moreover, insofar as the original moment of unreflective apprehension can be considered to explicate and unfold further dimensions of meaning through ongoing consideration of these duties as they continue in life, the original unreflective self remains hidden from oneself: dimensions of the original experience are not made exhaustively graspable to the self-reflecting subject, and the ultimate meaning is never therefore fixed.

Secondly, we shall transpose Dilthey's implicative continuity into a theological register. This will offer a further way to understand self-reflection as integrated in Christian life, without trespassing 'the hiddenness of the disciple' which Bonhoeffer considers fundamental to that life. In this case, it will be shown how reflections on oneself configure or affect direct consciousness, so those reflections become 'implicated in' or 'implicit to' unreflective lived-experience. The first step is to consider a facet of the lived-experience of Christian discipleship. For this, we can envisage acts of worship. Participating in acts of worship can be understood in the broadest possible sense as an acknowledgement, confession, declaration or proclamation of God's infinite majesty. As put in the words of the early Christian hymn, the *Te Deum*: 'We praise you, Oh God; we acknowledge you to be the Lord.' One can expect, secondly, that reflecting on one's own life in relation to God's infinite majesty, will impart or embed this acknowledgement into one's self-understanding, and thereby have some effect on life. One could mention here the apparent lowliness and insignificance of one's own life ('What is man that you are mindful of him?' Ps. 8.5) and a corresponding sense of immense personal responsibility resulting from being granted some recognition of, or sharing in, God's majesty ('yet you have crowned him with glory and honour' Ps. 8.6). But the important point, thirdly, is that, for one in whom these fruits of self-reflection have been accepted and assimilated, the explicit recognition of oneself *as* lowly and undeserving of sharing in the life of God is not present *to* consciousness as a clearly delineated element in every moment of life in which it is effective. Rather, this recognition should be considered as deeply embedded 'in' consciousness implicitly, as partially configuring one's engagement with life, without being perspicuously brought before consciousness in every instance where its consequences are active.

With Dilthey's 'implicative continuity', our self-reflections are always mediate and provisional. One's interpretation of oneself is always open to disruption in and by life. So while such reflections 'feed into' and configure unreflective lived-experience, they are still perpetually disrupted and reordered by that experience. To return to the above example, one finds oneself having to reconsider where one stands in relation to God's infinite majesty, one repeatedly falls short of living true to the 'glory and honour' one has been granted. For this reason, reflection on one's self as a disciple requires a concerted sense of provisionality, or better, humility. The true reality of one's life in God is never given to oneself as something that can be fully grasped, although it might be reflectively glimpsed and thereby 'feed into' and affect life. The reflective and unreflective thus exhibit a certain reciprocity, in which one's own discipleship remains essentially 'hidden'; so even armed with glimpses of oneself 'in Christ'; one can still only say of one's self: 'I do not know the man.'[60] That is, the self 'crowned with glory and honour'.

The third transposition of elements of Dilthey's philosophy into a theological register is on the practical side. The task here is to show how practical reflection can explicate moments of serving Christ (or obedience), as discerning how best to express the *Gestalt* of Christ. This will draw on Bonhoeffer's own use of the term *Gestalt* for referring to the personhood of Christ in *Ethics* (and elsewhere),[61] and what he terms Christ's 'formation' (*Gestaltung*) of the world. Using Bonhoeffer's terminology, the chapter aims to show, through a particular application of Dilthey's aesthetic receptivity, that approaching reflective discernment as deciding how best to enact Christ's *Gestaltung* of the world allows us to consider practical reflection as the evaluating of ends according to their appropriateness as expressing Christ's *Gestalt*. This attains a mode of practical reflection reconcilable with the unreflective, insofar as the singleness of intentionality or volitional oneness of 'simple obedience' is maintained, and there are not autonomously centred criteria for action (being aesthetically 'disinterested'), so the agent remains in 'purity of heart'.

This book closes with three broader implications arising from these three integrations of 'simplicity and wisdom'. First, there are implications of this integration for the interpretation of *Discipleship*; where the harmonious integration of simplicity and wisdom enables us to read Bonhoeffer's 'dangerous' assertions afresh. Claims such as 'knowing Christ means no longer knowing oneself' and

---

60. DBWE4, 86.
61. DBWE6, 79f.; DBWE12, 315f.

that our own will 'must die' in unreflective obedience can now be integrally interconnected with self-reflection and practical discernment, thus cohering with Bonhoeffer's later statement that 'only the one who combines simplicity and wisdom can endure'. The book's apparently 'dangerous' character means it still arguably tends to be 'stood by' with some difficulty, as an outlier on the more radical fringes of Bonhoeffer's thinking. Indeed, as Plant states, *Discipleship* is 'disturbing' because of its exclusivity, for 'it gives the impression there can be no other way of understanding Christian faith'.[62] But insofar as simplicity and wisdom have been shown to be mutually integral, the implication arises that, by concentrating so resolutely, uncompromisingly and forcefully on unreflective simplicity in *Discipleship*, Bonhoeffer was enabled to discover and unearth further dimensions of reflective wisdom, which, rather than recanting his uncompromising simplicity, actually foster and perpetuate it. As Bethge states, *Discipleship* was not a forsaking of the world, but 'a concentration' intended to issue in deeper worldliness and committed responsible action.[63]

Secondly, 'simplicity and wisdom' presents itself as a hermeneutical key for interpreting the Bonhoeffer corpus. Integrating simplicity and wisdom implies an interpretation of *Discipleship* which places the book at the centre of Bonhoeffer's work, showing how other elements of the corpus (the reflective) can be integrally located in relation to it. This integrating of hitherto uneasily related elements of the corpus implies that this hermeneutical key promises to offer a means of integrating other spheres of concern in Bonhoeffer scholarship beyond this book's focus on human subjectivity. Bethge holds that Bonhoeffer's theology involves a Christological mode of oneness which is neither 'diastasis' nor 'synthesis'.[64] Bringing this into dialogue with the integration of the duality of 'simplicity' and 'wisdom' of this book, we can suggest that the integration offered here of simplicity and wisdom promises to have broader implications beyond the unreflective–reflective tension. It will be seen in what follows that the *actus* distinction must tend towards diastasis in that the differentiation between each side of the duality is unavoidably stark (direct and reflective consciousness are, at bottom, mutually exclusive). Yet, as already mentioned, DeJonge's centralizing of the tensions between 'act' and 'being' as 'solved'[65] in the concept of person veers towards synthesis and threatens to undermine the enduring tension between the two. The integration of simplicity and wisdom offered here, however, avoids synthesis, while presenting a genuine 'oneness' through an integral interrelationship. Moreover, it avoids diastasis while holding firm to the unavoidable differentiation between the two, and so we suggest that 'simplicity and wisdom' offers an exemplary instance of what Bethge describes as Bonhoeffer's underlying pattern of thinking. This promises therefore to integrate and cohere different facets of Bonhoeffer's thinking beyond the unreflective and

62. Plant, *Bonhoeffer*, 98.
63. Bethge, 'Challenge', 48–50; see DBWE14, 89.
64. Bethge, 'Challenge', 74.
65. DeJonge, *Formation*, 96.

reflective and deserves further exploration as one of what Bethge calls elsewhere Bonhoeffer's 'creative formulas'.

Thirdly and finally, this holding together of two apparently conflicting sets of concerns, which, even when interrelated, can exhibit an ongoing, perpetually challenging dissimilarity, resonates with what we might term 'perennial tensions' which frequently reoccur in theology, being fundamentally grounded on abidingly perplexing aspects of the human relation to God. Arguably, the most fundamental of these is God's transcendence and immanence. It will be shown that the unreflective relates to what is termed God's transcendence, and reflection, to God's immanence. But reflection, conducted according to the three means of integrating simplicity and wisdom described by this book, promises to demonstrate how reflecting on encounters with God need not unwarrantedly ensnare God transcendent in the immanent. Rather, self-reflection as 'wisdom' is continually qualified, circumspect and measured, in order to perpetuate the 'perspectival shift' to God-centredness granted precisely *by* acknowledging God's transcendence. In short, wisdom as presented here offers 'dispossessed' modes of reflection, which – enabling us to reflect on our own life as 'hidden with Christ' in the God who stands at 'the centre of our existence' – deepen and intensify the relation to God as the radically transcendent source of life, given over to us in his fullness, that we might follow Jesus Christ.

Chapter 2

THE SIMPLICITY OF *DISCIPLESHIP*

This chapter analyses the four loci of the unreflective simplicity of *Discipleship* introduced in the previous chapter: 'seeing only Christ', the 'hiddenness of the disciple', 'simple obedience' and 'purity of heart'. The primary aim is to answer the challenge of the unreflective presented by *Discipleship*: to 'stand by' the uncompromising assertions therein (retaining the essentially unreflective core of the human response to Christ), while acknowledging the 'dangers' of the book (ensuring our understanding of human subjectivity 'in Christ' is not dislocated or ruptured with the reflective). This challenge confronts us particularly when we consider the fact that reflection is an unavoidable and necessary aspect of human life, and that Bonhoeffer is concerned to accommodate this unavoidability and necessity elsewhere in the corpus, precisely to avoid rupturing or fragmenting human subjectivity. Yet, in *Discipleship* he iterates a view of reflection that seems inherently to preclude or undermine life 'in Christ'. The first step in seeking to answer to the challenge of the unreflective, then, is to examine the loci of the simplicity of *Discipleship* more closely, to determine how each locus seems incommensurable with the reflective.

2.1 Discipleship: *Overview and simplicity as singularity*

2.1.1 Discipleship *in overview*

Bonhoeffer's *Discipleship* has long been regarded as supremely important for the trajectory of his life and work. Edwin Robertson calls it 'his most important book', which established him as a 'theologian',[1] Geoffrey Kelly and John de Gruchy note that it was the longest and 'most influential' book Bonhoeffer wrote during his lifetime, and Tietz states it is his 'most widely read book worldwide'.[2] The book is in two parts. In Part 1 Bonhoeffer describes discipleship (*Nachfolge*),

---

1. Edwin Robertson, in Wolf-Dieter Zimmerman and Gregor Ronald Smith (eds), *I Knew Dietrich Bonhoeffer*, translated from the German by Käthe Gregor Smith, London: Fontana, 1973, 10.
2. Gruchy and Kelly, in DBWE4, 1; Tietz, *Widerstand*, 70 (my translation).

or 'following after', in terms of an unquestioningly obedient response to the 'unconditional, immediate, and inscrutable authority' of Jesus Christ.[3] He argues on various fronts, most famously through his condemnation of 'cheap grace', which is contrasted with 'costly grace'. Grace is the unmerited redemptive gift of God in forgiving and justifying the sinner. To approach this grace 'cheaply' is, for Bonhoeffer, to take justification for granted, to 'assume' it as a 'presupposition' of Christian life,[4] and he considers this cheapening of grace to have had destructive consequences in 1930s German Protestantism. The key point is that if justification is *assumed* (if believers engage with life under the presupposition they are forgiven through 'faith alone' [*sola fide*]), then there seems to be no obligation to perform obedient action according to the commands of Christ, and Christ's 'unconditional authority' is thereby thwarted.[5] He responds with his well-known aphorism, 'only the believers obey, and only the obedient believe.'[6] This is not intended to mandate works righteousness, but rather to prevent the *sole fide* being misinterpreted as a presupposition which negates the need for concrete obedience. Bonhoeffer thus maintains that, although Christ's justification of the sinner can rest only on faith, obedience is still an equally necessary element of Christian life. The centrepiece of the book is Bonhoeffer's interpretation of the Sermon on the Mount in the second half of Part 1, which I will discuss later.

In Part 2 Bonhoeffer seeks to align his preceding discussion of discipleship and the authority of Christ with the Pauline doctrines of justification and sanctification. He is concerned here with showing that the traditions of the institutional church are in line with the view of following Christ in obedience (drawn from the Synoptic Gospels) that he outlines in Part 1. This extends Bonhoeffer's reservations voiced in the Christology lectures, about the split between the 'Jesus of history' of the Gospels and the 'Christ of faith' of Paul's letters, which was prevalent in liberal Protestantism.[7] This split tended to involve seeing the Gospels as the supremely authentic source for the study of the historical Jesus, allegedly enabling theologians to glimpse a historically verified 'kernel'[8] of Jesus's teaching, which is interpreted as a more credible or legitimate understanding of Christ than that presented by the more institutionally minded tenor of the supposed 'Christ of faith' of Paul. Given the Barmen and Dahlem declarations of the Confessing Church in 1933 and 1935, Bonhoeffer is concerned to establish the mandates of 'visible' institutional church organization, which he connects to his condemnation of cheap grace, by

---

3. DBWE4, 57 (translation altered).
4. Ibid., 51.
5. See DeJonge, *Formation*, 132.
6. DBWE4, 63.
7. DBWE12, 328.
8. For example, in Adolf von Harnack's *What is Christianity? Lectures Delivered in the University of Berlin during the Winter Term 1899–1900*, trans. Thomas Bailey Saunders, London: Williams & Norgate, 1902, 13.

presenting them as an outworking of discipleship as unconditional obedience.[9] As the focus of this book is the relation between the unreflective and reflective facets of human subjectivity in Bonhoeffer's theology, I will focus primarily on these aspects of *Discipleship* from here on.

2.1.2 Simplicity and singularity in Discipleship

Discipleship is the primary locus of the unreflective in Bonhoeffer's work and the place where the unreflective sits in the most acute tension with the reflective. Chapter 1 gave a preliminary indication of Bonhoeffer's frequent use of the terms 'simplicity', 'simple' and 'single-minded' as illustrative of the unreflective. He first utilizes the term 'single-minded' (*einfach*) in a 1928 Barcelona sermon,[10] which Green highlights as pointing forward to its use in *Discipleship*, where it is closely related to the terms 'simple' (*einfältig*) and 'simplicity' (*Einfalt*). Green calls these words 'technical terms' for Bonhoeffer's theology, describing *einfach* as meaning 'single, undivided, integrated, [and] of one mind', and simplicity as pointing to Bonhoeffer's concern for 'singleness of purpose'.[11] We shall see below how this 'singleness' presents us with a general characteristic of the unreflective simplicity of *Discipleship*, and we will amplify Green's summation of these words as technical terms by analysing the technicalities involved in their usage. It should be noted here that language of 'simplicity', although most prevalent in *Discipleship*, endures throughout Bonhoeffer's subsequent works. In *Ethics*, for example, we have highlighted the 'simplicity [*Einfalt*] and wisdom' passage that is central for this book, and moreover towards the end of his life Bonhoeffer gives these terms more detailed attention in *Letters and Papers*. There, he states that he has been led to differentiate between *einfältig* and *einfach* by his reading of Adalbert Stifter's novels, claiming *einfältig* means 'innocent' or 'naïve', while *einfach* denotes being 'simple' or 'uncomplicated'.[12] In *Discipleship*, written some years before this discussion, Bonhoeffer does not seem to have clearly differentiated between *einfältig* and *einfach*, for both seem to belong (in a relatively undistinguished fashion) to a semantic cluster broadly indicating what Green calls an 'undividedness' and 'singleness of purpose' between the believer and Christ.

---

9. See Tietz, *Widerstand*, 72.
10. DBWE10, 514.
11. Green, in DBWE10, 8.
12. DBWE8, 294. These comments about Stifter suggest that 'simplicity' is for Bonhoeffer not only theological but also closely related to wholeness and single-mindedness 'in the fullness of life'. This leads us to question Kaiser (*Becoming*, 37), who holds that simplicity is not an 'observable, psychological' reality but only a 'theological' truth, working from Bonhoeffer's comments in *Ethics* about mistaking 'psychic simplicity' for biblical simplicity (DBWE8, 320). Bonhoeffer's comments about Stifter suggest that he has in mind not only 'unobservable' theological facts but also something broader, and the fruitfulness of this broadness is amplified by our investigation of Dilthey in the later chapters.

The singleness involved in simplicity is of course particularly perceptible in German, due to the words being based on the component *ein*, close to *eins*, meaning one. This makes these words difficult to render into English while preserving the full richness of meaning, which could arguably have contributed to the difficulty of the reception of *Discipleship* in Anglo-American scholarship. In Fuller's 1948 translation of *Nachfolge* for example, he sometimes adopts 'spontaneous obedience'[13] for '*einfältiger Gehorsam*', which captures some of the 'exciting tempo' and 'breathtaking pace'[14] of Bonhoeffer's prose, albeit at the expense of a more precise meaning. Fuller also uses 'single-minded'[15] for *einfältig*, which is perhaps better for preserving a sense of singularity or oneness. The recent critical edition of *Discipleship* commonly uses the adjective 'simple' for *einfältig*, which, although it loses the resonance with oneness, does capture some of the broader semantic references Bonhoeffer would later highlight in Tegel, meaning plain, basic or uncomplicated.

The simplicity of *Discipleship* most basically involves an unreflective oneness between Christ and his disciples, and this pervades the whole book. This extends beyond *einfältig, einfach,* and *Einfalt*, and can be seen at numerous points elsewhere. For example, the relationship between the call of Christ and the disciple following is described as being 'one' (*in einem*),[16] and the command 'follow me', as '*eindeutig*', meaning 'clear'.[17] Jesus is described as being in 'complete unity' (*Einheit*) with the will of God,[18] which is mirrored in the disciple being in 'unity [*Einheit*] with Jesus'.[19] Bonhoeffer discusses 'the simplicity [*Einfalt*] of the eye'[20] and 'the simplicity [*Einfalt*] of the carefree life',[21] and also uses the nominal form *Einfachkeit* at various points, translated as 'simplicity' in the most recent edition.[22]

These words are closely linked with another cluster of terms contrasted with the first group, and which are also difficult to translate into English while preserving the full richness of meaning. This second group provides us with further orientation, in that Bonhoeffer links this second group with *reflective* subjectivity, and the words are invariably negative in character. This second cluster involves the component *zwei*, meaning two. It is a misinterpretation of Christ's call, we read, to reflect on it and consider it 'ambiguous' (*zweideutig*).[23] In reflection, the rich young man of Mt. 19.16–22 is said to let 'double-minded thinking' (*zweifältiges Denken*)

---

13. Dietrich Bonhoeffer, *The Cost of Discipleship*, London: SCM Press, 1959, 62.
14. Kelly and de Gruchy, in DBWE4, 3–4.
15. Bonhoeffer, *Cost*, 69f.
16. DBW4, 47.
17. Ibid., 64.
18. DBW4, 117; DBWE4, 117.
19. DBW4, 191.
20. Ibid., 168.
21. Ibid., 167.
22. Ibid., 202; DBWE4, 191.
23. DBW4, 58.

step 'into the place of the simple act' (*des einfältigen Tuns*).[24] We encounter the noun *Zweifel* (translated 'doubt'), arising when reflection tears disciples away from 'simple childlike obedience'.[25] The need for unreflective obedience is described as '*unzweifelhaft*', meaning 'unquestionable', and avoidance of it is said to bring *Verzweiflung* (despair). We also read that following Christ is completely focused on Christ alone, with no reflective 'ambiguity' (*Zweideutigkeit*),[26] and that 'simple obedience' pulls disciples out of the 'dichotomy' (*Zwiespalt*) of self-reflection.[27] Already, then, we see that the unreflective singularity of *einfältig*, *einfach* and *Einfalt* contrasts negatively with a reflective 'twoness', in words like *zweifältig*, *Zwiespalt* and *Zweifel*. In subsection 2.2 we shall discern exactly why reflection is related to 'twoness', but the point to be made here is that this contrast between *ein-* and *zwei-* words suggests the reflective is inherently negative, as the *zwei-* words invariably refer to undesirable consequences of reflection in Christian life.

2.2 The simplicity of Discipleship: Four loci

Each of the four loci below is focused on a particular mode of 'oneness' between the disciple and Christ, and can also be contrasted with a particular mode of the reflective 'twoness' which is presented as obviating genuine discipleship. The first two loci are centred on the cognitive domain, where unreflective simplicity means 'seeing' Christ as 'object' single-mindedly, and the reflective is approached as *self-reflection*, and beholding *oneself* as 'object'. The third and fourth pertain to the practical, where unreflective simplicity means acting in singular obedience to Christ, and the reflective is approached as evaluating intended actions to discern how to proceed.

2.2.1 'Seeing only Christ'

The first locus involves simplicity as a momentary oneness with Christ in unreflective encounter, which Bonhoeffer describes as 'seeing only Christ'.[28] Discipleship, says Bonhoeffer, means 'we see only' Christ, and the disciples are those who are 'fully absorbed in seeing God', and therefore 'their vision is simple [*einfältig*]'.[29] He states that 'the only thing [required] for us is to look away from ourselves' and 'to look to' Jesus Christ, whose 'image' (*Bild*) is 'always before the disciple's eyes', for in seeing only Christ, he says, 'I no longer cast even a single

---

24. Ibid., 62.
25. Ibid.
26. Ibid., 167.
27. Ibid., 67.
28. DBWE4, 161, 170.
29. Ibid., 86, 108, 161.

glance on my own life'.[30] As mentioned in the previous chapter, to look at oneself in thinking, to self-reflect, breaks this oneness most basically because in reflecting on oneself one cannot be seeing only Christ. In this elementary, foundational sense, the oneness between the disciple and Christ is a oneness between the disciple as subject and Christ as 'object',[31] a oneness of direct apprehension in which the subject is apprehending the 'object' and not explicitly aware of *him* or *herself* as a discrete 'object'. The reflective focus on oneself as discrete 'object' allows us to ascertain exactly how Bonhoeffer considers the singularity of 'seeing only Christ' to be 'split' or 'fractured' by self-reflection. This 'split' refers to a reflective 'twoness' on the part of the subject, between the 'I' that reflects and the 'I' as 'object' (or 'myself') which is then the focus of reflection. We can thus appreciate why Bonhoeffer considers that, in 'seeing only Christ', the disciple's 'vision' is singular or 'simple' (*einfältig*),[32] but in self-reflection there is a 'dichotomy' (*Zwiespalt*), which is a dichotomy between 'I and myself'.

The oneness of 'seeing only Christ', and its contrasting 'twoness' between 'I and myself', resonates across a broader range of discussion than Christian discipleship. Calling to mind the opening passage of *Act and Being* on transcendental philosophy, we can see Bonhoeffer drawing on philosophical discussions that resonate with this oneness and split, particularly in reference to Kant, post-Kantian German idealism, and pointing us, as we shall see in the later chapters, to Wilhelm Dilthey. In Chapters 4 and 5, I will give considerable attention to Bonhoeffer's distinction between the *actus directus* and *actus reflectus*, which we have already indicated refers first to a direct act of apprehension (*actus directus*), which is simply 'directed at' (*gerichtet auf*)[33] its object, so the subject 'sees' only that object and has no explicit awareness of him or herself. In this connection, Bonhoeffer uses a biological analogy in *Act and Being* with a quote from Johann Wolfgang von Goethe: 'the eye does not see itself',[34] meaning that just as the physical eye cannot see itself seeing, the 'I' of the subject cannot 'see' itself when it is directly 'seeing' an object; a line of Goethe Bonhoeffer also quotes in interpreting Matthew 6 in *Discipleship*, without citing it.[35] In the *actus reflectus*, the straightforward directedness to the original object of the *actus directus* is lost, and the acting subject becomes 'objectively conscious of itself in reflection'; the subject sees itself as 'object', and 'moves apart' into two.[36] The '*actus directus*' is described as 'utter

---

30. Ibid., 280, 281, 287.

31. Bonhoeffer uses the word 'object' in reference to Christ ('the object of faith is the person of Christ' [DBWE2, 126]), and we refer to Christ as 'object' with inverted commas to highlight Bonhoeffer's differentiation of Christ as 'object' from the usual meaning of object, on the basis of the former's 'personal objectivity', DBWE2, 128 (see Chapter 4, n1).

32. DBWE4, 161.

33. DBW2, 23.

34. DBWE2, 46.

35. DBWE4, 151; see DBWE11, 442.

36. DBWE2, 33.

intentionality' because it intends only the object of apprehension, whereas in the *actus reflectus* the subject is bifurcated, 'mirroring itself to itself'.[37]

However, when we examine *Act and Being* in Chapters 4 and 5, we shall see that Bonhoeffer explores how to conceive of a mode of self-reflection which sustains the singularity of intentionality 'at' Christ, while the 'I' is gazing on 'myself'. He undertakes this by investigating reflection on the self that is 'in Christ' or 'belongs' to Christ, and so self-reflection, in a sense, beholds Christ while looking at 'myself'. By pointing forward to this aspect of *Act and Being* here, we can appreciate that Bonhoeffer seeks to outline how the reflective twoness between 'I and myself' need not lead one into the apparently negative sounding 'dichotomy' he uncompromisingly assumes in *Discipleship*, but rather seems to accommodate the unavoidability and necessity of reflection for human subjectivity.

2.2.2 The 'hiddenness of the disciple'

In this second locus, Bonhoeffer envisages a more ambivalent dimension to self-reflection. Here, Bonhoeffer asserts that the 'I' of the disciple must always be 'hidden' from itself, because the drive to behold oneself is a drive for self-possession, a desire to bring one's life under one's own jurisdiction through understanding and interpreting oneself. Bonhoeffer considers this desire to be highly dubious, because for him life 'in Christ' involves belonging to 'Christ alone', meaning the interpretation of oneself is not at one's disposal, but is surrendered to Jesus. To reflect on oneself, for Bonhoeffer, means that one sees oneself 'out of' one's 'own power' and 'out of the flesh',[38] and self-reflection is therefore presented as unavoidably self-centred, while for a disciple, Christ should always be in the 'centre'.[39] To avoid this self-centredness we read, the disciple must remain 'hidden', for otherwise the disciple is plunged into what Bonhoeffer describes as 'ambiguity' (*Zweideutigkeit*).[40] This is the ambiguity of self-centredness, where the 'I' is in what Bonhoeffer considers a self-made world.[41] The life of a disciple must therefore be hidden, we read, because 'in the same moment I would desire to see it, I would lose it'.[42]

In this second locus of unreflective simplicity, it is not merely that the believer does not 'see' him or herself in focusing on Christ, but that the believer must guard against beholding him or herself as something apparently inherently problematic. This is particularly apparent in Bonhoeffer's interpretation of the Sermon on the Mount, specifically Matthew 6, in which he contrasts the hiddenness of the disciple ('the left hand does not know what the right hand is doing') with the visible aspects

---

37. DBWE12, 305.
38. DBWE4, 150.
39. Ibid., 93; see DBWE12, 324.
40. DBW4, 167.
41. DBWE10, 120.
42. DBWE4, 287–8.

of discipleship he discusses in Matthew 5 ('your light must shine in the world'). He calls the visibility of the disciples 'extraordinary', working from the Greek περισσον of Mt. 5.37, understood as the extraordinariness of the disciples manifesting Jesus to the world in their deeds. Yet, he argues Matthew 5 and 6 'collide hard against each other', because 'what is visible should be hidden at the same time'.[43] This is not a hiddenness of the disciples from the world, but a hiddenness of themselves from themselves. Only insofar as they do not reflect on themselves, he claims, can Christ remain in the centre. His thematic focus for the hiddenness of the disciple is ἁπλους from Mt. 6.22, meaning 'simple' or 'single', or 'pure', translated as *lauter* in the Luther Bible, referring to the 'pureness of the eye' that looks only to Christ.[44]

However, as with the first locus, the 'hiddenness' of the disciple promises to be elucidated through *Act and Being*. In Chapters 4 and 5 we shall see that the corresponding negative connotations of self-reflection align broadly with tendencies Bonhoeffer associates with what he calls 'post-Kantian idealism'.[45] This is based in part on his view that, for the idealist philosophers, there is no 'hiddenness' of the subject, that they claim to fully grasp the subject in self-reflection and posit (what Johann Gottlieb Fichte calls) an 'absolute identity'[46] between subject and object, or 'I and myself'. If one remains hidden from oneself, however, there can be no identification of the 'I' with 'myself', for the 'myself' is not given over to the reflective gaze. Bonhoeffer sees this supposition of an 'absolute identity' of subject and object as fundamentally flawed, being symptomatic of a human proclivity to surmount boundaries to thinking (in this case, the boundary of the self as 'hidden'), and self-reflection is thereby implicated in the construction by the subject of the allegedly 'self-made world' of the idealists, a world that is emblematic of the human desire for self-orientated mastery and all-encompassing jurisdiction. In his inaugural lecture in Berlin, he criticizes philosophers for whom 'the I becomes an object to itself by thinking its I',[47] and in a lecture in New York he connects this with idealism, where 'man knows himself immediately by the act of the coming of the ego to itself and knows through himself essentially everything', for then 'the ego stands in the centre of the world' which is created and ruled by it.[48] This unearths some of the background to why Bonhoeffer considers the twoness which contrasts to the unreflective 'hiddenness of the disciple' to be so deeply negative.

However, a question arises here which will be given more attention when we come to look at the philosophical Section A of *Act and Being*. In his discussion of transcendental philosophy, Bonhoeffer sharply differentiates what he calls 'genuine

---

43. Ibid., 149.
44. Ibid., 161f.
45. DBWE2, 34.
46. Johann Gottlieb Fichte, *Science of Knowledge*, Cambridge: Cambridge University Press, 1982.
47. DBWE10, 390.
48. Ibid., 471.

transcendentalism' from the misappropriations of 'post-Kantian' German idealism. In this differentiation, there are two alternative approaches to the split between 'I and myself', and in 'genuine transcendentalism' this split does not seem to be inherently undesirable or negative. Bonhoeffer defines genuine transcendentalism as maintaining the logical transcendence of the subject *qua* subject to thinking. This transcendentalism is 'genuine', in that it maintains the thinking subject can never be merely an object of thought, because 'subjectivity is that from which any activity of thought proceeds'.[49] This means most basically that any attempt to view oneself as 'object' cannot posit an 'absolute identity' between the two, for there is a boundary to self-reflection (the logical transcendence of the subject *qua* subject), and so there is always a dimension of subjectivity preserved in 'hiddenness' from the reflecting 'I'. In Chapter 4 we shall ask whether there can therefore be a split between 'I and myself' which does not lead into the 'ambiguity' (*Zweideutigkeit*) of all-encompassing self-mastery assumed in *Discipleship*; a 'twoness' which, by preserving hiddenness, means that disciples might somehow self-reflect while still heeding the admonition about their life 'in Christ', that 'in the same moment I would desire to see it, I would lose it'.

2.2.3 'Simple obedience'

The following two loci of the unreflective simplicity of *Discipleship* are practically orientated and are therefore contrasted with reflection as a discernment of the best course of action, self-consciously making decisions through evaluating possible ends. The third locus of 'simple obedience' (*einfältiger Gehorsam*) works from Bonhoeffer's assertion that to be a disciple is to stand under the admonition 'simply go and obey' and to practise 'simple, literal obedience' to the commands of Christ.[50] Deeds of 'simple obedience' are deeds that follow immediately from the command of Christ, and this obedience is 'simple' (*einfältig*) in exhibiting 'unity' (*Einheit*) with the will of Jesus Christ: 'the call goes out, and without any further ado the obedient deed of the one called follows.'[51] Bonhoeffer considers Christ to ground deeds of simple obedience and, insofar as these deeds are not thereby decided on by any agent-centred reflective evaluation, they are unreflectively 'single-minded'. This singularity is a volitional oneness, like that Green refers to as a 'singleness of purpose', where the agent unreflectively performs Christ's will.

The volitional oneness of 'simple obedience' is contrasted by Bonhoeffer with a practically orientated reflective 'twoness', which is a 'twoness' between oneself and one's intended actions. In this case, an agent is 'split' from his or her options and reflectively surveys them in the process of discernment. In contrast to simply obeying the apparently 'clear' (*eindeutig*) commands of Christ, reflectively

---

49. Paul D. Janz, *God the Mind's Desire*, Cambridge: Cambridge University Press, 2008, 108–9.
50. DBWE4, 181.
51. DBWE5, 57.

evaluating how to proceed is presented as throwing a disciple into 'doubt' (*Zweifel*) about the best course of action. Of course this leads us to question whether reflecting practically always involves 'doubt', and when we examine *Ethics*, we shall see that Bonhoeffer does not wish to dismiss all reflective deliberation tout court, but rather asserts that reflectively discerning how to proceed can be included within the movement of obedience. For example, he claims that followers of Christ 'have to examine, observe, judge, weigh, [and] decide' what to do,[52] and, as mentioned in Chapter 1, he outlines the disposition of 'wisdom' in which decision-making is described as 'seeking to obtain the best possible information about a course of events' prior to acting.[53] In examples like these, it is clear that Bonhoeffer considers that reflective deliberation can come into play in obedience and that there is some way of maintaining the volitional oneness of simplicity while reflectively discerning how to proceed.

Moreover, there are grounds to claim that investigating how reflective deliberation can be coordinated with 'simple obedience' would amplify and extend Bonhoeffer's intentions elsewhere in *Ethics*, for situating obedience within what he terms the 'fullness of life' (*Fülle des Lebens*) and the 'flow of life' (*Fluß des Lebens*), terminology which will prove important in the later chapters of this book. In 'The "Ethical" and the "Christian" as a Topic', Bonhoeffer argues that ethicists have severely missed the mark by their preoccupation with the 'so-called ethical phenomenon' of 'the experience [*Erlebnis*] of the ought', described as a situation involving a 'fundamental decision between' good and evil. It is not that Bonhoeffer considers such moments unimportant, for he states that 'the ethical conflict and its resolution ... certainly has its necessary time and place'. However, through being preoccupied with this conflict, he claims we downplay the fact that life is for the most part faced with intractable difficulties and unassailable complexities in the 'twilight' of apparently limitless shades of grey in everyday existence, not just an overt option for either good or evil. He writes, 'it is something else to cope with the small issues of daily life ... with the countless cases' in which we are '"frustrated" by what is peripheral, trifling, contrary and irritating'.[54] He therefore wants to extend the notion of the ethical to include the ambiguities of concrete existence in daily life, and he claims that a failure to do this causes the 'significant loss' to ethics, of 'the fullness of life'.[55]

Given Bonhoeffer's concern for 'the fullness' and 'the flow of life',[56] which he presents as undermined by reducing understandings of the ethical to exceptional moments of choosing between good and evil, we must ask what this implies for the 'simple obedience' of *Discipleship*. This is because 'simple obedience' is described in *Discipleship* as involving an explicit choice – between 'disobedience

---

52. DBWE6, 320 (translation altered), 283.
53. Ibid., 81.
54. Ibid., 364–5.
55. Ibid., 369.
56. Ibid., 369, 381.

or obedience'[57] – and thereby exhibiting a black-and-white bipolarity which is reminiscent of the 'ethical conflict' he discusses in *Ethics*. Moreover, moments of 'simple obedience' in *Discipleship* seem to pertain to 'boundary situations' ('being plunged into absolute insecurity'), while in 'The "Ethical" and the "Christian" as a Topic' he states, 'Jesus Christ embraces not merely ... the boundaries' but 'the centre and the *Fülle des Lebens*'.[58] Given that limiting 'simple obedience' to moments of explicit, overt decision for obedience would therefore seem to hold it open to the criticisms Bonhoeffer makes of reducing the ethical to moments of explicit conflict, we are led to enquire into how 'simple obedience' can be broadened so it pertains *both* to the 'boundary' and to 'the centre' in the 'fullness of life',[59] and insofar as this 'fullness' is connected with 'what is peripheral, trifling, contrary and irritating' this clearly means that 'simple obedience' needs to be open to reflection in the manifold perplexities of life.[60]

Indeed, there are further indications that we should explore the relation between reflection and the 'fullness of life' later in this book, arising from the letter in which Bonhoeffer says that 'he can see the dangers' of *Discipleship*, but 'stands by' what he wrote. In this letter, we learn he wrote *Discipleship* at the 'end of [the] path' in which he thought he 'could learn to have faith by trying to live something like a saintly life'. He states, 'Later on I discovered ... that one only learns to have faith' by 'living fully in the midst of life's tasks, questions, successes and failures, experiences, and perplexities'.[61] This suggests Bonhoeffer came to see the value of situating obedience firmly in the 'fullness of life', amid 'life's tasks' and 'perplexities', and these must invariably involve reflective activity. Therefore, we will revisit these comments on the 'fullness' and the 'flow' of life, as they are closely related to the problematic of this book.

2.2.4 'Purity of heart'

In this final locus, Bonhoeffer iterates a more questionable dimension to practically orientated reflection, in that the reflective split between an agent and intended actions is seen as naturally linked with a desire to establish transparent warrants for action which provide a self-legitimizing sense of ethical security. Belonging to 'Christ alone', for Bonhoeffer, means not being reliant on any self-validation of one's deeds, and he describes this as 'not knowing good and evil'.[62] To act in the unreflective simplicity of 'not knowing good and evil', he claims, is to act in 'purity of heart', for insofar as one is not acting on the basis of a desire for self-legitimization, one is 'purely' (as in 'singularly'), focused on Christ.

57. DBWE4, 74.
58. DBWE6, 381.
59. See DBWE12, 369.
60. DBWE6, 364–5.
61. DBWE8, 486.
62. See DBWE4, 106–7.

Reflecting on how best to proceed not only disrupts a volitional oneness between the disciple and Christ, but is also presented as obviating authentic discipleship through its innate proclivity towards establishing apparently secure warrants for acting. Bonhoeffer speaks of reflection tearing disciples 'away' from 'from simple (*einfältig*) childlike obedience' and into 'double-minded thinking (*zweifältiges Denken*)'.[63] The 'double-mindedness' here is a deepening of the reflective 'twoness' between an agent and his or her intended actions, which comes about through the agent *measuring* Christ's commands according to autonomous criteria, which, in exhibiting two centres of orientation for action (agent-centred deliberation and Christ's command), further bifurcates the volitional oneness of unreflective 'simple obedience'. This of course leads us to ask whether or not we might reflect on an obedient response in a way that is not grounded on an autonomous measure of good and evil; if we can 'split' into the 'twoness' of reflectively discerning how to proceed, without entering into the 'double-minded thinking' of autonomous evaluation. Again, there are strong indications elsewhere in the corpus that Bonhoeffer's theology that affirms this possibility. We shall see in Chapter 6 that in *Ethics* he states that there is a 'searching after the will of God which is certainly legitimate and necessary'.[64] This must involve a 'split' into the twoness of agent and options, but in not being centred on the agent (searching after the will of *God*) would not involve 'double-minded thinking'.

2.3 Summing up

The foregoing analysis delineates four loci of the unreflective simplicity of *Discipleship*, each exhibiting a 'oneness' which is contrasted with an apparently negative reflective 'twoness'. In 'seeing only Christ', there is a oneness of 'intentionality' between the believer and Christ, contrasted with the differentiation of 'I and myself' in self-reflection, and in the 'hiddenness of the disciple', the 'twoness' of 'I and myself' is linked with a desire for self-possession. In 'simple obedience' a volitional unity with Christ is contrasted with the separation of an agent from his or her options, and in 'purity of heart' this separation is deepened by reflecting on how to proceed with autonomously validating criteria for action. However, we have also seen that Bonhoeffer does not condemn all reflection tout court elsewhere in the corpus. In *Act and Being*, he points towards modes of reflective activity that can maintain the oneness with Jesus of 'seeing only Christ' and the 'hiddenness of the disciple' while entering into the reflecting 'twoness' of 'I and myself'. In *Ethics*, he gestures towards understandings of the reflective 'twoness' between an agent and his or her options, which sustain 'simple obedience' and 'purity of heart'.

---

63. DBW4, 62.
64. DBWE6, 320.

We have now gained a more detailed understanding of why reflection is presented as negative in *Discipleship* and, moreover, ascertained that each apparently negative aspect is viewed more positively by Bonhoeffer elsewhere in the corpus. This points us forward to Chapters 4–6, where the elements of *Act and Being* and *Ethics* discussed above will be examined in detail. The foregoing discussion now enables us to present these four loci of the unreflective simplicity in *Discipleship*, not as outright condemnations of all reflection per se, but rather as pointing us to 'requirements' or 'conditions' for modes of reflective activity that may not obviate genuine discipleship. If we can self-reflect while maintaining 'seeing only Christ' and the 'hiddenness of the disciple', and reflect practically in 'simple obedience' and 'purity of heart', then we will have made important gains in answering to the challenge of the unreflective in Bonhoeffer's theology; retaining the essentially unreflective core of the human response to Christ without fragmenting our understanding of human subjectivity 'in Christ'. Moreover, our discussion has gleaned some potentially fruitful terminology for this task, in that Bonhoeffer identifies the need to work with the 'fullness' and the 'flow' of life, where we are faced with unassailable complexities, and which must therefore involve reflective activity. Before examining the elements from *Act and Being* and *Ethics* mentioned above, it is necessary first to survey the relevant secondary scholarship, so we can build on interpretations of the simplicity of *Discipleship*.

Chapter 3

INTERPRETING THE SIMPLICITY OF *DISCIPLESHIP*

By bringing the four loci of simplicity in *Discipleship* into dialogue with other parts of the Bonhoeffer corpus, we gained indications of how Bonhoeffer seems to accommodate modes of reflective activity 'in Christ', where the fundamental characteristic of each locus is maintained. We therefore formulated these characteristics as *requirements* for reflective activity, which, if met, will show how reflection need not preclude Christ's 'immediate, unconditional and inexplicable authority'. That is, self-reflecting while still 'seeing only Christ' and remaining 'hidden' from oneself, and reflecting practically while retaining 'simple obedience' and 'purity of heart', promise to maintain the centrality of Christ in simplicity, without denying the unavoidability and necessity of reflection for human life. The first step in investigating this further is to study the secondary scholarship on *Discipleship* and draw on the work of Bonhoeffer's commentators to utilize their findings.

3.1 *The reception of* Discipleship *as detour or reiteration*

An abridged English translation of *Nachfolge* was published as *The Cost of Discipleship* in 1948, some eleven years after the first German publication. In 1954, a selection of material from *Widerstand und Ergebung* (*Resistance and Submission*) was also published in English, as *Letters and Papers from Prison*. The apparent contrast between these two publications, six years apart, seemed to provide two different views of Bonhoeffer himself, and the dissonance between each has arguably contributed to the tensions that have characterized *Nachfolge*'s reception. De Gruchy suggests that the image of a 'saintly martyr' held by the first readership of *The Cost of Discipleship* was thrown into question by the challenging formulations found in the *Letters and Papers*, with phrases such as 'religionless Christianity'. He also comments on the initial 'Anglo-Saxon' reception of the Bonhoeffer of *The Cost of Discipleship* as a man of 'great faith, courage and sanctity' who 'died a martyr's death'. In contrast, an image of Bonhoeffer was fostered in the 1960s of a 'radical theologian', which 'caused major upset for those for whom the testimony of the saintly martyr had struck such a deep chord'.[1]

The contrast between the two characterizations of Bonhoeffer seems to have contributed to the book's reception, which has tended to fall into two camps, depending on the degree to which the commentators subscribe to the dissonance in question. These two camps are broadly resonant with Bonhoeffer's now familiar comment: 'I can see the dangers of that book, but I stand by what I wrote.' For those who detect a 'detour' in *Discipleship*, the emphasis is more on the 'dangers' of the book, while for those tending towards a continuous view of the corpus, the emphasis is on 'standing by' it. Those who take their primary lead from the Bonhoeffer of Tegel, most famously Hanfried Müller, consider *Discipleship* as the product of a 'detour',[2] in the sense that Bonhoeffer is seen as diverging in *Discipleship* from his earlier concerns in *Sanctorum Communio* and *Act and Being*, before revisiting those earlier concerns definitively in the *Ethics* and *Letters and Papers*. The detourists thus argue that on the way to the summation of his thinking in Tegel prison, he was sidetracked into ('dangerous') theological positions he would later recant, directly or indirectly. The second broad camp includes those who emphasize the homogeneity of the Bonhoefferian corpus and argue that Bonhoeffer's thinking exhibits developmental continuity and thematic unity. The introduction to the most recent translation of *Nachfolge*, for example, firmly 'stands by' the work, describing it as 'a reiteration, in some form, of almost everything Bonhoeffer has previously written', which 'far from being a detour' actually 'explains the steps' that led him from academia to imprisonment.[3] As specified in Chapter 1, our concern is to follow Bonhoeffer in both acknowledging the 'dangers' of the book and 'standing by' it, and so our study of *Discipleship*'s reception will examine the reasoning behind both responses to the book, to advance our attempt to follow Bonhoeffer's own two-sided stance to the book.

Before looking at these tensions, two preliminary remarks should be made. First, this chapter is focused primarily on English-language scholarship on *Discipleship*. This is because the problems with the book's reception have been particularly acute in the Anglo-American sphere, especially in the earlier decades of Bonhoeffer scholarship, following the success of John Robinson's *Honest to God*, which fostered an image of Bonhoeffer that was deeply inimical to the impression given by *Discipleship*.[4] Although Robinson's interpretation is almost unanimously accepted now as a creative misreading, the apparent gulf between *Letters and Papers* and *Discipleship* which he helped to foster characterized Bonhoeffer interpretation for some time. The second preliminary remark is that the tension between unreflective and reflective in *Discipleship* has not tended to be the primary focus of many of Bonhoeffer's commentators. This is partly because this problematic is not

---

1. John W. de Gruchy, *Daring, Trusting Spirit*, London: SCM Press, 2005, 118, 138.
2. Bethge, 'Challenge', 44, 64–5.
3. Geoffrey B. Kelly and John D. Godsey, in DBWE4, 17, 21.
4. Robinson, *Honest to God*, see 64ff.

something centrally thematized by Bonhoeffer himself, and also because the main concern of Bonhoeffer research in the decades immediately following his death was the relationship between the church and world, so *Discipleship*'s ecclesiology and alleged unworldliness dominated its academic reception. Nonetheless, matters related to the four loci we met in Chapters 1 and 2 do arise in these discussions, albeit not always explicitly, but at least as subsidiary elements which we shall draw out chronologically in the following section.

3.2 The trajectory of interpreting the simplicity of Discipleship

3.2.1 Eberhard Bethge: 'The Challenge of Dietrich Bonhoeffer's Theology' (1967)

3.2.1.1 Background and overview The term 'detour' originates from a reference made by Hanfried Müller, in his 1956 work *Von der Kirche zur Welt*.[5] Müller uses the term with reference to Bonhoeffer's *Life Together*, but in his Alden-Tuthill lecture from 1961 (published in 1967) Bethge extends the term by referring as 'detourists' to those who sought both to downplay the significance of all Bonhoeffer's mid-1930s writings, especially *Discipleship*, and to emphasize instead the 1940s writings.[6] Before examining Bethge's 'Challenge' lecture directly, it is necessary to point out that the first full-length theological analysis of Bonhoeffer in English is Godsey's *The Theology of Dietrich Bonhoeffer*. The 'detourist' debate had begun in German scholarship, between Müller and Bethge, although Müller's book had not yet been published in translation. Godsey's work responds by iterating the homogeneity and cohesiveness of the corpus, using a tripartite classification of Bonhoeffer's development. The first period from *Sanctorum Communio* to 1933 he terms 'theological foundation', the second of 1933–39 'theological application', and the third period 'theological fragmentation'.[7] As these subheadings suggest, Godsey does not see any break, or shift, between the first and second periods.[8] He states that *Discipleship* is 'a reiteration, in some form or another, of almost everything the author had hitherto written',[9] a statement reproduced almost verbatim in the introduction to the 2001 translation of *Nachfolge* he co-edited.[10] While Godsey acknowledges that the key issue for Bonhoeffer scholarship is the relation between the first two periods and the third, he presents a case that, viewed thematically, the corpus is unified. He undertakes this by arguing that Bonhoeffer's Christology is the 'unifying element' binding the body of work together,[11] stating

---

5. Müller, *Von der Kirche zur Welt*.
6. Bethge, 'Challenge', 52.
7. John D. Godsey, *The Theology of Dietrich Bonhoeffer*, London: SCM Press, 1960, 80.
8. Ibid., 51.
9. Ibid., 151.
10. DBWE4, 17.
11. Godsey, *Theology*, 261.

that it is Bonhoeffer's *understanding* of the revelation of God in Jesus Christ which develops' and 'thus provides the real clue to his development'.[12] Three periods of Bonhoeffer's work are then classified as, first, an exposition of 'Jesus as the revelational reality of the church'; secondly, 'Jesus Christ as the Lord of the Church'; and thirdly, 'Jesus Christ as the Lord of the World'.[13]

Godsey thus uses Christology to maintain continuity between Bonhoeffer's views on the relationship between the church and world, but he does not touch on the unreflective–reflective problematic. Godsey does discuss what Bonhoeffer calls 'the hidden character of the Christian life' in *Discipleship*, which might seem related to our concern with the 'hiddenness of the disciple'; he connects this hiddenness with the concept of the 'arcane discipline', which is prominent in the prison writings.[14] He considers the arcane discipline to offer continuity between the second and third periods, but, beyond broad thematic resonances surrounding the concept of 'hiddenness', there is no fundamental link between the *disciplina arcani* and the hiddenness of the 'I' to self-reflection, because the former is not concerned with self-reflective hiddenness, but with preserving aspects of Christian life and practice as hidden – particularly the exposition of the Creed, for example.[15] For this reason, we can leave Godsey's discussion of hiddenness aside and focus on Bethge.

In 'The Challenge of Dietrich Bonhoeffer's Theology', Bethge gives an overview of Bonhoeffer's theology, and he seeks to establish continuity between the work of 1933–39 and the 1940s.[16] Like Godsey, Bethge offers a threefold scheme for Bonhoeffer's work, the first period as 'foundation', the second as 'concentration', and the third as 'liberation'.[17] He states that he wants to challenge those who see the years after 1933 as 'a detour', specifically in the sense of being 'an unpleasant and legalistic narrowing of the pass, producing fundamentalists of a sort'.[18] Bethge points to individual examples of continuity to make his point. Two of these impinge on the unreflective–reflective tension, and will be discussed in the following two subsections, and each functions for Bethge in showing that the period of 'concentration' is not a 'temporary aberration' but is rooted in themes which occur earlier.[19]

3.2.1.2 *'The child' in* Act and Being Bethge's citing of conceptualities that are suggestive of continuity does not involve a detailed discussion of each, they are essentially mere pointers. The first of these, 'the child' in *Act and Being*, certainly

---

12. Ibid., 265.
13. Ibid., 266.
14. See DBWE8, 364–5, 373.
15. DBWE14, 554–6.
16. Bethge, 'Challenge', 48–50.
17. Ibid., 22, 44, 70.
18. Ibid., 44.
19. Ibid., 50.

seems to provide a direct resonance with the simplicity of *Discipleship*. The child arises at the end of the *Habilitationsschrift* and points to a disposition whereby the believer is caught up in beholding Christ with no sense of a past, and thus replicating the simple, direct awareness of a child.[20] To speak of a 'pure orientation to Christ', with no awareness of the past, is reminiscent of the first two cognitive loci discussed in Chapter 2: 'seeing only Christ' (being caught up in beholding Christ) and the 'hiddenness of the disciple' (one's past as 'hidden'). Bethge thus provides a valuable indication that in seeking to understand the simplicity of *Discipleship*, we should look closely at *Act and Being*'s 'the child'.

However, calling to mind our discussion of 'seeing only Christ' and the 'hiddenness of the disciple' in Chapter 2, it is worth noting that Bethge makes no mention of Bonhoeffer's 'transcendental attempt' from Section A of *Act and Being*, where we found resonances with these loci of the simplicity of *Discipleship*. It was in the 'transcendental attempt' that the *actus directus* is described as simply 'directed at' (*gerichtet auf*)[21] its object, so the subject 'sees' only that object, and where Bonhoeffer criticizes the allegedly full possession of the subject by the self-reflective gaze in 'post-Kantian idealism'. Bethge's interpretation of the simplicity of *Discipleship* makes recourse only to the theological Section C of *Act and Being* and not the philosophically orientated Section A. When he speaks of 'deadly reflection', he is offsetting reflection only with direct consciousness as *faith*, stating the 'the *believing* ego must not reflect', for that 'kills faith'.[22] However, this book contends that the simplicity of *Discipleship* has philosophical resonances that are worthy of further investigation, and so we shall note here that this can be taken as an omission of some potentially important material for this book's concerns.

3.2.1.3 Reflection as 'bedevilled' in Creation and Fall Bethge also claims there is a foreshadowing of *Discipleship* in *Creation and Fall*'s (1933) discussion of what Bethge terms the 'bedevilled nature' of reflection.[23] There are certainly elements of *Creation and Fall* that are directly reminiscent of the simplicity of *Discipleship*. For example, Bonhoeffer discusses the 'unity' and 'unbroken obedience'[24] of prelapsarian humanity, and states that after the Fall, Adam and Eve undergo a 'split' (*Zwiespalt*) and are thrust into 'disunion' (*Entzweiung*).[25] He therefore connects the twoness of *Zwiespalt* and *Entzweiung* with the 'knowledge of good and evil', which we have seen in Chapter 1 is explicitly connected in *Ethics* with reflection. Bonhoeffer also points to a connection between the dividedness of 'knowing good and evil' with self-centred autonomy, claiming that with the

---

20. DBWE2, 157f.
21. DBW2, 23.
22. Bethge, 'Challenge', 36 (my italics).
23. Ibid., 50.
24. DBWE3, 113, 98.
25. Ibid., 88.

knowledge of good and evil, humankind is 'acting out of its own resources' and is 'lord of its own world'.[26]

However, in *Creation and Fall* the link between the twoness of *Zwiespalt* with *reflection* itself is much more tangential than in *Ethics*. Bonhoeffer does speak generally in the earlier work about 'thinking'; claiming that 'with all their powers of thinking' fallen human beings are 'tied to [the] torn apart world [of knowing good and evil], to antithesis, to contradiction',[27] but this is not drawn out in terms of self-reflection and practical discernment of how to proceed. For this reason, our enquiry will concentrate primarily on *Ethics* in our pursuit of modes of reflection that can sustain 'simple obedience' and 'purity of heart'.

In summary of Bethge's discussion, we have an example of 'standing by' *Discipleship*, by citing thematic convergences with other elements of the corpus, which challenges the 'detourists' by implying that the 'dangers' of the book should not be seen as 'unpleasant' and 'producing fundamentalists', but as the result of a 'concentration' on themes that occur earlier in the trajectory of Bonhoeffer's thought.[28] It is worth noting here that approaching the apparent exclusivity of unreflective simplicity over reflective wisdom in *Discipleship* as a 'concentration' perhaps offers a way to 'stand by' the challengingly 'dangerous' assertions without taking them as absolute and total for the entirety of Christian life; to 'concentrate' on a certain ('dangerous') aspect of life (the unreflective) does not inherently preclude this aspect of life being seen as continuous with other aspects (the reflective), and so we shall revisit this approach to *Discipleship* as a 'concentration' in the subsequent chapters.[29]

3.2.2 Clifford J. Green: The Theology of Sociality (First Edition 1972)

3.2.2.1 Overview Between Bethge's lecture and Clifford Green's work, the former published a key historical–biographical work: *Dietrich Bonhoeffer: Theologian, Christian, Man for his Times*.[30] In his book, Bethge discusses a personal event in Bonhoeffer's life, which characterizes Green's interpretation in a way that touches on the apparent unsustainability of 'simple obedience' discussed in Chapter 2, for challenging assertions, such as 'my own will … must be killed' in following Christ,[31] are explained by Green with this personal event. In the biography, Bethge

26. Ibid., 113, 142.
27. Ibid., 92.
28. Bethge, 'Challenge', 50.
29. See Chapter 12, Section 4.
30. Between Bethge and Green was John A. Phillips's *The Form of Christ in the World: A Study of Bonhoeffer's Christology*, London: Collins, 1967. This does not mention the themes of this book, but Phillips provides one of the most stridently 'detourist' interpretations, arguing that Bonhoeffer's earlier interests were 'discarded' at Finkenwalde, where he exhibits 'sectarian overtones' (110).
31. DBWE4, 154.

shows that many of themes of *Discipleship* were already high on Bonhoeffer's agenda before the church struggle took hold in 1933, and he concludes that *Discipleship* 'arose out of the course of development that Bonhoeffer had been pursuing long before' the *Kirchenkampf*.[32] He considers this course of development to have been instigated by 'something [which] occurred' in Bonhoeffer's 'personal life ... that it is hard for us to see clearly, though its effects are plain'.[33] This refers to a marked point of deepening and enrichment in Bonhoeffer's faith and sense of personal calling, which Bonhoeffer himself refers to subsequently as 'becoming a Christian' or 'turning from the phraseological to the real'.[34] This event is generally thought among commentators to show itself in the more devotional tenor and increasingly biblical focus of his writings from *Creation and Fall* onwards. Bethge's views on these events thus give more basis to his earlier statement that *Discipleship* is not merely an 'aberration'.[35] Green's 1972 book is deeply influenced by Bethge's biography, and, relevant for our purposes, he argues that 'simple obedience' is fundamentally rooted in the personal event Bethge describes.

Green's work is focused on what he terms 'the theology of sociality'. It need only be briefly summarized, to show how it contributes to a homogeneous reading of the corpus. Green works from an opening statement to *Sanctorum Communio*, which he considers programmatic for the corpus *in toto*: 'The more theologians have considered the significance of the sociological category for theology, the more clearly the social intention of all the basic Christian concepts has emerged.' These basic concepts include '"Person", "primal state", "sin", and revelation"' which are seen as 'fully understandable only in relation to sociality'.[36] By presenting this as 'programmatic'[37] for all of Bonhoeffer's work, Green broadly challenges the 'detourists', through highlighting an underlying, continuous concern and pattern of thinking, in which Bonhoeffer consistently presents basic theological items of concern – like 'revelation' or 'sin' – as properly understood only through their inherent embeddedness in human interrelatedness. He thus claims that *Discipleship* '*adds* to' the theology of sociality, and '*presupposes* it',[38] indicating his general stance towards the corpus as continuous, a stance which has continued to develop in the work of many commentators until the present day. However, Green's general move in this direction is arguably not fully borne out, as his reading of some aspects of *Discipleship* still leave it sitting relatively awkwardly within the corpus as a whole.

---

32. Eberhard Bethge, *Dietrich Bonhoeffer: Theologian, Christian, Man for His Times*, Minneapolis: Fortress Press, 2000, 159.
33. Ibid., 130.
34. DBWE14, 134; DBWE8, 358.
35. Bethge, *Bonhoeffer*, 377.
36. DBWE1, 21.
37. Green, *Sociality*, 1. Green's 1972 original was revised and republished in 1999.
38. Ibid., 3 (original italics).

3.2.2.2 'Simple obedience' and the abrogation of the will Green is orientated by what he terms 'the autobiographical dimension', giving significant emphasis to the 'turning point' in Bonhoeffer's self-understanding, calling it 'a personal liberation' which results in an 'existential commitment to faith and the church'.[39] He then argues that this event explains certain problems he finds in *Discipleship*, problems which touch on one of our practical loci of simplicity: simple obedience. Green states that *Discipleship* is 'the direct theological expression'[40] of the turning point Bonhoeffer underwent, which is described as Bonhoeffer turning from cultivating his own ego strengths (ambition, learning, and influence over others) to submitting to Christ's will and seeking to serve the church.[41] This alleged submission to the will of Christ leads Green to interpret *Discipleship* as indicative of a personal struggle in which Christ is the dominant victor. For this reason, he claims *Discipleship* is stipulated on a 'power Christ',[42] whereby disciples are commanded to submit their egos to the domineering force of Jesus. This immediately calls to mind the challenging statements from *Discipleship* aforementioned, that 'my own will ... must die, must be killed' in following Christ.[43]

Green questions Bonhoeffer's emphasis on a 'power Christ', by arguing that he had not learned to distinguish healthy ego strength from selfish, domineering ego strength. The result is that Christ dominates the autonomous ego completely in *Discipleship*, and the disciple is ultimately violated. The Christ of *Discipleship* is thus presented 'as a mighty *power* who defeats the strong self-will of the powerful, autonomous human ego'. But Green argues that had Bonhoeffer distinguished between human 'dominating power' and 'mature strength', he would not have made this error and would not have 'unwittingly' negated positive human 'strength as well as self-serving power'.[44] Green undergirds his argument by drawing on the prison theology, where we find an affirmation of the strength of human maturity, approached Christologically.[45] This is taken by Green as a theological affirmation of the value of 'healthy ego qualities', which need not be 'overruled' by Christ, and which, in being affirmed, can avoid the danger of violating the human in following Christ.

Green claims this tension in *Discipleship* is indicative of Bonhoeffer's inner conflict: 'he is overreacting against his own past', we read, in an internal 'power struggle'.[46] He connects this with what he considers violent language in the text, such as Bonhoeffer's reference to Christ as an 'angry power', of humans being 'subdued'

---

39. Ibid., 3, 40.
40. Ibid., 3.
41. Ibid., 39f.
42. Ibid., 40.
43. DBWE4, 154.
44. Green, *Sociality*, 195.
45. DBWE8, 366–7.
46. Green, *Sociality*, 197. Green also highlights an apparent contradictoriness between the 'power Christ' who dominates the self-willed disciple, and a Christ of 'weakness', in *Discipleship*.

(*überwinden*) by grace, and being the salt of the earth or being 'annihilated' (*vernichten*), and of Christ (and the church) engaging in 'hand-to-hand combat' with the world.⁴⁷ The rootedness of *Discipleship*'s challenging formulations in Bonhoeffer's personal 'power struggle' lead him to argue that the book is – in this particular respect – an 'unfruitful digression' which interrupts the otherwise clear connection between the 'early theology of sociality and that of the *Letters*'.⁴⁸

Green's evaluation presents us with a problem, connected to the unreflective– reflective problematic. Green accounts for the uncompromising elements ('dangers') of *Discipleship* – which are closely related to the challenging statements we connected to the unreflective in Chapters 1 and 2 – by denying their worth as valid theological formulations, seeing them instead as an unfortunate consequence of personal factors.⁴⁹ However, Bonhoeffer's concern for simplicity endures beyond *Discipleship*, and in *Ethics*, for example, his discussions still feature language that Green might class as domineering. For example, he speaks of an 'overcoming [*Aufhebung*]' by Christ, where there is 'no room for application and interpretation, but only for obedience or disobedience', and in which moreover, human beings renounce 'any self-justification', which would include, presumably, justifying oneself on the basis of Green's 'healthy ego strengths'.⁵⁰ We can therefore conclude that Bonhoeffer's 'dangerous' assertions in *Discipleship* have theological substance for Bonhoeffer and cannot be explained solely by an internal 'power struggle'. Because Green sidelines the challenging assertions of *Discipleship* (notwithstanding his broader contribution to establishing the continuity of the corpus), we shall be led to investigate Bonhoeffer's comments on 'simple obedience' in *Ethics* in Chapter 6, to seek resources enabling us to 'stand by' *Discipleship* more effectively.

3.2.3 *Ernst Feil: The Theology of Dietrich Bonhoeffer (1985)*

3.2.3.1 Overview Ernst Feil's monograph is widely recognized as one of the most important contributions to the field.⁵¹ His overall aim, like Green and Bethge, is to counter the view that there is a significant break in Bonhoeffer's thinking, which he claims 'represents a sustained unity'.⁵² As with Green, Feil's study is best understood in relation to Bethge's biography, for, as Feil's translator Martin Rumscheidt states, it is intended to be the biography's 'theological complement'.⁵³ This section will show that Feil continues in the same direction as Green, by moving towards continuity, and introduces a new mode of argumentation, which we have

---

47. Ibid., 198.
48. Ibid., 329.
49. Ibid., 338: 'What Marx and Freud long ago saw about the roots of thought in social and psychic life has now come to roost in the nests of the theologians.'
50. Ibid., 40.
51. See Plant, *Bonhoeffer*, 153.
52. Feil, *Bonhoeffer*, xx.
53. Martin Rumscheidt, in Feil, *Bonhoeffer*, xii.

touched upon in Chapter 1 and to which we will return in Chapter 12: using a particular 'couplet' or 'duality' as a hermeneutical key for unifying the corpus; in this case, the *actus directus* and *reflectus*. However, it will also be shown below that Feil seems to downplay the theological substance of *Discipleship*, perhaps through considering it primarily as a devotional text, and – like the other commentators we have covered – he does not give any attention to the 'transcendental attempt' in seeking to amplify *Discipleship*, despite the fact that his primary hermeneutical key of the *actus* distinction is actually first made by Bonhoeffer at precisely this juncture of *Act and Being*.

To give an overview of Feil's centralizing of the *actus* distinction, we should bear in mind that he sees the theology of the prison letters arising from preoccupations of Bonhoeffer's which can be detected at the outset of his academic career: namely, his concern to challenge the legacy of German idealism in theology, which was still extant to some degree in the Berlin milieu in which Bonhoeffer trained. Feil observes this concern manifesting primarily in Bonhoeffer's need to 'define the relation of praxis and theory'. He states that Bonhoeffer was 'convinced that he came out of a tradition' which was unable to accommodate this distinction 'on account of a false (idealistic) hermeneutic'.[54] He goes on to present the distinction between the *actus directus* and *reflectus* as indicative of an overarching concern to place 'praxis', 'faith' or 'life' (*actus directus*) at the centre of theology as opposed to 'thought' and 'reflection' (*actus reflectus*).[55] As we have seen in Chapter 1, broadly applying a 'creative formula' or particular 'opposing pair' for interpreting the Bonhoefferian corpus has been taken up by commentators since Feil, and his contribution to the field is therefore of considerable importance. However, when we look at the detail of his argument, and the implied approach to the simplicity of *Discipleship* therein, we are presented with a two-sided omission, which is both theological and philosophical.

3.2.3.2 Omitting the theological subtext to Discipleship In Part One of Feil's book, there are grounds to argue that he downplays the specifically theological subtext to *Discipleship*, a subtext we have seen both Godsey and Bethge seek to highlight, seeming to stand closer to René Marlé, who calls the book 'a sermon'.[56] Feil discusses 'praxis' at length, with very scant reference to *Discipleship*, although *Discipleship* is generally acknowledged as the place where Bonhoeffer's practical concerns are utterly central. As Part One focuses on methodology, his key text is *Act and Being*. He highlights the connection between the *actus directus/reflectus* distinction, and Bonhoeffer's description of 'knowing as believer' (which is 'act' or praxis), on the one hand, and 'knowing in preaching/theological knowledge' (which is reflection), on the other.[57] He then goes on to argue that this distinction

---

54. Ibid., 5 (original parentheses).
55. Ibid.
56. René Marlé, *Bonhoeffer: The Man and His Work*, New York: Newman Press, 1968, 75.
57. Ibid., 14.

undergirds Bonhoeffer's approach to theology as an academic discipline and argues convincingly that the *actus directus* lies at the basis of theology for Bonhoeffer, with the *actus reflectus* as a secondary movement, able only to approximate to the genuine encounter with Christ of the *actus directus* and never lay full claim over it. A similar point is made by Hans-Jürgen Abromeit, who states that for Bonhoeffer, 'thought is always poorer than life'.[58] That is, theology (as reflective) is seen as secondary to the more primary 'believing way of knowing',[59] which reflection should therefore never ground or replace. Feil thus holds that the *actus* distinction is 'an essential indicator of how Bonhoeffer understands things', being 'clearly present in his entire work and therefore ... at the very centre of his theology'.[60]

Despite the value of Feil's contribution to Bonhoeffer scholarship, he neglects to draw out the implications of his centralizing of the *actus* distinction for interpreting the simplicity of *Discipleship*, which we have seen is closely related to it. If the *actus directus*, the believing way of knowing, and its broad analogue 'praxis' are understood as foundational, fundamental and irremovably central to Bonhoeffer's oeuvre, then this leads naturally to the view that *Discipleship*, with its strong resonances with the theological *actus directus* (as acknowledged by numerous commentators[61]), is similarly deeply significant for the corpus as whole. The scarcity of Feil's references to *Discipleship* in Part One of his study thus feels at times like a significant omission. He mentions that, for Bonhoeffer, 'knowledge which mediates God's word is dependent ... upon obedience, and not vice-versa', that 'action' takes primacy over 'word', that 'theology has as its basis discipleship and its task is to give expression to that discipleship', and finally the assertion that 'what is paradigmatic in Bonhoeffer' is that 'he both experienced and thought about discipleship as the heart of faith in its nonmanipulative character'.[62] Yet, in with these statements there is no discussion of the simplicity of *Discipleship* and its connection to the *actus directus*. We can conclude, then, that Feil omits to give full weight to the importance of the simplicity of *Discipleship* in Bonhoeffer's thought, although his analysis would seem to imply this as an obvious corollary.[63]

3.2.3.3 Omitting the philosophical subtext to Discipleship The omission of the theological subtext of *Discipleship* is related to another omission in Feil, in that the *actus* distinction is not first made by Bonhoeffer with reference to theological methodology, but arises in his discussion of transcendental *philosophy*. Although

---

58. Hans-Jürgen Abromeit, *Das Geheimnis Christi*, Neukirchen-Vluyn: Neukirchener Verlag, 1991, 11.

59. DBWE2, 126.

60. Feil, *Bonhoeffer*, 29.

61. For example DBWE4, 150 (n169).

62. Feil, *Bonhoeffer*, 50, 49, 24, 53.

63. Feil does discuss *Discipleship* at length in Part Two, but not the unreflective–reflective issues, and focuses on Christology, while interpreting the book largely as pertaining to issues of 'praxis' (78).

Feil makes the *actus* distinction absolutely central, he makes no mention of the fact that the distinction originates in the philosophical Section A of *Act and Being*. Although the terminology of *actus directus* and *actus reflectus* was borrowed by Bonhoeffer from a piece of Lutheran dogmatics, his discussion of it is initially conducted in a purely philosophical framework.[64] Bonhoeffer does of course extend the notion theologically, but Feil sidesteps the philosophical origin of the distinction entirely. He describes the distinction in terms of being between 'faith and reflection' and related to Bonhoeffer's seeking 'to discern "the interrelation of *belief* as act and *revelation* as being"'.[65] This is of course correct for Section B of *Act and Being*, but not the philosophical Section A, as we saw in Chapter 2. Feil thus joins Bethge in interpreting the *actus* distinction purely theologically, when its genealogy would seem somewhat broader, thus providing further impetus to examine Section A of *Act and Being* in Chapter 4, to discern if the simplicity of *Discipleship* would benefit from being brought into dialogue with the passage in question.

3.2.4 Michael DeJonge's Bonhoeffer's Theological Formation *(2012)*

In this section, we make a sizeable chronological leap from Feil (1985) to our next interlocutor, Michael DeJonge (2012). Scholarship on *Discipleship* remained largely unchanged for the two decades after Green's and Feil's work, as is shown in an essay by de Gruchy from 1987, which summarizes the debates surrounding the work in a way which could have been written in the mid-1970s.[66] Nonetheless, this section demonstrates that the field has now changed somewhat, through a continuation of the moves towards continuity and 'standing by' the book instigated by Bethge and Godsey, then extended by Green and Feil, along with an increased awareness of the detail of *Discipleship*'s relatedness to the theology of *Act and Being*. Valuable moves in this direction were made in 1996 with Charles Marsh's *Reclaiming Dietrich Bonhoeffer*. Marsh sets out to reclaim Bonhoeffer 'for contemporary theological inquiry'[67] and focuses on his 'use of philosophy', which, he claims, has been granted 'precious little scholarly attention'.[68] In this regard, Marsh gestures towards an approach to *Discipleship* which is promising for this book. He takes issue with those who have construed *Discipleship* (and *Life Together*) as 'pietistic and naïve',[69] maintaining that there is a 'complex theological grammar' to these books, with 'important subtextual discussions with Bonhoeffer's philosophical

---

64. DBWE2, 28.
65. Feil, *Bonhoeffer*, 10.
66. John de Gruchy, 'The Development of Bonhoeffer's Theology', in John de Gruchy (ed.), *Dietrich Bonhoeffer: Witness to Jesus Christ*, London: Collins, 1987, 1–42 (7–8).
67. Charles Marsh, *Reclaiming Dietrich Bonhoeffer*, Oxford: Oxford University Press, 1994, vii.
68. Ibid., ix, n6.
69. Ibid., x.

conversation partners'.⁷⁰ Notwithstanding the promise of these statements for our concerns, Marsh does not give *Discipleship* sustained attention.⁷¹ Nonetheless, Marsh's indication of a 'complex theological grammar' to *Discipleship* perhaps aptly summarizes the more recent work of Christiane Tietz, Michael DeJonge and Florian Schmitz, upon whom we shall now focus in this section.

Before examining DeJonge directly, it is necessary to mention a commentator who highlights what we might term a 'complex theological grammar' to *Discipleship*, and whose work DeJonge himself builds on, Christiane Tietz. In a 2005 paper, Tietz argues that the aphorism 'only the believers obey, only the obedient believe' formally and structurally parallels the coordination of 'act' and 'being' in Section B of the *Habilitationschrift*. Act in this context means the act of faith, and being refers to the continuity of a 'haveability'⁷² to faith, in which one's believing is an enduring facet of the self. The problem, as Tietz describes it elsewhere, is whether the apprehension of revelation (believing as act) is 'merely something that happens again and again' and is therefore 'unstable', or pertains to being, so that believing constitutes something 'lasting' and 'determinate' in one's self-understanding.⁷³ In *Act and Being* Bonhoeffer presents 'being in Christ in the church' as coordinating both sides to this duality, arguing that the church provides a 'haveable' continuity for the believer, which presupposes the act of faith; while at the same time, the act of faith presupposes being in the church, where one is brought 'again and again' to believing. Tietz argues that this relationship of mutual interdependence is mirrored, in part, by the relationship between believing and obeying in Bonhoeffer's aphorism in *Discipleship*, in that to believe, she claims, Bonhoeffer argues that followers of Christ must obey, and yet to obey he argues they must believe. A full critical evaluation of Tietz's work is beyond the scope of this chapter, but it should be noted that she points to the considerable theological depth to *Discipleship* hitherto only gestured towards by Godsey, Bethge and Marsh, and somewhat neglected by Feil.

Michael DeJonge builds on Tietz's work in his monograph *Bonhoeffer's Theological Formation*, which takes the 'oppositional pair' of 'act' and 'being' and – as we have seen – uses their coordination in Bonhoeffer's 'distinctive concept of person' as the hermeneutical key for the whole corpus. As regards *Discipleship*, specifically, he is in broad agreement with Tietz on the structural parallels between

---

70. Ibid.
71. Marsh's almost total omission of *Discipleship* from his analysis is striking. For example, in a discussion of 'the call of the disciple' in Mk 8:34 and Lk. 9:23, both of which are key texts in *Discipleship*, the book itself is not mentioned, and Marsh states that we are not to see 'the voice of Jesus' as 'the subjection of the ego of the disciple', without reference to *Discipleship*, although this is precisely the sort of language we find there. Ibid., 144.
72. See '*habbar*', DBW2, 85.
73. Tietz, *Widerstand*, 27–8.

the coordination of act and being and the believing–obedience aphorism.[74] DeJonge claims that the aphorism is intended to challenge two misconstruals of the relationship between faith and works, which he calls 'legalism' and 'pseudo-Lutheranism'. The former could also be termed 'works righteousness', the view that by performing certain deeds (obedience) one is made righteous, which, as he puts it, 'reduces faith to the result of humanly possible works',[75] bringing it within human capacities. 'Pseudo-Lutheranism' could be approached using Bonhoeffer's term 'cheap grace', which refers to the prioritizing of Christ's unmerited redemptive work by faith alone to such a degree that obedience becomes 'peripheral to faith'.[76] DeJonge argues that, just as 'faith is the precondition of being in the church, and being in the church is the precondition of faith' in *Act and Being*, in the *Discipleship* the aphorism 'a situation (being [obedient]) that makes faith (act) possible, … is simultaneously made possible by faith'.[77] With both Tietz and DeJonge, then, a move towards uncovering the theological depth of *Discipleship* is perceptible, thus further demonstrating that *Discipleship* does not constitute a 'detour', and can be 'stood by'.

However, if we seek to apply DeJonge's analysis to the unreflective–reflective problematic, we encounter an issue similar to that touched upon in our discussion of his work in Chapter 1. It will be recalled that DeJonge's presentation of Christ as a unity between act and being that 'solves' the opposition was seen as veering towards synthesis, whereas we are taking our lead from Bethge's comment about a 'oneness established by Christ', which is 'neither synthesis nor diastasis'. DeJonge veers towards synthesis in his analysis of the *Discipleship* aphorism, by arguing that the call of Christ creates both believing and obeying, and so 'Bonhoeffer's own theological thinking works to get back behind this split by attention to the person of Christ as a logically prior unity'.[78] Moreover, he connects this with a hermeneutical methodology, which he associates with Wilhelm Dilthey. He claims that Bonhoeffer's work exhibits a Diltheyan 'thought-form', in seeking to 'interpret parts in terms of the whole',[79] in this case the 'whole' as the unity of Christ, and the parts as 'believing' and 'obeying'. DeJonge's application of Dilthey's thought to Bonhoeffer's theology will be covered in Chapter 8, but here the point needs to be made that, in locating the 'whole' or the 'unity' between opposing pairs through what he describes as getting 'back behind' the 'split' to something 'logically prior'

---

74. They differ on the interpretation of the 'first step', for Tietz argues that there is a shift from *Act and Being* to *Discipleship*, as in the former, entering what she terms the 'circle' of mutual presupposition (of act and being) is entirely passive, whereas in *Discipleship* the disciple must make the 'first step', but DeJonge counters that this 'step' still presupposes faith. Cf. DeJonge, *Formation*, 132–3, n11.

75. Ibid., 132.

76. Ibid.

77. Ibid., 133.

78. Ibid., 135–6.

79. Ibid., 9.

to the opposition, he threatens to veer, again, towards synthesis. That is, if we were to apply this 'logically prior' unity of Christ to the unreflective and reflective, we would not be acknowledging the 'dangers' of *Discipleship*, for the uncompromising stance towards the interrelation of the two in the book would be undermined.

Before summing up this chapter, there is one remaining commentator to mention – Florian D. Schmitz – who has written the only monograph focused almost entirely on *Discipleship*: *Nachfolge: Zur Theologie Dietrich Bonhoeffers*. Schmitz's text is impressive, and a full evaluation of it is beyond the scope of this project, insofar as he does not thematize the unreflective–reflective problematic, although we shall draw on some elements of his work in Chapter 6. Here, we need only point to one of his key aims in the book, as indicative (along with Tietz and DeJonge) of a general move towards continuity in recent years, and more specifically, his way of 'standing by' *Nachfolge*. Schmitz sets out to argue that the understandings of the world in *Discipleship* and *Ethics* are essentially continuous and harmonious, against much secondary interpretation, which – as we have seen – has often posited a certain unworldliness in the former. He highlights that this unworldliness is often connected by commentators with Bonhoeffer's comments about *Discipleship* being written at 'the end of the way',[80] and argues convincingly to the contrary that in both works, 'Christ is the redeemer of the *whole* world, which demands from Christians a life *in the world*'.[81] What is particularly distinctive about Schmitz's approach is that he argues against the notion there was an 'exclusivization' (*Exklusivierung*) of Christ and his followers to something limited to the 'space of the church-community', but rather a way which focused on the 'purity' of the church community, and this was the 'way' Bonhoeffer reached the end of, before entering the conspiracy. His second key aim beyond joining *Discipleship* and *Ethics* together is to offer a closely contextual reading of Bonhoeffer's theological development in moving away from this 'purity'. As is evident from the foregoing, the unreflective–reflective problematic is not his concern, but it is worth noting that – in pointing to the 'inner connection' (*inneren Verbindung*) of *Discipleship* and *Ethics* – we are given further impetus to examine *Ethics* in Chapter 6, to see if this 'inner connection' might be applicable to our concerns in this book.

3.3 Summing up

We can now situate our examination of the unreflective–reflective problematic in relation to the work of the commentators discussed in this chapter. First, because the two cognitive loci of 'seeing only Christ' and the 'hiddenness of the disciple' have largely evaded explicit analysis in terms of the resonances with

---

80. DBWE8, 486.
81. Florian Schmitz, *Nachfolge: Zur Theologie Dietrich Bonhoeffers*, Göttingen: Vandenhoeck & Ruprecht, 2013, 14 (my translation).

the 'transcendental attempt' highlighted in Chapter 2, the need for a detailed study of this section of *Act and Being* has been intensified with the foregoing analysis. Secondly, because Bethge, Tietz and DeJonge connect *Discipleship* with theological elements from *Act and Being,* we are given further impetus to examine the theological sections of the *Habilitationsschrift* to assess what resources might be found there to apply to our concerns. Thirdly, following Schmitz's comments about an 'inner connection' between *Discipleship* and *Ethics,* and the fact that Green's critique of 'simple obedience' would benefit from consulting the latter text, we shall be led to conduct a thorough examination of *Ethics* in Chapter 6, paying particular attention to the continuity between the two works, particularly in terms of the simplicity of *Discipleship*.

Moreover, Bethge's use of the term 'concentration' as a way to interpret the apparent exclusivity of the unreflective in *Discipleship* is promising in offering a sense of single-mindedness or sharp focus to the text, which does not intrinsically preclude incorporation into a broader picture, and we have some first pointers from DeJonge towards the promise of exploring Dilthey's philosophy, in that he gestures towards Diltheyan resonances in Bonhoeffer's work. Overall, it is evident from this discussion of Bonhoeffer's commentators that the reception of *Discipleship* has not been straightforward, although there is a general move towards unifying and integrating the corpus. This book seeks to build on this general directionality (in seeking integration). Nonetheless, it is clear that, insofar as the 'dangers' of *Discipleship* have tended to be associated with the alleged unworldliness of the text, they have not so much needed to be 'stood by' but actually challenged, as seen from Bethge right up to Schmitz. Associating the simplicity of *Discipleship* as exhibiting 'dangers', however, our reading of *Discipleship* promises to enable *both* a 'standing by' it *and* an acknowledgement of its 'dangers', more closely mirroring Bonhoeffer's own two-sided stance to the book.

Chapter 4

SIMPLICITY AND THE TRANSCENDENTAL ATTEMPT

Chapter 2 indicated that the cognitive loci of the simplicity of *Discipleship*, 'seeing only Christ' and the 'hiddenness of the disciple', have important background in the philosophical Section A of *Act and Being*. Moreover, we discerned in Chapter 3 that this background has gone largely unacknowledged by *Discipleship*'s commentators. This chapter examines relevant passages of *Act and Being*, particularly the 'transcendental attempt', to ascertain more precisely how the philosophical material found there can contribute to reconciling unreflective simplicity with the reflective. This contribution will involve first an understanding of how self-reflection can maintain a 'directedness' to Christ, thus adhering to the requirement of 'seeing only Christ', which will prove important in Chapter 5. This promises to contribute to understanding how self-reflection can be reconciled with the demands of *Discipleship*, where we read that Christ is 'always before the disciple's eyes'.[1]

Secondly, we shall be pointed towards understanding how self-reflection can preserve the 'hiddenness of the disciple'. The 'transcendental attempt' presents a particular construal of a 'hiddenness' (as 'limit'[2]) on the part of the subject, which promises to serve as a coordinate or parameter of self-reflection, without granting full self-possession to the reflective gaze. This 'limit' will be seen to be something on which the difference between what Bonhoeffer terms 'genuine' and 'post-Kantian' transcendentalism partly hinges, which leads us to discern that the self-reflective differentiation of 'I and myself' as something inherently negative (implied by *Discipleship*) is best understood as connected with problems Bonhoeffer finds with self-reflection in post-Kantian transcendentalism, namely, the 'I' raising 'itself to the position of lord' through self-possession.[3] This finding will prove important, for it suggests that the self-reflective split as it is understood in genuine transcendentalism is not inherently negative, and in understanding exactly why this is the case, gains are made towards understanding how self-reflective activity

---

1. DBWE4, 280–1, 287.
2. For a full discussion of the background to Bonhoeffer's use of the term 'limit' (*Grenze*), see Kirsten Busch Nielsen, *Die Gebrochene Macht der Sünder*, Leipzig: Evangelische Verlagsanstalt, 2010, 34f.
3. DBWE2, 39.

can fulfil the requirement of our second locus of simplicity; how one can self-reflect while, 'no longer knowing oneself'.[4]

4.1 Act and Being: *Philosophy in relation to theology*

4.1.1 Aims of Act and Being

Act and Being has famously been perceived as 'an uncharacteristically dense and opaque tome', and Bonhoeffer's 'most inaccessible' book.[5] Being an academic dissertation, it certainly lacks the readability of his later works, and this inaccessibility has been intensified for English-language readers by confusion arising from errors in both the 1962 and 1996 translations, where some points even 'fully invert' the original German even in the critical edition.[6] Moreover, some of Bonhoeffer's own terminology is particularly given to being misread, and the structure and nature of the argument show points of 'youthful unevenness'.[7] Nonetheless, it remains a work of key importance in Bonhoeffer's development, despite being his 'most neglected' book,[8] and it has moments of startling brilliance in its own right. Most importantly for this project, it also directly analyses the themes of human self-understanding and self-reflection.

Bonhoeffer's overall aim in *Act and Being* is to locate and describe what he calls elsewhere, a 'genuine theological epistemology',[9] which means a truthful and accurate way to understand what it is to know God, along with knowing the human being and the world in light of God, or in light of the knowledge of God. Bonhoeffer's concern is primarily methodological; he is seeking to describe how we know the matters discussed in theology. As Wayne Whitson Floyd Jr puts it, this dissertation 'evidences Bonhoeffer's ... concern to find for theology a methodology adequate to its unique subject matter'.[10] With this overall aim in mind, however, it may be surprising that the interlocutors in the opening chapters (Kant, Hegel, Husserl, Heidegger, et al.) are exclusively philosophical. Floyd suggests that Bonhoeffer's most 'distinctive contribution' in *Act and Being* is this dialogue with contemporary philosophical trends,[11] evincing his desire for 'theology to speak with all the resources of modern thought'.[12] The sustained

---

4. DBWE4, 86.
5. Wayne Whitson Floyd, Jr, in DBWE2, 6; DeJonge, *Formation,* 6.
6. Janz, *Desire,* 104–5, n3.
7. Ibid., 105.
8. Ibid., 102.
9. DBWE10, 454; see Wayne Whitson Floyd, Jr, in DBWE2, 17.
10. Wayne Whitson Floyd, Jr, in DBWE2, 7.
11. Wayne Whitson Floyd, Jr, *Theology and the Dialectics of Otherness: On Reading Bonhoeffer and Adorno,* Lanham, MD: University Press of America, 1988.
12. Wayne Whitson Floyd, Jr, in DBWE2, 7.

attention Bonhoeffer gives to philosophical interlocutors in Section A suggests his acute sensitivity to the distinctive challenges of theological epistemology in no way subtracts from his willingness to engage fully with epistemological discussions from the philosophical arena.

The main issue for the text is the relationship of act and being, which we touched on as a theological issue in Chapter 3, but which is also – importantly – 'the most basic and most broad of all *philosophical* polarities'.[13] Approached philosophically, 'act' refers to the human exercise of thought. First, (in the 'transcendental attempt'), Bonhoeffer examines the act of thinking as an attempt to understand the 'being'[14] which performs that act. This 'being' belongs to the 'I' of the human being, which is 'logically prior' to thought, for, as Paul D. Janz states, it is the '*thinking being* out of which thinking proceeds'.[15] As Bonhoeffer puts it, in transcendental philosophy, 'the I intends to understand itself by regarding itself'.[16] Secondly, (in the 'ontological attempt'), Bonhoeffer discusses the attempt of the act of thinking to understand the being of that which is exterior to it, or to quote Janz: 'the being of that into which thinking enquires outside of itself (the world)'.[17] This attempt is *also* an enquiry into human self-understanding, because the thinking 'being' which conducts the act of thinking shares the world of the being of that which is exterior to it, so to arrive at the truth of being which is exterior to the act would also contribute to arriving at the truth of the thinking 'being' which conducts that act. Common points of confusion among the book's readers include misreading 'the transcendental attempt' as dealing only with act (thinking) and 'the ontological attempt' as dealing only with being. Bonhoeffer is dealing with the self-understanding of the human 'being' in *both* attempts, although the manner of approach is, of course, different in each. It is the 'transcendental attempt', however, which includes thorough and explicit discussion of *self*-reflection, for the act of 'the I intend[ing] to understand itself by regarding itself',[18] is, of course, an act of self-reflection. The transcendental attempt is, therefore, the passage of *Act and Being* on which we shall focus.

4.1.2 Philosophy and theology in Act and Being

Before going into the detail of the transcendental attempt, some preliminary remarks are required to show why Bonhoeffer's philosophical writings have been

---

13. Janz, *Desire*, 102 (my emphasis).
14. Following Bonhoeffer, we place subjective 'being' in inverted commas and not objective being, because 'the term *being* is already an *objective* ontological (or ontic) category and as such cannot really be used properly to express the inherently subjective pre-theoretical "I"', (see Janz, *Desire*, 106).
15. Janz, *Desire*, 105–6.
16. DBWE2, 33.
17. Janz, *Desire*, 106.
18. DBWE2, 33.

somewhat neglected by *Discipleship*'s commentators and also to present some key conceptualities for understanding genuine transcendentalism. Bonhoeffer's interlocution with his philosophical conversation partners closes with an assessment of both the transcendental and ontological attempts. Commentators on this discussion frequently quote Bonhoeffer's more strident epithets about the problems of autonomous philosophical thought, but rarely give full weight to the subtlety of his position.[19] Because this book contends that Bonhoeffer's discussion of the 'transcendental attempt' is of key importance in orientating his subsequent theological explorations of 'act' and 'being' in Sections B and C of the text, and that this discussion can contribute to the overall concerns around human subjectivity, it is necessary to discuss the nuances of Bonhoeffer's assessment of philosophy. That these nuances are often overlooked can be seen, for example, even in commentators generally sensitive to the value of Bonhoeffer's engagement with philosophy, such as Floyd, who concludes that Bonhoeffer considers all philosophical attempts to gain self-understanding 'a failure'.[20]

Bonhoeffer states that both the transcendental and ontological attempts tend to result in a 'system confined in the I' in which 'the I understands itself through itself and can place itself into the truth'.[21] Calling to mind his aim of uncovering a 'genuine theological epistemology' (with particular reference to human self-understanding), Bonhoeffer makes clear that this aim cannot be achieved autonomously or philosophically, because theology understands 'human existence as essentially determined by guilt or by grace'.[22] Exactly what Bonhoeffer means by this will require further discussion in Chapter 5, but here it suffices to mention that the understanding of the human being as 'determined by guilt or by grace' depends, for Bonhoeffer, on 'the viewpoint of revelation',[23] meaning a viewpoint given externally, by the communication or disclosure of God transcendent, and therefore by definition a viewpoint unable to be arrived at autonomously. To bring revelation into philosophical discussion, he claims, would involve 'bursting'[24] the framework of that discussion, implying that the structure of a philosophical enquiry into the self cannot bear the weight of revelation, as it is conducted with an entirely different framework.

However, Bonhoeffer is not merely sweeping aside all philosophical attempts at human self-understanding. There are two ways Bonhoeffer presents philosophical enquiry as valuable for theology, the second of which is rarely given sustained attention. The first is shown in his statement that philosophy makes 'a contribution to the understanding of the problem of act and being within the concept of

---

19. See for example, Clifford J. Green, *Bonhoeffer: A Theology of Sociality* (revised edition), Grand Rapids, MI: Eerdmans, 1999, 77.
20. Wayne Whitson Floyd, Jr, in DBWE2, 11.
21. DBWE2, 76.
22. Ibid., 77.
23. Ibid.
24. Ibid.

revelation'.²⁵ This means that, even with a foundational shift into the acceptance of revelation, our understanding of the issues at stake is constructively informed by the discussions of act and being which stem from a purely philosophical context. The transcendental attempt thus offers valuable resources to theology, notwithstanding the commitment to revelation as a 'unique subject matter'. This is because the basic coordinates of his philosophical discussion, like the 'act' of the subject, and aspects of objects that transcend thinking as 'being', are still found in the theological realm, even if deeply reconfigured by theological concerns. Insofar as philosophy offers the fruits of a highly focused and sustained investigation of basic parameters of autonomous human cognition, it offers resources Bonhoeffer finds useful in seeking to understand theologically orientated cognition.[26] This provision of basic coordinates by philosophy leads DeJonge to state that Section A has a 'preparatory constructive function' for the subsequent sections, in presenting 'philosophical concepts that, once recast in light of revelation', will 'help' Bonhoeffer articulate his theological undertaking.[27]

Secondly, however, Bonhoeffer points to a more substantial and pressing way in which philosophical thinking impinges on the theological sphere, going beyond this application of relatively discrete elements like understandings of act and/ or being. Bonhoeffer claims that 'questions concerning the interpretation of act and being can be put to revelation in the sharpest possible manner' by genuine transcendentalism, because this approach offers an acute assessment of the human capacity for self-understanding. In his introductory overview of the book, he opens by saying 'the *heart of the problem* [of act and being] is the struggle with the formation of the question that Kant and idealism have posed for theology'.[28] This 'question' is that of the transcendental attempt, the question of the degree to which 'the I' can 'understand itself by regarding itself'.[29]

In order to elucidate this question more fully and amplify how it is 'posed for theology', we need to note an important aspect of what Bonhoeffer considers 'genuine' transcendentalism. The authenticity of 'genuine' transcendentalism refers to what we might term 'classical' or 'orthodox' Kantian epistemology, which denotes what Bonhoeffer considers the correct interpretation of the intention of certain elements of Kant's *Critique of Pure Reason*. Bonhoeffer considers this 'genuine' Kantianism to place firm limits on the jurisdiction of reason, on the potential of autonomous thinking to place the 'I' into the truth about itself, or rather, about the degree to which 'the I' can 'understand itself by regarding itself'.[30] He values what he considers to be Kant's position, that 'autonomous [self-] understanding' is presented by an 'internal contradiction' with the 'I' being unable

---

25. Ibid., 79.
26. Ibid., 27.
27. DeJonge, *Formation*, 22.
28. DBWE2, 27 (my emphasis).
29. Ibid., 33.
30. Ibid.

to think of itself, and therefore 'being deeply called into question by knowledge'.[31] For my purposes, the key aspect to this alleged 'internal contradiction' is a 'limit' or 'boundary' Kant places on cognizing the 'I'. This presents a 'contradiction', for the faculty of reason, which inherently seeks after knowledge, arrives at an insurmountable gap *to* knowledge, which cannot be fully known, or rather cognized, without contravening the way it is conceived. This point will be explained fully in the following section, but the point to bear in mind here is that Bonhoeffer admires this aspect of Kant's work and claims it shows the '*primordial legitimacy*' of autonomous human thinking.[32] This 'primordial legitimacy' poses questions to revelation in the 'sharpest possible manner', we read, because it shows that even thinking from revelation, there always stands a danger that what are held to be theological limits, like God's transcendence, might actually be limits placed on thinking from within the movement of human thought and which are actually surreptitiously autonomous, and not therefore genuinely theological after all.[33] Indeed, he finds this danger in what he calls Barth's 'formalism', particularly regarding the latter's construal of God's freedom, and his response to this can aptly be considered an example of what Tom Greggs has called Bonhoeffer's 'being more Barthian than Barth'.[34]

Bonhoeffer's comments on the 'primordial legitimacy' of autonomous thinking demonstrated by Kant tend to be overlooked by interpreters of *Act and Being*. This is arguably because Bonhoeffer also claims that even a 'genuine' transcendental philosopher will find the 'internal contradiction' unsustainable. Limits to knowledge provided by thinking, we read, are always 'thought away [*werden zerdacht*] until they are no longer genuine limits'.[35] Nonetheless, his guarded endorsement of this 'legitimacy' shows that Bonhoeffer understands the relation of philosophy and theology as more than simply employing discrete elements of philosophical discussion within the domain of theological criteria. He goes on to use the insights of genuine transcendentalism as what we might term 'checks and balances' on theological enquiry, to ensure that, even with a foundational orientation to revelation, theology stays within proper 'critical limits', some of which remain defined in philosophical terms. In Chapter 5, we shall see how Bonhoeffer's theological undertaking proceeds on the basis that philosophy poses questions to theologians 'in the sharpest possible manner', and actually lies at the 'heart' of the demands placed on theological epistemology.

---

31. Ibid., 36.
32. Ibid., 35 (my italics).
33. See Jürgen Boomgaarden, *Das Verständnis der Wirklichkeit*, Gütersloh: Kaiser, Gütersloher Verl.-Haus, 1999, which claims Bonhoeffer's engagement with philosophy in Section A provides him with the 'only possible access to a fundamental, systematic problem with Protestantism' (my translation), 34.
34. Tom Greggs (speaking specifically about *Offenbarungspositivismus*) in *Theology against Religion*, London: T&T Clark, 2011, 61.
35. DBWE2, 45; DBW2, 48.

4.2 The transcendental attempt

4.2.1 'Genuine transcendentalism'

Bonhoeffer introduces his discussion of transcendental philosophy with a description of the 'basic posture of transcendental philosophers'. He states, 'all thinking refers to something transcendent in two ways.'[36] The first 'way' is the 'thing-in-itself' (*Ding-an-sich*), which as understood in Kant's *Critique of Pure Reason* is '*logically* transcendent' of human cognitive capacities.[37] The 'thing-in-itself' is logically transcendent of sensible intuition, because it is arrived at when all the perceptible attributes of a 'thing' have been stripped away through philosophical analysis. This means, claims Bonhoeffer, that it cannot be cognized, as it offers no material to be classified by the concepts of the understanding (see Chapter 7). The second way in which 'thinking refers to something transcendent' is more important for this study, and is what we shall focus on. This involves the pre-theoretical thinking 'being', which is also understood as 'logically transcendent' to thought, for it is the ground, or 'being', from which the very act of thinking is conducted and thus cannot be brought into, or enclosed within, the remit of that act. That is, the thinking 'being' is presented as logically having to be prior to the act, in the sense that were there no 'being' there could be no act; for if there were no 'I', there could be no 'I regarding itself'.

The thinking 'being' in genuine transcendentalism is considered by Bonhoeffer to be unable properly to behold its own self-thinking, for if it tries to, it finds that which is beheld is not the thinking 'being' itself, but a thought of itself or an idea of itself. More exactly, that which is strictly transcendent to the act is the actual *execution* of the act of thinking by the thinking 'being'. This cannot be fully grasped *by* thinking, for each grasping act of thought must be undergirded by a further originating execution of thought, and so on ad infinitum. The execution itself, then, is always beyond that which can be beheld by the subject. Any reflection on or of oneself in thought is always grounded by an unreflected level of 'pure act'[38] which transcends the self-reflective gaze. We can thus discern that the thinking 'being' can never be an 'object' of thought because 'subjectivity is that from which any activity of thought proceeds'.[39] The recognition of this fact constitutes what genuine transcendentalism considers a 'limit' to thinking. This is a limit, insofar as the thinking 'I' acknowledges that, in seeking to 'understand itself by regarding itself',[40] there is a dimension of its own subjectivity that cannot be fully 'regarded' or possessed by the self-reflective gaze and which thus limits the parameters of the act itself.

---

36. DBWE2, 34.
37. Janz, *Desire*, 108.
38. DBWE2, 38; see 35, 56.
39. Janz, *Desire*, 108–9.
40. DBWE2, 33.

However, an objection could be raised here, that because everything the 'I' knows of itself is known *by* thinking, that thinking is actually prior to the 'I'. This response characterises Bonhoeffer's understanding of idealism, but before studying that it should be noted that Kant attempts to foreclose this line of argumentation through his definition of the subjective transcendent 'limit' as the 'transcendental unity of apperception'.[41] The word 'transcendental' means this limit is the condition of the possibility of thinking, which implies that thinking cannot be prior to it, for it is the necessary structural framework that makes thinking possible. More exactly, Bonhoeffer references Kant as holding that there is a necessary condition which makes self-consciousness possible, namely, that any conscious process is recognized as belonging to the same 'I'. This explains the word 'unity' in the transcendental unity of apperception; the fact that any phenomenon of consciousness appears to a unified subject, in the sense of pertaining to the same consciousness. In Kant's own words, the transcendental unity of apperception 'produces' the 'I think'.[42] That is, to say that *I* think something, presupposes that all my objects of thought necessarily belong to me, otherwise there could be no sense of an 'I'. Bonhoeffer considers this to counter the suggestion that thought is prior to the 'I', for he holds that the activity of an 'I' thinking can only pertain where there is a prior unity accompanying thought. This, again, shows what Bonhoeffer goes on to call the 'primordial legitimacy' of human reason: that by arriving at the transcendental unity of apperception, thinking can place a 'limit' on itself from within thinking.

When Bonhoeffer states that the 'basic posture of transcendental philosophers', is that 'all thinking refers to something transcendent in two ways',[43] he is referring to a two-way transcendence of 'limit'; between the thing-in-itself and the transcendental unity of apperception. It is by adhering to these limits, he claims, that transcendental philosophy is 'genuine'.[44] He thus describes genuine transcendental thinking as 'pure act', in that it restlessly moves between these two 'poles'[45] and cannot settle in either, rebounding against limits which prevent it claiming full jurisdiction and possession of either pole. As Bonhoeffer states: 'one may speak of genuine transcendentalism so long as ... the thing-in-itself and transcendental apperception are understood as pure limiting concepts.'[46] For Kant, says Bonhoeffer, human self-understanding 'is characterised' as 'self-knowing "in reference to" (*in Bezug auf*)', that is, self-knowing strictly within the 'act', 'suspended between' (*eingespannt zwischen*) two limits, as called by Floyd, a 'method of suspended dialectic'.[47]

---

41. DBWE2, 37, 50 (transcendental unity of apperception will be discussed in detail in Chapter 7).
42. CpR, 246.
43. DBWE2, 34.
44. Ibid., 33.
45. Ibid., 35.
46. Ibid.
47. Ibid.; Floyd, *Dialectics*, 64.

4.2.2 'Post-Kantian transcendentalism'

The 'genuine' transcendental attempt is distinguished from what Bonhoeffer calls 'transcendentalist philosophy as understood by post-Kantian idealism'.[48] This refers to specific developments in the transcendental tradition after Kant, which Bonhoeffer considers to have failed to maintain the 'suspended dialectic' outlined above. Bonhoeffer describes a philosopher as having two options when faced with Kant's delineation of the two poles of transcendence. The first option is for thinking to 'suspend itself' (*hebt es sich selbst auf*), or rather 'suspend' its drive for all-encompassing knowledge, and accept its limitations. This is the approach of 'genuine transcendental philosophy'. The second option is for thinking to surmount the limits of the 'I' and/or the 'thing-in-itself', which Bonhoeffer connects with post-Kantian idealism. Maintaining our focus on the subjective 'pole', Bonhoeffer claims that, if thinking does not submit to the limit of the transcendental unity of apperception, the human being has raised 'itself to the position of lord',[49] meaning that it has full jurisdiction, ownership of the terrain, and it is therefore master over itself.

This self-possessive grasp of the 'I' occurs if the prior subjective synthesis undergirding all conscious activity is no longer a 'limit'. Bonhoeffer holds that idealist philosophers are guilty of this, by considering that because the 'I' *is* known only in the act of thinking, the 'being' of this 'I' is actually constituted *by* thinking. That is, by maintaining that the 'I' can entirely only know itself in thought, thought is presented as actually *constituting* the 'I'. In adopting this approach, thinking is then logically prior to the 'I', and the 'I' that constitutes itself in thought becomes what Bonhoeffer calls elsewhere (following Fichte), the 'creative ego'.[50] This is where Bonhoeffer invokes one of his philosophical applications of Luther's *ratio in se ipsum incurva* (reason turned in upon itself), saying that 'spirit' (*Geist*, meaning self-conscious mind) is then 'turned in upon itself'.[51] This is reminiscent of Hegel's description of a 'point at which *Geist* gets rid of ... being burdened with something alien',[52] such as the dimension of subjectivity transcendent to thinking in genuine transcendentalism. So, in genuine transcendental philosophy, self-knowledge is faced with an insurmountable limit. In 'post-Kantian idealism', this limit is surmounted and claimed by the act of thought, the act has come to rest and no longer rebounds against a pole it cannot possess.

---

48. DBWE2, 33.
49. Ibid., 39.
50. DBWE10, 471.
51. DWBE 2, 41.
52. Quoted by Floyd, *Dialectics*, 111, n108; see Ferenc Lehel's introduction to *Dietrich Bonhoeffers Hegel-Seminar 1933*, ed. Ferenc Lehel and Ilse Tödt, München: Chr. Kaiser, 1988, for a discussion of Bonhoeffer's engagement with Hegel.

4.3 Transcendentalism and the simplicity of Discipleship

4.3.1 Subject–'object' singularity

The Kantian 'transcendental unity of apperception' as limit constitutes a 'hiddenness' to subjectivity which will be seen to have important resonances with the 'hiddenness of the disciple' in *Discipleship*. Now, we shall turn our attention to an aspect to transcendental philosophy which promises to resonate with *Discipleship*'s 'seeing only Christ', by looking at the *actus directus* and *reflectus* as described in the 'Transcendental Attempt'. In the first place, attention will be given to how Bonhoeffer's discussion of transcendental philosophy enables us to speak of the unreflective as exhibiting a 'subject–object singularity'.

The *actus* distinction is first made in the opening pages of *Act and Being* when, in introducing the problem of act and being, he claims, 'given that the act [of thinking] takes place in consciousness, we must distinguish between direct consciousness (*actus directus*) and reflective consciousness.'[53] The 'direct consciousness' of the *actus directus* is described as 'pure intentionality',[54] meaning primarily that the act of thinking intends *only* its object, it 'sees' only the object on which it is focused or to which it is 'directed'. In the 'pure act' of direct consciousness, he claims, there is consciousness only of the object, so it is 'pure' in the sense of exhibiting an unadulterated singularity of directedness.[55] Moreover, Bonhoeffer considers this singleness of directionality 'at' the object to be the defining feature of the *actus directus*, which is thus described as 'purely "outwardly directed"', in 'intentionality pure and simple'.[56]

Moreover, because the *actus directus* 'sees' only the object, and, with Bonhoeffer's quoting of Goethe, 'the eye does not see *itself* seeing',[57] the sense of singularity between the 'act' and the object it intends can be extended to pointing towards a singularity between the acting *subject* and the object. That is, insofar as the subject, or 'I', has no explicit awareness of itself in the *actus directus*, but is aware only of the object it singularly intends, this 'I' is caught up solely with the object, and so we can speak of this facet to the *actus* distinction as a 'subject–object singularity' in which the subject 'sees' only the object being apprehended and has no explicit consciousness of itself 'within' the movement of the act itself. As the *actus directus* is 'directed', 'intending' or 'seeing' *only* the object of apprehension, it calls to mind

---

53. DBW2, 23 (my translation).
54. This use of the word 'intentionality' in *Act and Being* differs from other well-known usages of the term, such as Edmund Husserl's, which is much broader, and includes aspects of unreflective and reflective consciousness, whereas for Bonhoeffer it specifically linked to the unreflective only, to simply 'intending' an object. Cf. Edmund Husserl, *Logical Investigations Volume 1*, trans. J. N. Findlay, London; New York: Routledge, 2001.
55. DBWE2, 38.
56. Ibid., 28, 43.
57. Ibid., 46.

the singularity of 'vision' or intention of 'seeing only Christ', about which we read that the disciples 'always' see 'only him', which is why their vision is called 'simple (*einfältig*)',[58] meaning *singular*; focused 'purely' on Christ alone. Also, to speak of 'direct consciousness' as subject–object singularity also calls to mind the unity Bonhoeffer describes in *Discipleship* between those who 'see only Christ' and Christ himself. In simplicity, we read, the disciples belong 'entirely and undivided to Christ', with whom there is an 'absolute bond' [*Bindung*], described as involving 'deliverance [*Entbundensein*] from one's own I'.[59]

In order to point to how this will contribute to our search for a mode of self-reflection reconcilable with 'seeing only Christ', it needs to be borne in mind that, by this description, when consciousness is 'directed at' oneself, the original directedness to the object of the *actus directus* is lost. That is, to 'consider' or 'regard' oneself, 'interrupts' or 'displaces' the singularity of directedness 'at' the original object of the *actus directus*. For this reason, he writes, 'the intentionality of the act is displaced by reflection' and reflection is 'suspended' in 'intentionality'.[60] As it stands, we are not yet at the juncture where the potential of this for contributing to our concerns can be brought fully into view. Nonetheless, this aspect to Bonhoeffer's discussion should be noted here, for we shall see in Chapter 5 that he works from this to embark on a line of argumentation which is promising for our endeavour. Bonhoeffer goes on to enquire into possible modes of self-reflection that do not 'interrupt' or 'displace' the subject–object singularity of the *actus directus*. He goes on to argue that 'the essence of the [theological] *actus directus* lies [in] … its intentionality toward Christ' and explores how, by considering this as its essence, he can then describe a 'reflection on the self' which is 'included within the intentionality toward Christ'.[61] Put differently, he works from the observation that the unreflective *actus directus* is primarily defined as a subject–'object' singularity and scrutinizes how 'I and myself' might move apart into two, without interrupting or displacing the focus on Christ, thereby promising to show us how we can understand self-reflection as reconcilable with the locus of simplicity, 'seeing only Christ', whereby we can look on ourselves, yet 'always' have Christ before our 'eyes'.[62]

4.3.2 The hiddenness of the 'I'

In this final subsection we shall discuss a second aspect to the transcendental attempt which connects it to our analysis of *Discipleship*: the 'hiddenness of the disciple'. The claim that the preservation of a dimension of subjectivity as 'limit' constitutes a form of 'hiddenness' is relatively self-evident from Section 4.2. To

---

58. DBWE4, 11, 281, 161.
59. DBW4, 107, 136 (my translation).
60. DBWE2, 28, 32.
61. DBWE2, 156–7.
62. DBWE4, 280–1, 287.

consider that the originating execution of the act of thinking is always transcendent *to* thinking is to consider it hidden *from* thinking, for it cannot be brought under the self-reflective gaze. The transcendental unity of apperception stipulates that there is a necessary condition of self-consciousness (a unified 'I'), but this condition is not an object for thinking, but a limit to thinking, a point beyond which thought cannot go. Again, insofar as the transcendental unity of apperception is preserved as 'limit', the possibility of reflecting on oneself while preserving 'hiddenness' as a coordinate of thinking is opened up. That is, in genuine transcendentalism, self-reflection involves a certain humility, an acceptance of 'limit', a dimension of oneself which is not fully known.

As this limit cannot be objectified by self-reflection, it is sharply contrasted with the apparently boundless parameters of self-reflection in idealism. Looking more closely at this here will enable us to show how *idealist* self-reflection, specifically, seems close to the criticisms of self-reflection in *Discipleship*. Genuine transcendentalism seeks to foreclose the objectification of the 'I' through a 'pure limiting concept', and this preserves the *subjectivity* of the 'I', its status as subject *qua* subject being inherently distinct from what can be beheld as object ('myself'). By maintaining that the execution of the act of thinking cannot be beheld *by* thinking, and is 'logically prior' to it, that which conducts the act (the 'I') is firmly differentiated from that which is thought (the self-reflective 'myself'). Bonhoeffer claims the 'I' 'must be thought of as something in process', but in idealism, he contends, it 'becomes something completed as myself'.[63] The idealist 'myself' is 'complete' because it is entirely given over and possessed by the self-reflective gaze, with no dimension transcendent to it, for something with a hidden dimension can only be understood 'incompletely'.

Interestingly, this shows there are two different ways to construe self-reflection in genuine transcendentalism and idealism respectively. We have seen in Chapter 2 that Bonhoeffer connects self-reflection with 'twoness', the duality of 'I and myself'. But, on the basis of the foregoing analysis, it is apparent that the split into 'I and myself' is importantly different in genuine transcendentalism from idealism, because only in genuine transcendentalism is there a genuine differentiation between an 'I' and 'myself'. That is, in not preserving the undergirding execution of the act as transcendent or hidden in idealism, there is for Bonhoeffer no 'I' (or 'something in process') – no subject *qua* subject – but rather only an object: 'myself'. The 'I' that thinks itself in idealism is thus construed as absolutely identical with the thought of itself, and the 'internal contradiction' of genuine transcendentalism is apparently resolved. In idealism, thinking has full jurisdiction over (what is taken to be) the thinking 'being', for it is entirely captured as 'myself'. On a superficial level, idealism might seem less contradictory, for thinking seems to have gained the knowledge it seeks. From the perspective of genuine transcendentalism, however, idealism actually evinces a profound *rupture* between 'I and myself'. This is because the genuine 'I' which undergirds every act of thinking has fallen out of

---

63. DBWE2, 38.

view, and the self-reflecting self is only viewing its own thought of itself, and not actually acknowledging the 'I' that executes the act of thinking at all. The 'I' proper, a sheer dynamism of 'pure act', is thus alienated from itself, and in this sense, in idealism, the 'I' is 'mirroring *itself* to itself',[64] and seeing only its reflection.

These two different approaches to self-reflective twoness offer us valuable material for interpreting the apparently inherently negative twoness of self-reflection as inherently self-centred in *Discipleship* (indicated by words such as *zweifältig, Zweideutigkeit* and so on). That this negative 'twoness' is reminiscent of the rupture of idealism can be seen in *Creation and Fall*, where the fallen human being (who is described as 'split apart' (*im Zwiespalt*) 'in itself'), is said to act 'out of its own resources, in its aseity, in its being alone'.[65] That is, Bonhoeffer connects the problematic self-reflective twoness with isolation and self-centredness, which is clearly related to the self-absorbed and self-referential idealist 'creative ego' which only mirrors 'itself to itself'. Moreover, Bonhoeffer writes in his inaugural lecture in Berlin that 'the I is unable to capture itself', and so he criticizes philosophers for whom 'the I becomes an object to itself by thinking its I'.[66] In New York, he connects precisely this move with idealism, where 'man knows himself immediately by the act of the coming of the ego to itself and knows through himself essentially everything', and then 'the ego stands in the centre of the world' which is then 'created and ruled by it'.[67]

The transcendental attempt thus offers us two construals of the self-reflective split, one of which Bonhoeffer finds far preferable to the other: opting for a relatively neutral or ambivalent 'split' between 'I and myself' in genuine transcendentalism, in which 'I and myself move apart' as 'the I intends to understand itself by regarding itself'.[68] In *Act and Being* this is not presented as inherently problematic, insofar as the 'I' is construed as a 'limit', and the 'I' is not given over to the self-possession of the reflective gaze thereby. Yet, the self-reflection of idealism, in which the 'I' 'becomes something completed as myself',[69] leaves the 'I' standing 'alone' in a self-made world with itself in the centre. This second construal is closer to the self-reflection criticized in *Discipleship*, which lacks the 'primordial legitimacy' of autonomous thought evinced by the self-limitation of genuine transcendentalism.

4.4 Summing up

So, in contrast to the commentators on *Discipleship* we covered in Chapter 3, such as Feil and DeJonge, the foregoing analysis has made clear that the philosophical

---

64. DBWE12, 305 (my emphasis).
65. DBWE3, 89 (translation altered), 113.
66. DBWE10, 390.
67. Ibid., 471.
68. DBWE2, 33.
69. Ibid., 38.

Section A of *Act and Being* provides key points of orientation for interpreting the simplicity of *Discipleship*, perhaps even demonstrating what Marsh calls the book's 'important subtextual discussions with Bonhoeffer's philosophical conversation partners'.[70] Moreover, we have two findings to pursue in Chapter 5. First, Bonhoeffer offers an interpretation of the unreflective *actus directus* centred on subject–object singularity, a singularity 'interrupted' by the *actus reflectus* focusing on the subject itself. We shall see in Chapter 5 how this leads him to investigate the possibility of presenting an *actus reflectus* which somehow maintains the singularity of the *actus directus*. This promises to aid our own objective of understanding how self-reflection can be reconcilable with 'seeing only Christ', in which the 'I and myself' move apart, yet still 'always' keeping Christ before the subject's 'eyes'. Our second finding is that the self-reflective split as it is understood in genuine transcendentalism is not inherently negative, because it preserves a dimension of subjectivity as 'hidden' from the reflective gaze. Insofar as this points us towards understanding how one can self-reflect while 'no longer knowing oneself',[71] this clearly promises to advance our enquiry. We are thus led to enquire in Chapter 5 how subject–object singularity and 'hiddenness' as limit function in *Act and Being*'s theological discussions.

70. Marsh, *Reclaiming*, x.
71. DBWE4, 86.

Chapter 5

THE *ACTUS REFLECTUS* AS WISDOM: RECONCILING THE UNREFLECTIVE AND REFLECTIVE IN *ACT AND BEING*

This chapter focuses on aspects of the theological sections of *Act and Being* to enquire into how approaching the unreflective by focusing on its subject–object singularity, and construing a 'hiddenness' pertaining to the subject as 'limit', are each developed to inform the theological content of the *Habilitationschrift*. This enquiry is driven by two concerns for responding to the challenge of the unreflective in *Discipleship*. First, to understand a mode of self-reflection which maintains the subject–object singularity of the unreflective and, secondly, to ask how the genuinely transcendental preservation of a dimension of subjectivity as 'limit' might similarly be brought into play while self-reflecting. With the first concern, we make significant gains in this chapter, for Bonhoeffer presents two modes of self-reflection intended to maintain the 'directedness' to the 'object' of the *actus directus* (subject–'object' singularity), the 'object' of which here is, of course, Christ.[1] Bonhoeffer calls these modes of self-reflection 'self-understanding-in-remembrance' and 'the Christian conscience', and to bring these into view we need to examine *Act and Being*'s critique of Karl Barth. This is because Bonhoeffer arrives at these 'Christ-directed' modes of self-reflection through seeking to address his unease with Barth's alleged sequestering of the unreflective 'I' as a 'heavenly double'. Bonhoeffer's responses go some way towards approaching self-reflection as 'wisdom'; a self-reflection which, in maintaining subject–'object' singularity, promises to be harmonious with 'seeing only Christ' in *Discipleship*.

With the second concern, however, the degree to which the construal of a 'hiddenness' pertaining to the subject as 'limit' from genuine transcendentalism informs Bonhoeffer's discussion is more limited, for this aspect of the

---

1. Bonhoeffer's referring to Christ as 'object' means what he terms Christ's 'personal objectivity', which involves the recognition that Christ as person cannot be objectified: a 'person is a unity over and above "entity" and "nonentity"'. When Christ is spoken of as 'object' in this book, this caveat should be borne in mind, so I use inverted commas for the word 'object' in referring to Christ. DBWE2, 126.

transcendental attempt does not seem to perdure into the theological sections of *Act and Being*. Indeed we shall see that, in 'self-understanding-in-remembrance' and 'the Christian conscience', notwithstanding the move towards continuity (or 'wisdom'), there is an apparent 'resurfacing' of language of subjective fragmentation and dislocation which seems to arise through not making adequate room for a subjective 'hiddenness' in self-reflection, even though a particular construal of 'hiddenness' is central to the transcendental attempt.

5.1 Bonhoeffer's presentation of Barth in Act and Being

Barth's work is highly resonant for Bonhoeffer's overall aim in *Act and Being*: to locate and describe a 'genuine theological epistemology'.[2] We have seen that Bonhoeffer concludes Section A by saying he wants to investigate human self-understanding through 'the concept of revelation'.[3] Barth is, of course, the theologian whose very raison d'être was to re-establish theology on a proper footing regarding revelation, understood as the 'communication'[4] of God transcendent. In *Act and Being*, we see the general pattern of Bonhoeffer's reception of Barth which arguably endures throughout his life, whereby he critically challenges certain aspects to Barth's work, while being consistently orientated by the Barthian project. To quote Greggs, Bonhoeffer and Barth 'travelled along the same trajectory', or according to Bethge, Bonhoeffer always 'criticised [Barth] as an ally', or as DeJonge states, he 'develops his alternative to Barth on the very road that Barth clears'.[5] This is aptly demonstrated in *Act and Being*, where Bonhoeffer is deeply sympathetic to Barth's attempts to re-found the theological endeavour on the basis of revelation, but still poses highly pertinent questions to these attempts.

---

2. DBWE10, 454. This book focuses only on Bonhoeffer's presentation of Barth in *Act and Being* and not on the separate questions of how accurate this presentation is, how Barth's later work might have reconfigured this presentation, nor Bonhoeffer's reception of Barth elsewhere. It should be borne in mind that *Act and Being* draws particularly on Barth's *Der Römerbrief* (reprinted as *Der Römerbrief 1922*, Zürich: Theologischer Verlag, 2010), the essay 'Schicksal und Idee in der Theologie' (in *Zwischen den Zeiten* 7 (1929): 309–48), and *Die Christliche Dogmatik im Entwurf*, München: Chr. Kaiser Verlag, 1927). For a discussion of the Barth–Bonhoeffer relationship, see Andreas Pangritz, *Karl Barth in the Theology of Dietrich Bonhoeffer*, Grand Rapids, MI: Eerdmans, 2000, 29–40, and Greggs, *Religion*, 32ff.

3. DBWE2, 76.

4. On Barth's approach to revelation as 'communication', see Paul D. Janz, *The Command of Grace: A New Theological Apologetics*, London: T&T Clark, 2009, 45–7.

5. Greggs, *Religion*, 10 (referring to Bonhoeffer's and Barth's respective critiques of religion specifically), 58–9; DeJonge, *Formation*, 113.

5.1.1 Holy Spirit as subject and the 'believing I'

To discuss *Act and Being*'s critique of Barth we must first provide some preliminary orientation. Bonhoeffer focuses on the act-centred nature of dialectical theology. However, in doing so, he moves into very different territory from his preceding philosophical investigations. Whereas Bonhoeffer's discussion had previously considered 'act' as the human act of thinking, now act is understood as the act of God.[6] Moving from the philosophical to the theological domain, the bold assertions of Barth's which Bonhoeffer quotes in the opening pages of Section B are somewhat jarring, causing the reader to want to critically interrogate Barth's warrants for making such declarations. But, in a sense, this is to misread the overall thrust of the Barthian project, which Thomas F. Torrance describes (in reference to Barth's *The Epistle to the Romans* (1922)) as 'let God be God and man ... be man',[7] or as put by Bonhoeffer: an enquiry not into 'how' revelation exists, but '*that*' it exists'.[8] These quotes provide a basic point of Barthian orientation, namely, that to account, or give grounding warrants, for the veracity of God's revelation undercuts the central pivot of theology itself. To establish through human endeavour *that* God has revealed himself is seen as undermining the enquiry from the outset, for what is communicated by God transcendent is then only what human enquiry can establish as communicable. In short, God would then be seen by Barth as no longer freely revealing himself, but as limited by human capacities of being communicated to. To 'let God be God and man be man', then, is to take heed of this central point and not reduce God to the level of human capacities.

The key 'act of God' for Barth – the '*that*' of which we cannot ground – is the 'act of faith'. This is a cognition of the communication of God, in which this communication is believed. However, this believing is different from the way we believe things in non-revelatory cognition, for that which is revealed is by definition considered to be utterly beyond unaided human comprehension. As Barth states elsewhere, 'we ought to talk of God' but 'we are human and so we cannot talk of God'.[9] To believe in God's revelation, then, is not something Barth thinks we can generate for ourselves, but is entirely God-given. As presented by Bonhoeffer, God is 'the subject of cognition of revelation',[10] meaning that Barth declares that the person of God 'acting' in us when we believe is the Holy Spirit: 'the subject of understanding is God as Holy Spirit.'[11] So when one believes in

---

6. DBWE2, 84, 92–3.

7. Thomas F. Torrance, *Karl Barth: An Introduction to His Early Theology, 1910–1931*, London: SCM Press, 1962, building on Barth's slogan, 'Let God be God', 52.

8. DBWE2, 126.

9. Quote from a Göttingen lecture in Eberhard Busch, *Karl Barth: His Life from Letters and Autobiographical Texts*, Philadelphia: Fortress Press, 1976, 140.

10. DBWE2, 92.

11. Ibid., Greggs, *Religion*, 33f., for a discussion of related points from the pneumatology of the later *Church Dogmatics*.

the revelation of God transcendent, the act of faith is presented as almost being 'implanted' into the cognitive apparatus of the human being. Barth thereby seeks to safeguard God's self-revelation by ensuring it is not understood as something *possessed* by human beings. So it is not only unattainable *by* thinking but also once given, still transcendent, to some degree, *for* or *to* thinking. Both aspects to this, its unattainability and its remaining beyond full possession, are seen by Barth as offering an alternative to much of nineteenth-century liberal Protestantism, which, he maintains, fails to ensure that revelation does not become something under human jurisdiction.[12] Before looking at the relevant critical issues this presents, it is necessary first to study an element of it which provides a crucial backdrop for understanding what Bonhoeffer presents as the differing emphases of the *actus* distinction in genuine transcendentalism and Barth's theology respectively.

Bonhoeffer presents Barth as holding that it is not the case that God as 'subject' simply supplants human cognition as such. Rather, we read, Barth posits a (human) 'believing I' as involved in cognizing revelation. This 'believing I' is never given to us as some locatable facet of ourselves, which we can attain or possess: 'the I of faith ... can never be something one just comes across.'[13] This is confusing, for it is hard to see how God can be the 'subject' of the act of faith, as well as there being a human 'believing I' undergoing the cognition of revelation. Bonhoeffer leaves this unclear and simply states that Barth posits this 'believing I' as 'given' *along with* the act of 'God-understanding-God's-self'.[14] The 'believing I' offers Barth a point of contact between human and divine, while still maintaining God's being 'wholly other' (*ganz anders*).[15] That is, if God as Holy Spirit were merely 'implanted' into cognition, then God's self-communication would have to be either completely beyond understanding in every sense (and therefore not proper communication) or, if understood, then in danger of being brought under human jurisdiction. By positing a 'believing I' which is given along with every act of 'God-understanding-God's-self', there is a sense in which communication occurs (human subjectivity is present 'in' or 'to' the act), but this is not enclosed by limits of human understanding, for the human element is not locatable or even attestable by human endeavour. This throws up many critical issues, but before moving on to these, it is necessary first to discuss how Bonhoeffer situates Barth as offering a form of theological transcendentalism.

---

12. Cf. Barth's 1922 correspondence with von Harnack, where he criticizes the latter's notion of an 'ascent of God' through 'culture, historical knowledge, morality and so on' in Busch, *Karl Barth*, 147.

13. DBWE2, 93.

14. Ibid.

15. Karl Barth, *The Epistle to the Romans*, trans. Edwyn C. Hoskyns, Oxford: Oxford University Press 1968, 49, 107; Barth, *Römerbrief 1922*, 27.

5.1.2 Barth's theology as transcendentalism

Bonhoeffer classifies Barth as a theological counterpart to transcendentalism, most basically because it is in an *act* that the 'object' is cognized. But there is more detail to Bonhoeffer's classification, which enables us to discern why he claims that, in Barth, the 'original transcendental approach comes into its own'.[16] Bonhoeffer holds that, in Barth, there is a clear distinction between how the *actus directus* and *reflectus* are each related to the 'act of faith'. In order to keep the act of faith safe from human jurisdiction, Barth holds that it cannot be reflected on without ceasing to be faith proper: faith is beyond self-reflection, for God is no longer acting when the human being reflects on the act of faith, or rather, believing is entirely unreflective.

This clear demarcation between the act of faith and reflection on faith interests Bonhoeffer because it aligns with his prior discussion of the *actus directus* and *reflectus* in the transcendental attempt. If we maintain that the free transcendence of God's revelation must be preserved by understanding the Holy Spirit to be the subject of the act of faith to which the 'believing I' is present, then there is an abrupt differentiation between direct consciousness in that act of faith and the reflective consciousness involved in looking *at oneself* as believer. As Bonhoeffer states, to 'make God the content of my consciousness means to understand God as an entity'.[17] To reflect on the moment of saying 'I believe', then, is to focus on what Barth calls in *Romans* an 'empty canal' or 'burnt-out crater',[18] a mere vessel in which God may have acted but in which the revelatory act itself is no longer occurring. But, notwithstanding the general shared orientation he finds between 'genuine transcendentalism' and Barth's thinking, there is an important difference in Bonhoeffer's presentation of the emphases of their respective *actus* distinctions, which as we shall see shortly becomes the cornerstone of his critique.

In genuine transcendentalism, it will be recalled, the emphasis of the move from the *actus reflectus* to the *directus* is on the loss of subject–'object' singularity, in which the subject 'sees' only the object and not its own 'seeing', and there is no explicit self-awareness as such. In the *actus reflectus*, however, self-awareness is explicit, and the singular focus of direct consciousness on the original 'object' is thereby lost. In Bonhoeffer's presentation of Barth, he points to a subtle, but important, difference of emphasis to the *actus* distinction from that of genuine transcendentalism. Bonhoeffer sees the emphasis of the Barthian approach to lie not so much in reflection breaking the subject–'object' singularity of the *actus directus*, but rather in its cancelling out of the divinely 'given' subjectivity of the 'believing I', thought to be present 'in' or 'to' God 'understanding-God's-self in the act of faith'. The emphasis in Barth is therefore a loss of one subject to another, a precluding or contravening of the unreflective 'believing I' by the 'empirical I' that reflects. For Barth, the *actus reflectus* ensnares the divinely 'given' subjectivity of

---

16. DBWE2, 97.
17. Ibid., 92.
18. Barth, *Romans*, 65.

the 'believing I' within the parameters of human cognition and thus undercuts the free transcendence of God's self-revelation, negating or abrogating the 'believing I' by operating under one's own self-reflective capacities.

5.1.3 Bonhoeffer's critique of Barth

Bonhoeffer states that, in Barth, it 'remains problematic' how the human being 'can be perceived as something that has continuity'.[19] That is, if knowledge of God's revelation is intangible to the 'I' that reflects, it does not perdure or continue in 'the flow of life'. This concern for continuity applies to two facets of Bonhoeffer's discussion of Barth, the second of which is closely related to our own concern to integrate the unreflective and reflective aspects to human subjectivity 'in Christ'. To set out this second facet in detail, we need briefly to discuss the first, Bonhoeffer's concern for the continuity of the 'believing I'. This concern arises from the view that, if the 'believing I' comes into being and then disappears according to entirely free and unaccountable acts of God, it is unclear how it can 'be thought of as a unity'.[20] It is not easy to discern concretely what Bonhoeffer means by this 'unity' of the 'new existence', but the point seems to be that, in God's self-communication, the 'believing I' needs to be understood as being the same 'I' in every case. In being posited as something present in the act of faith 'ever anew',[21] there is no consistency between each instance of faith. This is problematic, as for genuine communication to occur, the 'I' that says 'I believe' needs to be the same 'I' in every case, for otherwise that which is cognized is simply lost immediately after each momentary instance of believing.

Bonhoeffer's second concern is for the continuity of what he calls the 'whole I' or the 'empirical total I',[22] which relates directly to our objective to integrate human subjectivity 'in Christ'. The 'empirical total I' is the subjectivity of the human being in its entirety, including the unified subjectivity of a mind–body unit *and* the 'believing I'. In short, given the lengths Barth takes to ensure that the 'believing I' cannot be drawn under human jurisdiction, this also threatens to undermine the notion of God communicating from the 'earthly', or empirical, side. Because that which is given to the 'empirical I' is utterly differentiated from the 'I' that says 'I believe', the 'total' unity of the human subject seems to be undermined. Again, without a unified consciousness there can be no communication as such, so Bonhoeffer is keen to acknowledge Barth's concern for God's free transcendence without rupturing the 'empirical total I' into what threatens to appear as two separate subjects.[23] Bonhoeffer is thus faced with something of a tightrope, between wanting to ensure the merely *human* act of trying to cognize

---

19. DBWE2, 97.
20. Ibid., 98.
21. Ibid., 90.
22. Ibid., 97.
23. See ibid., 93–8.

God is properly differentiated from the act of faith, yet also that there is a genuine encounter between the human and God, so there are not two parallel but separate acts occurring somehow 'in' the same consciousness.

Bonhoeffer's first concern for the continuity of the 'believing I', he claims, is suitably met by Barth. A full discussion of why this is the case is beyond the scope of this chapter, but for present purposes it will suffice to point out that Bonhoeffer understands Barth to present the 'believing I' 'formally' as the 'non-being' of the 'empirical I': it 'is the non-being of the first world [of the empirical I] which forms the being of the second world [of the believing I]'.[24] This alleged continuity is opaque and abstract, at least in Bonhoeffer's presentation of it. Here, we need only note that he is confident that the continuity of the 'believing I' is established by Barth, but argues that it comes at a high price, rendering the second concern for the continuity of the 'empirical I' more acute: 'the continuity' of the 'believing I' comes 'at the expense of the continuity of the total I'. This can be seen most basically as a straightforward corollary. If the 'believing I' is that which the 'empirical I' is not, then that which the 'empirical I' actually knows of the 'believing I' is so remote and abstract that the unity *between each* 'I' falls out of view.

This critical issue is rendered more severe, in that Bonhoeffer sees Barth as presenting the 'second world' (to which pertains the believing I) as 'supra-temporal'. Again, there is much going on in Barth's situating of the 'kingdom of heaven' as supratemporal that is outside the ambit of this study.[25] The key point for present purposes is that Bonhoeffer understands Barth to safeguard the transcendence of God's self-communication by holding that, if one can look on a moment in which one believes and consider the 'believing I' to have been at work specifically *then*, this makes the 'believing I' a possession of one's consciousness. If, however, one considers the moment of believing as thoroughly 'not-I', then the loss of one human subject to another is taken to an extreme point where the act of belief is so separate from human cognition that it is seen as not occurring 'in' time at all: Bonhoeffer states, the 'believing I' then 'has its continuity in the supratemporal'.[26] But, if the empirical total cannot say 'I believed *then*', the act of faith itself is ruptured from the subjectivity of the 'empirical total I' existing in the 'flow of life'.

Bonhoeffer therefore takes Barth to task on this, asking: 'Is the new I to be thought of in unity with the empirical total I, or does it remain its heavenly double [*himmlischer Doppelgänger*]?' The heavenly double is thus the supratemporal

---

24. Ibid. Exactly what this involves requires considerable discussion that cannot be entered into here, except to note that Bonhoeffer approaches the Barthian dialectic as a *Denkform*, while maintaining that this mutual negation is effective insofar the 'proviso made by dialectical theology is not a logical one that might be cancelled by the opposite' but 'a real one in each case' (ibid., 85). With this he chimes with recent interpretations of a *Realdialektik* in Barth by Michael Beintker and Bruce L. McCormack, cf. McCormack, *Karl Barth's Critically Realistic Dialectical Theology*, Oxford: Clarendon, 1997, 11.

25. See Barth, *Römerbrief*, 73, 84–5.

26. DBWE2, 99.

'believing I'. Bonhoeffer responds to this by claiming that, despite being 'utterly supratemporal' the 'act' of the 'believing I' 'has to be thought on the horizontal plane as well as from the infinity of the vertical perspective'.[27] This reference to verticality calls to mind one of the most oft-repeated Barthian statements that God acts 'perpendicularly from above' (*senkrecht von oben*).[28] In bringing the 'horizontal' into view here, Bonhoeffer is saying that the act of faith needs to be thought of as occurring on the level of tangible human consciousness in the temporal 'flow of life', bearing a point of reference in time, and thus perceptibly 'in' the consciousness of the 'empirical total I'. To make our way to studying Bonhoeffer's constructive alternatives, we must first examine how this critique of Barth is importantly orientated by the transcendental attempt discussed in Chapter 4.

5.1.4 Bonhoeffer's critique of Barth based on the actus *distinction*

In establishing how Bonhoeffer's critique of Barth is orientated by his discussion of philosophical transcendentalism, it should be pointed out that he is not denying Barth's position outright. He does not argue that there is no 'vertical perspective', but claims 'the act of the new I ... has to be thought on the horizontal plane *as well*.'[29] He brings the 'horizontal plane' into his response, by changing the emphasis of the *actus* distinction, from a focus on the loss of one human subject to another (the 'I' to the 'not-I') to something close to its central facet in genuine transcendentalism, the loss of subject–object singularity. Bonhoeffer says of Barth's view of revelation that 'what is revealed is called Christ, and the subject of understanding is God as Holy Spirit'.[30] In his response to the 'heavenly double', he focuses his attention on the aspect of *Christ* being 'what is revealed'. The spotlight is thus put on the loss of the directedness to this 'object' in moving from the *actus directus* to the *reflectus*, and not the loss of the pneumatologically instituted subjectivity of the 'believing I'. If the central element for understanding the cognition of revelation is the 'object' of apprehension (Christ), Bonhoeffer considers that this allows us to understand the saying of 'I believe' to occur in time. As he writes, 'we maintain that the essence of the *actus directus* lies not in its timelessness, but in its intentionality toward Christ.' He thus puts the dialectical framework of Barth's discussion aside, with the implication being that, if the 'object' of belief is the incarnate Christ, revelation occurs in time.

By rendering the moment of saying 'I believe' more tangible through affirming its temporality, the danger of ensnaring revelation in human capacities threatens to resurface, for if we can say 'I believed *then*', the self-revelation of God is made something we can point to in our own experience, and it would be thereby under

27. Ibid.
28. Barth, *Römerbrief*, 84.
29. DBWE2, 99 (my italics).
30. Ibid., 92.

human jurisdiction. Bonhoeffer responds to this by stating that the 'intentionality' is 'not repeatable because it is freely given by God'.[31] This means first that whether or not one genuinely beholds Christ in the *actus directus* is entirely at God's disposal ('freely given by God'). In reflecting on oneself as believing, then, reflection is not revelatory: the 'object' Christ 'cannot be pointed to in a here-and-there open for exhibit'.[32] But, although the givenness of the revealed 'object' is entirely at God's disposal, this does not mean that the apprehending of Christ itself does not occur in time. 'Nothing could be more mistaken', he claims, 'than – on the basis of the fact that everything is accessible to reflection only in reflection … to dispute that there is an *actus directus* in time'.[33] That is, the 'object' is actually given to the consciousness of the 'empirical I', for he states, 'the *essence* of the *actus directus* lies in the way Christ touches upon existence, in its historical, temporal totality'.[34] This de-emphasizes the 'vertical perspective' and concentrates on the 'horizontal'.

Insofar as one can reflect on apprehending Christ in a way which is harmonious with the original 'intentionality to Christ' of the *actus directus*, Bonhoeffer considers we can understand the *actus reflectus* as not merely tearing the subject away from God. This means that the unattainable and unpossessable moment of apprehension is something given to self-understanding, it can be reflected on authentically, although reflection is not itself revelatory. Bonhoeffer's shift of emphasis still involves a 'loss': no act of reflection can find the 'object'. Yet, he holds that the 'object' could be 'open' to reflection insofar as one can reflect properly on having apprehended it. Bonhoeffer writes, 'the *actus directus* is not accessible to the demonstrative "here and there"', but, 'it occurs in concrete, conscious, psychic events that are *substantially open to reflection*', so 'it is not that the *actus directus* offers no material to reflection'.[35] In the following subsection I will discuss how Bonhoeffer constructs his two instances of theologically orientated reflective subjectivity on the basis of this reorientation, or rather, how we can approach self-reflection on the basis that the *actus directus* is 'substantially open' to reflection and 'offers material' to it.

Nonetheless, there is an unanswered question in Bonhoeffer's critique, regarding what role, if any, the 'believing I' plays. That Bonhoeffer states that the horizontal view must be thought of 'as well' as the vertical shows that he does not wish to discard the 'believing I', but to complement it with a change of emphasis. In doing so, he leaves unanswered the issue of whether there is still a 'believing' *and* 'empirical I' in his view of things. This point should be noted here, for we shall revisit it in Section 5.3.

31. Ibid., 100.
32. Ibid., 128.
33. Ibid., 128–9.
34. Ibid., 100.
35. Ibid.

5.2 'Self-understanding-in-remembrance' and the 'Christian conscience'

Bonhoeffer's emphasizing of the 'object' of the *actus directus* rather than its subject leads him to envisage reflecting on oneself as having apprehended the 'object', although the genuine 'presence' of the 'object' is not reflectively attainable. Bonhoeffer works from this insight to describe two forms of reflective subjectivity for theological enquiry, which are intended to extend the *that* of revelatory communication into a broader range of human self-understanding, and which will advance our enquiry by moving us towards understanding the reflective as 'wisdom'.

5.2.1 'Self-understanding-in-remembrance'

In order to examine 'self-understanding-in-remembrance' directly, it must be situated as an aspect to what Bonhoeffer calls 'the theological way of knowing'. This is contrasted by Bonhoeffer with the 'believing way of knowing',[36] which pertains to the unreflective *actus directus*, where 'there is simply no reflection', for 'faith carries itself forward in "direct consciousness" [and] ... cannot be reflectively reproduced'.[37] He goes on to state that the 'moment of faith' is 'the concrete event of being taken hold of (*Angegriffen*) by Christ'.[38] His mention of concreteness is related to his concern for the 'horizontal perspective' mentioned above, for a purely 'vertical' (supratemporal) perspective is inherently abstract, meaning at bottom non-spatial and non-temporal, whereas concreteness points conversely to spatio-temporal situatedness. Bonhoeffer considers that concretizing the *actus directus* of faith with the 'horizontal perspective' renders it (*contra* Barth) 'substantially open to reflection'. He explores this openness by outlining how we reflect on the 'concrete event' of apprehending Christ, which occurs within what he calls the 'theological way of knowing'. The theological way of knowing is the epistemological mode in which human beings investigate matters pertaining to God's revelation, but not God's self-revelation *itself*, the communication of which still resides entirely with God. Human beings can enquire into matters like Scripture, ecclesiology and so on, and indeed, as Bonhoeffer comments, this is necessary in order to engage in activities like preparing to preach. In reflecting on, say, the word of Christ in the Gospel, he holds that one is not encountered by Christ, for Christ's presence is entirely at Christ's own disposal. Reflecting on the Scriptures and being 'taken hold of' by Christ are thus firmly differentiated by the presence or non-presence of Christ as revealed 'object'. In reflection, Bonhoeffer states, 'Person and word have separated',[39] meaning the words 'about' Christ and Christ's own 'personal objectivity' have 'moved apart', and one is focused on words

36. Ibid., 124–6.
37. Ibid., 133.
38. Ibid., 128.
39. Ibid., 129.

'about' Christ, while the 'object' proper is not actively 'taking hold of' the reflecting subject. But – importantly – he argues that reflection can evince what we might call a 'pointedness' towards that 'object', meaning that it is concerned with the 'object' and seeks to represent it reflectively as authentically as possible. This pointedness is not 'directed at' the 'object' in a strict sense, for the genuine presence of Christ must be entirely at God's disposal. As Bonhoeffer writes, the words available to reflection are mere 'assertions' taken 'from the memory of divine happenings' and the 'creative word' of 'Christ they cannot speak'.[40] In this way of knowing, says Bonhoeffer, we are thus reflecting 'on entities', insofar as the God's free disclosure in Christ is represented as objects in the '"here and there" open for exhibit'; meaning attainable and possessable by human endeavour, and not the 'living person'.[41]

As it stands, there is thus very little to differentiate Bonhoeffer's distinction of the 'believing' and the 'theological' ways of knowing from Barth. Bonhoeffer indirectly acknowledges this by stating that 'in light of what we have said, theological thinking is in principle indistinguishable from profane thinking'.[42] However, Bonhoeffer goes on to state that, although in reflection 'the living person of Christ remains a reference in thought', 'any genuine reference ... is not made possible by a theoretical method, but by holding fast in humility to the word that has been heard'.[43] This is a difficult formulation because the term 'genuine reference' is something we would expect to occur only in the *actus directus*, in that only in direct consciousness are we understood to be genuinely directed at the actual, living person of Christ. Despite his choice of language being confusing and misleading, we can elucidate Bonhoeffer's meaning by applying the term 'pointedness' instead. Bonhoeffer means that reflection can be genuinely pointed 'at', or rather, 'in the direction' of Christ, although the living person is not revealing himself. Bonhoeffer then indicates how we might ensure this pointedness reflects Christ as authentically and accurately as possible: 'by holding fast in humility to the word that has been heard.' This means staying firmly focused on what *was* the 'object' proper of the *actus directus*, the living person of Christ, and staying resolutely mindful (in 'humility') of the fact that the actual living person of Christ is not given to reflection. In short, we have a broad way to account for reflective consciousness as commensurable with the unreflective here, but before examining how this advances our enquiry, it is advisable to mention how it differs from Barth. Bonhoeffer acknowledges this difference by stating: 'in the obedience of thinking, the scholarly discipline of theology *does* differ from everything profane',[44] which while seeming to contradict his prior statement that theological thinking is 'in principle indistinguishable from profane thinking' subtly demarcates itself from it. The key words are 'in principle'. This means that, although the 'object'

---

40. Ibid.
41. Ibid., 130–1.
42. Ibid.
43. Ibid., 131.
44. Ibid.

is in a *principled* way never given to reflection, the theological way of knowing (occurring 'in humility') is a form of reflection which can maintain a pointedness to the 'object', although the living person of Christ cannot be present to it. That is, there is an *actus reflectus* here which is an authentically Christ-orientated activity, insofar as it is performed in humility, performed with this distinction ever in view. Now we can examine how this is extended by Bonhoeffer into a corresponding mode of self-reflection.

In Bonhoeffer's approach, although the *actus reflectus* is under human jurisdiction, it can ('in humility') share a pointedness to the same 'object' 'at' which the unreflective *actus directus* is 'directed' (Christ). With the example given above of reflecting on the Scriptures, this pointedness is relatively straightforward to envisage. When thinking about self-reflection, however, it seems more abstruse or even contradictory to envisage reflectively focusing on oneself while one's activity is also somehow 'pointed at' Christ. Nonetheless, Bonhoeffer presents an attempt to do just this, which he calls 'self-understanding-in-remembrance'.

Bonhoeffer seems to hold that there is an implicit or unthematized sense of oneself as believer which is given along with the unreflective apprehension of Christ. He writes that there is a 'self-understanding "in faith"', which arises when 'Christ assails my existence',[45] but – building on the distinction between the believing and theological ways of knowing outlined above – it is clear that to reflect on this implicit and unreflective sense of oneself as believer can be, as he describes it, 'preserved for thinking only in "remembrance"' (*im Gedächtnis*).[46] This means reflecting on oneself as one who *has* been 'assailed', mirroring to oneself the sense that one was 'taken hold of', which – as reflective – evinces the moving apart of 'word and person' in that Christ is not the 'object' proper. This differs from Barth insofar as the act of faith of the 'believing I' was for him something one could never reflect on in any circumstances, remaining always transcendent to reflective subjectivity. For Bonhoeffer, one can view oneself as having been addressed by Christ, although the *that* of the address remains at God's disposal, meaning one cannot establish whether or not the living person of Christ was really present at the point being remembered.[47] However, one can look at a moment of saying 'I believe' and *understand oneself* to have 'believed *then*', and the unreflective apprehension of Christ can be reflected on authentically thereby. As this pertains to reflecting on the memory of an unreflective moment, Bonhoeffer refers to understanding oneself in this fashion as 'self-understanding-in-remembrance'.

The key question remains, nevertheless, of how looking back at oneself in memory, a pointedness to the original 'object' Christ is maintained. Bonhoeffer only touches on this very briefly, and perhaps the brevity of his discussion on this point contributes to the problems discussed in the following section. Bonhoeffer states that 'only in the church', where Christ's 'living person is at work – is it

---

45. Ibid., 135.
46. Ibid.; DBW2, 133.
47. DBWE2, 133.

understood that a thinking which wants to serve the concrete church in reality also serves, as autonomous thinking, the law of Christ'.[48] Here, Bonhoeffer is making a distinction of motive which, he holds, determines the pointedness of self-reflection. If one is reflecting on oneself as having apprehended the revealed Christ as an act of 'thinking which wants to serve the concrete church', he considers this orientates self-reflection authentically towards Christ. He is not explicit about why this is the case, but we can surmise that the directedness to Christ of the original act of direct consciousness is maintained because self-reflection in the service of the church is somehow protected from the self-centred or self-possessive tendencies it otherwise involves.

Bonhoeffer gives us no examples of what he has in mind with 'self-understanding-in-remembrance', but the example he gives of the 'theological way of knowing', preparation for preaching, would hold for *self*-reflection as well, insofar as one may be led to reflect on one's own experiences of the apprehension of Christ in order to serve Christ in the church. That is, before preaching, it may be beneficial to reflect on moments of 'being assailed' or 'taken hold of' by Christ, to evaluate the points one wishes to make. Although Bonhoeffer does not spell this out, the point seems to be that this is different from reflecting on oneself for its own sake, out of curiosity or perhaps more insidiously and pridefully. So, it is not the act of self-reflection itself which is important here, but rather the end to which it is put. Before evaluating how this advances our discussion, we should note that underlying 'self-understanding-in-remembrance' is the emphasis of the *actus* distinction from genuine transcendentalism, namely, a shift of emphasis (from Barth's 'believing I'/'empirical I' dialectic) back to the loss of the original directedness of the object in reflection. By maintaining that engaging in self-reflection in the service of Christ presents 'autonomous thinking' which serves Christ,[49] Bonhoeffer offers an *actus reflectus* which maintains the subject–'object' singularity of the *actus directus* in which one is pointed towards the same 'object' as the actus *directus* in self-reflection. This basis in genuine transcendentalism also characterizes the second mode of reflection commensurable with the unreflective, which we will now discuss.

5.2.2 The 'Christian conscience'

Bonhoeffer's second mode of a commensurable self-reflection is called the 'Christian conscience',[50] and it is one of two forms of conscience he mentions in his final Section C of *Act and Being*. The first involves the self-reflection of one who is 'in Adam', meaning unredeemed, and, insofar as Bonhoeffer considers that it is only by being 'taken hold of' by Christ that one knows one is a sinner, conscience

---

48. Ibid., 134.
49. Ibid.
50. Ibid., 158.

'in Adam' is seen as intrinsically self-justifying.[51] For one who is redeemed, however, Bonhoeffer considers conscience to function differently, and he calls this 'the Christian conscience'.

Bonhoeffer states that, if 'being-in-Christ means being orientated towards Christ, reflection on the self is obviously not part of that being' and 'here lies the problem of Christian conscience'.[52] The issue seems to be that, as with 'self-understanding-in-remembrance', being 'orientated towards Christ' means being 'directed at' the 'object' proper, which pertains only to the unreflective. This presents a 'problem' as regards conscience, because conscience is an intrinsic feature of being human and to deny it would trespass human integrity. Bonhoeffer therefore needs to establish how we can reflectively evaluate ourselves 'in Christ' although *that* we are 'in Christ' cannot be grounded *by* reflection. Furthermore, if we could not reflect 'in Christ', then our being 'in Christ' would be completely reflectively ungraspable, and Bonhoeffer would be veering towards the discontinuity of the 'heavenly double'. For this reason, he outlines a 'reflection on the self' which is 'included within the intentionality toward Christ', mirroring the same approach of 'self-understanding-in-remembrance' in that it *points to* the 'object' which is only properly present to the unreflective.

The 'Christian conscience' involves a process of self-reflective moral evaluation, but the actual evaluation of one's moral standing is entirely under the preserve of Christ's forgiveness. That is, in conscience one reflects on one's own conduct, but in 'Christian conscience', one does not hold jurisdiction over the judgement of that conduct. Bonhoeffer describes this in terms of intentionality, for he holds that to see oneself as 'pardoned' is to see oneself in Christ, because the qualification of oneself as 'pardoned' can only be granted *by* Christ, and one is still then, in a sense, 'directed at' Christ. Bonhoeffer writes, 'I see my sin' within 'forgiveness through Christ'.[53] In this way, then, human beings look 'back' on themselves and maintain a pointedness towards the object at which the unreflective consciousness of faith is directed: Christ in his personal objectivity or, as Bonhoeffer puts it, 'reflection as such [the Christian conscience] can no longer break the intentionality towards Christ'.[54]

5.3 Towards the actus reflectus as 'wisdom'

We learned in Chapter 1 that, in *Ethics*, Bonhoeffer gestures towards a permitted and endorsed understanding of reflection in Christian life, which he sets out as continuous or harmonious with unreflective simplicity, and even as inalienably bound up in it, and that he refers to this reflection as 'wisdom'. In order to evaluate

51. Ibid., 139.
52. Ibid., 155.
53. Ibid., 156.
54. Ibid., 156–7.

how Bonhoeffer's two modes of self-reflection in *Act and Being* outlined above can also be considered to constitute wisdom, our task is to assess how they meet the cognitive requirements of the loci of the simplicity of *Discipleship*: maintaining the singularity of vision of 'seeing only Christ' and preserving the 'hiddenness of the disciple'.

5.3.1 'Self-understanding-in-remembrance' as wisdom

In 'self-understanding-in-remembrance', Bonhoeffer holds that the 'empirical I' reflects authentically on a moment of believing and points that reflection towards Christ through engaging in self-reflective activity through a motive of serving Christ. In assessing how far this continuity meets the requirement of 'seeing only Christ', Bonhoeffer clearly provides us with some important gains. First, the moment of belief is brought into reflection, and reflection does not intrinsically negate or preclude believing. More specifically, by differentiating between apprehending the 'object' proper and reflecting on an implicit sense of oneself as believer given along with that apprehension, Bonhoeffer sets out a framework in which reflection does not merely 'tear one away' from Christ, insofar as we can consider that sense to be given 'from outside' (in apprehending Christ as revealed 'object') and therefore not self-generated as such. This means that although self-reflection comes under human jurisdiction, and is non-revelatory thereby, the focus of self-reflection, arguably, 'belongs' to Christ, meaning generated or instigated by Christ, and by focusing on oneself in this fashion one can be considered to still be 'seeing' Christ in his effects. Moreover, although in 'self-understanding-in-remembrance' the 'I' is made an object of thought in reflection, this is intended to maintain intentionality to Christ through being directed in his service.[55] This informs our endeavour considerably, because the pointedness of self-reflection towards Christ is shared with the 'object' of the *actus directus* in this mode of self-reflection, and therefore there is an alignment of orientation between the unreflective and reflective in 'self-understanding-in-remembrance'. This offers us a way to approach self-reflection in a way in which – by maintaining the subject–'object' singularity of the *actus directus* in genuine transcendentalism – an addressee of revelation maintains the requirement of 'seeing only Christ'.

Nevertheless, there are two problems with 'self-understanding-in-remembrance' that require attention. First, it offers a relatively narrow and highly specialized arena for self-reflection (with an explicit desire to 'serve Christ in the church', such as when 'preparing to preach'). Calling to mind our discussion in Chapter 1, this renders its gains for the overall aims of this book to be relatively limited, in that we are working from an acknowledgement that self-reflection is unavoidably crucial for being human in the broadest possible sense, and so it seems unrealistic to

---

55. Bonhoeffer does not give any examples, but his earlier discussion of preparing to preach could serve as an example of someone looking back on being 'assailed' in order to 'serve the concrete church'.

permit self-reflection only when it adheres to these conditions. This narrowness is no doubt a consequence of the fact that *Act and Being* was written for a readership of 'professional theologians'[56] when this terminology was applied only to ministry in the church.

The second problem arises through drawing our attention to the fact that, notwithstanding Bonhoeffer's concern for continuity, his discussion of 'self-understanding-in-remembrance' still assumes considerable *dis*continuity between the *actus directus* and *reflectus*. For example, he states that 'human beings, when they understand themselves in faith, are entirely wrenched away from themselves',[57] meaning that any self-reflectively gleaned knowledge of oneself is always undone in the unreflective consciousness of faith, which '*creates our Dasein again and again*'.[58] This is problematic, because 'self-understanding-in-remembrance' is explicitly intended to set out a mode of self-reflection from which we need not be 'entirely wrenched away' in the unreflective, because it shares an orientation to the same 'object' of unreflective consciousness. Arguably, Bonhoeffer lapses into language of fragmentation and dislocation here, because the differentiation of 'I and myself' in genuine transcendentalism has not fully perdured into his theological undertaking. That is, he seems to consider in the transcendental attempt that genuine transcendentalism preserves a dimension of subjectivity as transcendent to the self-reflective gaze, and thus he avoids full objectification of the 'I', insofar as the 'I' itself cannot be fully beheld as 'myself'. To preserve hiddenness as limit promises to offer us a way to establish a mode of self-reflection from which we need not be '*entirely* wrenched away', because the possessive gaze of self-reflection has not laid full claim over the 'I' by rendering it a mere object as 'myself'. Indeed, this promises to offer a broader understanding for the place of 'humility' in self-reflection than Bonhoeffer's approach to this virtue in 'self-understanding-in-remembrance', as something evinced by only engaging in self-reflection to serve Christ in the church.

5.3.2 The 'Christian conscience' as wisdom

On the 'Christian conscience', Bonhoeffer again offers some considerable advances as regards the maintaining of the subject–'object' singularity of the *actus directus* in self-reflection. By looking at oneself as 'pardoned', and bearing in mind that this 'pardon' cannot be self-generated, one is – in a sense – 'looking at' Christ, or as Bonhoeffer puts it, reflecting 'on the self' in a way 'included within the intentionality toward Christ'. As above, the focus of self-reflection in this case 'belongs' to Christ, meaning it is generated or instigated by Christ, and by focusing

---

56. Clifford J. Green comments (DBWE8, 232, n32) that *Der Theologe* for Bonhoeffer would mean an ordained pastor.
57. DBWE2, 134.
58. Ibid., 132.

5. The Actus Reflectus as Wisdom

on oneself in this fashion one can be considered still to be 'seeing' Christ in his effects, even though reflection stands under human jurisdiction.

Nonetheless, the fact remains that Bonhoeffer again still assumes a measure of fragmentation and dislocation in this discussion. This can be seen in the fact that he offsets this 'backward'-looking self-reflection of Christian conscience with what he terms 'the child', a disposition of Christian life described as 'being defined by the future alone' in which one is in a state of 'purity' or 'simplicity', which mirrors the momentary, direct awareness of the child, uncharacterized by the accumulation of past experience. He describes this 'mode of being' as a 'pure orientation towards Christ'[59] and claims it is 'beyond' any reflection.[60] The distinction between the 'Christian conscience' and 'the child' is problematic for us, because the former is explicitly set out as a mode of self-reflection which is orientated to Christ, so it remains unclear how this 'pure orientation' to Christ which is 'beyond' reflection is to be demarcated from the prior attempt to outline a mode of self-reflection 'included within the intentionality to Christ'. Moreover, it is difficult to discern how there can be continuity between 'the child' and the 'Christian conscience', if the former has no sense of a past. If we take the Christian conscience as the self-reflection of the 'empirical I' 'in Christ', there seems to be genuine rupture here, insofar as the 'empirical I' is unavoidably affected by the past and so must be abruptly split from the 'I' of 'the child', which is 'defined by the future alone'. This observation is intensified in that he describes the child as a state in which human beings are 'wholly detached from themselves in contemplation of Christ', which 'expresses the personality in relation'.[61] Again, we must ask here how a 'personality' can pertain to an 'I' with no awareness of the past, especially given Bonhoeffer's prior outlining of a mode of reflection on past sin 'in Christ'.

Arguably, Bonhoeffer's lapses into language of fragmentation and dislocation is a consequence of a residual presence of the Barthian 'vertical perspective' in his thinking. This is, of course, implied by his express desire to think of the horizontal perspective 'as well' as the vertical. So, unreflective subjectivity in Bonhoeffer's discussion still bears traces of supratemporality, which of course, renders any attempt at continuity deeply challenging, for the 'empirical I' (that reflects) is always unavoidably temporal. Put differently, Bonhoeffer's leaving unanswered of the question of whether there is a 'believing I' created 'ever anew' in every (unreflective) act of faith, resurfaces through a residually supratemporal 'believing I' lurking in his discussion. Now, calling to mind our earlier discussion of a mode of hiddenness as 'limit' in genuine transcendentalism, we can ask if employing the preservation of hiddenness from that discussion could avoid this residual fragmentation. In the transcendental attempt, Bonhoeffer is clear that genuine transcendentalism preserves a dimension of subjectivity as transcendent to the self-reflective gaze, and if we were to bring this into the theological domain, it

---

59. Ibid., 157.
60. Ibid.
61. Ibid.

promises to serve as a coordinate or boundary for self-reflection which avoids full objectification, but is present 'to' or 'in' reflective consciousness – and not therefore simply 'beyond' all reflection as such.

5.4 Summing up

With the 'Christian conscience', valuable gains have been made in Bonhoeffer's maintaining of the directedness of the *actus directus* in self-reflection, which will inform our subsequent chapters, insofar as he offers a mode of self-reflection 'in Christ' and therefore not incommensurable with the unreflective. With 'self-understanding-in-remembrance', again Bonhoeffer's maintaining of the subject–'object' singularity of the *actus directus* offers us a valuable pointer for approaching a mode of reflection that maintains 'seeing only Christ'. However, although this moves us towards wisdom , it does not seem to offer the broadness of scope which Bonhoeffer himself suggests when he states that 'only the one who combines simplicity and wisdom can endure', for he maintains that subject–'object' singularity is maintained through only engaging in self-reflection in parameters which seem unhelpfully narrow. It can be concluded therefore that, although we have moved towards 'wisdom', we shall need to construe self-reflection more broadly than 'self-understanding-in-remembrance'.

More negatively, however, the preservation of a subjective 'hiddenness' 'in' self-reflection from genuine transcendentalism seems to have fallen out of view in both of Bonhoeffer's attempts to establish continuity. In 'self-understanding-in-remembrance' he seems to assume that self-reflection can always only objectify the 'I' as 'myself', rather than be orientated or configured by the awareness of a 'hidden' 'I' in self-reflection. In the distinction between the 'Christian conscience' and 'the child' moreover, this 'limit' or boundary promises to enable us to understand how the 'empirical I' that reflects can have an awareness of the unreflective 'I' as hidden, so unreflective consciousness is not merely 'beyond' all reflection. Moreover, insofar as the unreflective 'I' is, in the strictly limited sense of genuine transcendentalism, present 'to' or 'in' self-reflection, this promises to offer us a way to construe the unreflective 'I' not as 'defined by the future alone' but as present 'to' the temporal without being fully given over the self-reflective gaze. For this reason, in Chapter 7 we shall investigate more closely the particular construal of subjective 'hiddenness' as 'limit' in genuine transcendentalism by examining certain pertinent aspects of the foundational text of transcendental philosophy, Kant's *Critique of Pure Reason*. Before embarking on that examination, however, we must turn our attention to the practical side of our enquiry and explore Bonhoeffer's *Ethics*.

Chapter 6

TOWARDS PRACTICAL DISCERNMENT AS WISDOM: UNREFLECTIVE AND REFLECTIVE AGENCY IN *ETHICS*

Chapters 1 and 2 indicate that the practical loci of the simplicity of *Discipleship* can be constructively elucidated through Bonhoeffer's *Ethics*. There, we learned first that *Discipleship* presents 'simple obedience' (a volitional oneness between Christ and the disciple in unreflective agency) as 'interrupted'[1] by reflection, but in *Ethics* Bonhoeffer permits and endorses activities of practical, reflective discernment in Christian life. Secondly, we learned that 'purity of heart' (unreflectively acting without self-orientated criteria) is sharply juxtaposed with reflection in *Discipleship* as something inherently linked to the 'knowledge of good and evil', but in *Ethics* Bonhoeffer describes Christ-centred practically orientated activities of reflection in which an agent is said to be 'freed from the knowledge of good and evil'. Further impetus to examine *Ethics* has also been given through study of *Discipleship*'s reception in Chapter 3, for example from Schmitz, who claims there is an 'inner connection' between *Ethics* and *Discipleship*. Our discussions which have touched on the practical domain in the previous chapters, then, combine to point us to *Ethics*, and insofar as this text will move us towards understanding modes of reflection continuous or harmonious with the unreflective, we shall, again, have moved towards 'wisdom', reflection as commensurable with unreflective simplicity.

6.1 Gestaltung *and the reflective*

6.1.1 Ethics *and* Discipleship

Ethics, collated posthumously from unpublished manuscripts, was seen by Bonhoeffer as highly significant for his own intellectual legacy, indicated by his comment, I 'sometimes think my life is more or less behind me, and all I have left

---

1. DBW4, 62 (my translation).

to do is finish my ethics',[2] leading Green to call the book his '*magnum opus*'.[3] As indicated above, *Ethics* evinces links with our areas of concern from *Discipleship*, most obviously through Bonhoeffer's comments about 'unreflective doing' in the manuscript 'God's Love and the Disintegration of the World'. But, importantly, Bonhoeffer also exhibits a stance towards reflection which seems much broader than *Discipleship*'s, in 'God's Love', again, and also in 'History and the Good' and 'Ethics as Formation', where our hermeneutical key of simplicity and wisdom is found. Indeed, this consonance and dissonance with *Discipleship* influenced early arrangements of the *Ethics* manuscripts, as Bethge's 1963 arrangement sought a chronological ordering and placed 'God's Love and the Disintegration of the World' as the first chapter, classing it as belonging to the earliest 'Cost of Discipleship' stage of writing the book.[4] Green's painstaking analysis resulted in the arrangement of the 1998 edition, which seeks to replicate Bonhoeffer's own intended structure and also shows that 'The Ethical and the Christian as a Topic' was actually the last manuscript written, suggesting that simplicity ('unreflective doing') remains centrally important for Bonhoeffer's thinking long after Finkenwalde. Now we will examine 'unreflective doing' in *Ethics*, with a view to exploring subsequently how reflection can be commensurable with this 'doing'.

6.1.2 'Unreflective doing' and 'simple obedience' as Gestaltung

Bonhoeffer speaks of 'unreflective doing' as something arising from a 'knowledge of Jesus', which he says is 'transformed into doing, without any self-reflection whatsoever'. Moreover, he claims that, for followers of Christ, 'doing has become unquestioning' and so these followers are 'completely dedicated to and absorbed by it', and so look 'only at Jesus Christ'.[5] This 'doing' is unreflective, in the sense that there is a unity between agent and intended action, and, insofar as Bonhoeffer holds that Christ himself is 'incarnated' or 'becomes human' (*menschwerden*) in the deeds of his followers, this is presented as a unity between the agent and Christ. Language of being 'entirely absorbed' in the performance of Christ's will, and 'looking only' at him, obviously resonates with the unreflective simplicity of *Discipleship*, and the unity between an agent and Christ of 'unreflective doing' aligns closely with the volitional unity of the 'simple obedience' of *Discipleship*. Moreover, *Discipleship*'s apparent exclusivity between 'simple obedience' and reflection seems at first glance to be carried over into *Ethics*, for *un*-reflective

---

2. DBWE8, 222. Bearing in mind that Bonhoeffer did not plan to call this project *Ethics*, but had a working title of 'The Penultimate and Preparing the Way', we have not capitalized the word ethics in this quote (in German it would be capitalized either way).

3. Green, in DBWE6, 1.

4. Harold Lockley, *Dietrich Bonhoeffer*, Swansea: Phoenix Press, 1993, 67; cf. Appendix III of DBWE6, 477 and Green in same volume, 27.

5. DBWE6, 318.

doing is by definition exclusive of reflection, occurring 'without any self-reflection whatsoever'.[6]

However, as this 'doing' is understood as Christ's own 'becoming human' in the world, it is related to another key term from *Ethics*, to which considerable attention will be given in this chapter: *Gestaltung*. This is usually translated as 'formation', but it is important to bear in mind that it does not only include Christ's formation of the human being,[7] but also his 'formation of the world' 'through' or 'in' the deeds of his followers. As he states, 'the *Gestaltung* of a world reconciled with God' proceeds 'only from the form (*Gestalt*) of Christ'.[8] *Gestaltung* thus includes Christ's forming of the world according to his own form, Christ's will being performed *through* human action, thus involving a volitional oneness between the human agent and the will of Christ himself, thus broadly correlating with the 'simple obedience' of *Discipleship* and the volitional oneness indicated there by the *ein*-words discussed in Chapter 2.

Importantly for our purposes, approaching unreflective agency as an instance of *Gestaltung* (as both sharing a volitional unity between an agent and Christ) offers a conceptual key for understanding how reflection can sustain volitional unity with Christ. *Gestaltung* seems to offer a commensurability with reflection, insofar as we can envisage reflecting 'within' *Gestaltung*, discerning how one's deeds might form the world according to Christ's form, or best approximate to Christ's will, and this is harder to envisage with *un*-reflective doing. We can thus approach reflection 'within' *Gestaltung* as involving the 'moving apart' of an agent from his or her intended actions, but without 'splitting' an agent from Christ's will, insofar as these actions are approached as Christ's 'taking form', or Christ's own action. As discussed in Chapter 2, *Discipleship*'s 'simple obedience' is said to issue in deeds which have their sole 'ground' (*Begründung*)[9] in Jesus. To examine whether or not a 'reflective *Gestaltung*' will sustain 'simple obedience', then, we need to establish how it can similarly lead to deeds 'grounded' only on Christ. To answer this question, we shall need to look closely at the term *Gestaltung* and its semantic cognate *Gestalt*.

---

6. Ibid.
7. Bonhoeffer presents Christ's formation as involving *both* the formation (or 'con-formation') of human beings and the formation of the world. As the usual Anglo-American meaning of 'formation' in theology is humanly focused, this side to Bonhoeffer's presentation tends to dominate the literature, for example, Kaiser, *Becoming*; Geoffrey B. Kelly and F. Burton Nelson, *The Cost of Moral Leadership*, Grand Rapids, MI: Eerdmans, 2003; Lisa E. Dahill, *Reading from the Underside of Selfhood*, Eugene, OR: Pickwick Publications, 2009. Joseph McGarry suggests formation is a 'by-product' to discipleship, 'Formed While Following: Dietrich Bonhoeffer's Asymmetrical View of Agency in Christian Formation', *Theology Today* 71, no. 1 (2014): 106–20.
8. DBWE6, 92.
9. DBW4, 45.

6.1.3 Gestaltung *and* Gestalt

Gestaltung's root term *Gestalt* has a large and complex semantic field, encompassing different aspects of German language philosophy, psychology and literature. Focusing in this subsection on why Bonhoeffer uses *Gestalt* will provide us with important background for asking whether or not a 'reflective *Gestaltung*' can sustain 'simple obedience' subsequently. Bonhoeffer first employs *Gestalt* extensively in his *Christology* lectures of 1933,[10] where it provides him with a means to articulate his key concern with the 'present Christ' in the 'here and now' (*hic et nunc*).[11] *Gestalt* exhibits qualities which allow him to strike a balance between avoiding some of the consequences he sees following from the understandings of Christ's presence in both liberal and Barthian theology. On the one hand, Bonhoeffer connects the trajectory of liberal Protestant Christology with a tendency to see Christ as a historical figure, whose ethical teaching is passed through the ages by the medium of Scripture. He finds this unsatisfactory, because he is indelibly marked by the dialectician's conviction of the 'infinite qualitative difference'[12] between humanity and God, and considers the liberal approach to undermine this difference by enclosing God's revelation in a human framework of history. That is, by emphasizing Christ as teacher rather than revealer, and seeing his teaching as transmitted through human activity in temporal channels of dissemination, Bonhoeffer holds that Jesus is reduced to a mere historical figure and not vitally present *hic et nunc*. To speak of the *Gestalt* of Christ, however, seems to offer Bonhoeffer some conceptual armoury for an understanding of Jesus as really present among human beings in the here and now.

Before looking at why this is the case, it should be pointed out that, although Bonhoeffer is orientated by the Barthian-dialectical critique of liberal Protestantism, he is also dissatisfied with some consequences of that critique. Barth avoids a liberal domestication of Jesus into a merely historical figure by emphasizing the historical Jesus as something akin to one of Barth's 'burnt-out craters',[13] because historical enquiry is orchestrated and conducted by human beings. As we have seen, God's act of revelation is held by Barth to be entirely under the preserve of God, and so apprehending Christ as the revealed Son of God is not something attainable by historical research. To recall terminology we met in *Act and Being*, Bonhoeffer speaks of Barth's theology as involving a 'vertical perspective' linked to 'supratemporality', involving a 'wholly otherness' intended to avoid ensnaring revelation in what human beings can generate for themselves. This purely 'vertical perspective' applies also to Bonhoeffer's construal of Barth's accounting for Christ's presence, for he considers that God's act of revealing himself is protected by Barth

---

10. For an extensive discussion of the genealogy of *Gestalt/Gestaltung* in Bonhoeffer's work and a review of secondary interpretations of its significance, see Kaiser, *Becoming*, 85–102.
11. DBWE12, 310f.
12. Barth, *Romans*, 10, 335.
13. Ibid., 65.

from being something humans can instigate or stimulate by investigating historical remnants of Jesus' life to disclose his ethical teachings. Rather, revelation is seen as communicated only by the 'God who acts perpendicularly from above'. For Bonhoeffer, to sequester Christ's presence as pertaining to momentary impositions on the here and now 'from above' undermines Christ's enduring presence in the here and now 'for me' ('*pro me*').[14] Bonhoeffer develops the theme of Christ's 'being-there-*pro-me*' to challenge theologians who have divorced Christ's person from his effects or works, arguing therefore that insofar as Christ is 'there' (in his person) he is there 'for me' in his works.[15] With a purely 'vertical perspective' however, the 'givenness' of Christ *to* human beings is undermined. To elucidate the present Christ further, then, Bonhoeffer wants to avoid both the liberal and dialectical options. He wants to avoid the 'low' Christology of the liberal tradition, in which Christ is captured in a linear, temporal framework. But he also wants to avoid the allegedly intangibly 'high' Christology of Barth, in which Christ is so aloof from the temporal ('horizontal') that his being here 'for me' is compromised by the 'infinity' of the 'vertical perspective'.[16]

Gestalt offers Bonhoeffer useful terminology for avoiding both options. The word derives from the past participle of the verb *stellen*, meaning 'to be stood' or 'placed'. It has been used commonly in German philosophy to translate the Latin *forma*, and in this connection refers to the 'spatial' and 'intuitable' appearance of a thing.[17] Moreover, in psychology and the study of literature, the word is used to mean 'character' or 'personality',[18] and thus has a strong dimension of 'presentness', insofar as these associations point to the concrete world of human life and interaction. These factors combine to suggest that the appeal of the word *Gestalt* to Bonhoeffer arises from its strong resonances with the concrete, to intuitability in space and time, and thus its avoidance of the dangers of intangible supratemporality he finds in Barth. But – as tangibly concrete – we need to ask if this slips into the problems of liberal Protestantism, understanding Christ within a humanly attainable framework. Here, we find the word *Gestalt* has complementary characteristics to those given above, which promise also to avoid the consequences of liberal Protestantism about which Bonhoeffer is uneasy. *Gestalt* refers to a *whole*, meaning a 'characteristic unity'[19] which is not merely a sum of parts. This points to a sense of openness in the word, in that a *Gestalt* cannot be divided into components and then understood through reductive analysis, by being broken down and reconstructed from constituent, causal elements. The 'characteristic

---

14. See P. Ziegler, 'Christ For Us Today', *International Journal of Systematic Theology* 15 (2013): 25–41, for a full discussion of Christ's 'promeity' in Bonhoeffer.
15. DBWE12, 310f.; note '*habbar*', DBW2, 85.
16. DBWE2, 99.
17. Arnim Regenbogen and Uwe Meyer, 'Gestalt', in *Wörterbuch Der Philosophischen Begriffe*, Hamburg: F. Meiner Verlag, 2013, 260–1.
18. See Plant, *Bonhoeffer*, 120f.
19. Regenbogen and Meyer, *Wörterbuch*, 260–1.

unity' is something beyond the jurisdiction of this sort of analytical approach, which resonates with Bonhoeffer's criticism of understanding Christ through breaking him down into constituent elements in his *Christology* lectures.[20] For Bonhoeffer, to 'break down' the person of Christ into 'components', like historically verified items of data, and then 'reconstruct' Christ's person *from* these components, ensnares the divinely revealed Son of God into a framework of human rationality.[21] The 'openness' of the term *Gestalt* thus promises to ensure that understandings of Christ's person are not to be *brought to completion* or enclosed by human activity.[22]

Having given important background to *Gestalt*, we can now approach *Gestaltung* directly. Of course, *Ethics* is not concerned with theoretical Christology, but the semantic background to *Gestalt* proves important, for again it strikes something of a balance between liberal Protestant and dialectical approaches, but this time in the sphere of ethics. Some of Bonhoeffer's earliest reservations about the Barthian project were based on his concern that ethics, or practical action, appears to be sidelined through overemphasizing the 'absolute qualitative difference' between God and the world.[23] In very basic terms, if God is utterly remote from our existence, acting 'perpendicularly from above' at his own disposition, Bonhoeffer asks what this implies for our understanding of how we are to behave, or why Scripture demands certain actions over against others. On the other hand, however, some examples of the liberal approach (e.g. arguably Albrecht Ritschl)[24] could be seen as guilty of reducing the distance between God transcendent and human beings through making the central pivot of God's dealings with humans hinge almost entirely on the ethical, on the human attempt to adhere to the teachings of Jesus. Again, this threatens to reduce God's revelation to being under human jurisdiction.

20. DBWE12, 311–12.

21. This is connected to Bonhoeffer's criticisms of asking 'how' rather than 'who' in Christology, DBWE12, 301–6.

22. This presentation of Bonhoeffer's use of *Gestalt* for understanding Christ's person differentiates this book from DeJonge's centralizing of the concept of 'person' in distinction to Barth's 'subject' in *Act and Being*. Although *Gestalt* and DeJonge's presentation of 'person' share an emphasis on intrinsic unity, the inner dynamics of Christ's personhood ('act' and 'being') are 'broken down' and analysed in DeJonge's approach (*Formation*, 71), and he presents 'person' as offering a 'logically prior' (98) unity and a 'conceptual foundation' (77) for understanding Christ. Insofar as *Gestalt* is understood as always historically instantiated, inextricably intertwined with concrete exteriority, and not reducible by conceptual analysis, it promises to be more effective as the 'third option beyond subject and object' (71) which DeJonge sees Bonhoeffer pursuing, as would seem to be evinced by Bonhoeffer's utilization of *Gestalt* from 1933 onwards.

23. Friedrich Schlingensiepen, *Dietrich Bonhoeffer 1906–1945*, London: T&T Clark, 2010, 77.

24. See Albrecht Ritschl, *Die christliche Lehre von der Rechtfertigung und Versöhnung Volume 1*, Bonn: Marcus, 1888.

The word *Gestaltung* enables Bonhoeffer to respond constructively to these difficulties. As *Gestalt* refers to the spatial, and the intuitably concrete, the *Gestaltung* of Christ has a pressing sense of referring to the lived world of human beings in the here and now, a sense that Christ demands to be given form in present human action. However, insofar as *Gestalt* refers to a 'characteristic unity'[25] which is not merely a sum of constituent elements, this avoids correlating human actions or ethical programmes too closely or confidently with Christ in the world. In short, as Christ's *Gestalt* is not something we can orchestrate, conduct or complete through our own endeavours, we cannot control or claim his *Gestaltung* of the world as lying entirely under our jurisdiction. In this sense, Bonhoeffer can say *Gestaltung* 'is not primarily concerned with the formation of the world by planning and programmes', but with 'the unique *Gestalt*' of Christ.[26] To bring our own objective for this section back into view, our task now is to ask how this contributes to our pursuit of a mode of reflective discernment which sustains the 'volitional unity' of 'simple obedience'.

6.1.4 *Commensurability with the reflective*

To evaluate the commensurability of *Gestaltung* with reflective discernment, we should first call to mind Bonhoeffer's offsetting of 'simple obedience' with reflection in *Discipleship*, on the basis that 'simple obedience' issues in deeds not decided upon *by* the disciple, but proceeding directly from Christ. The issue here is that deeds decided upon by an agent do not belong to 'Christ alone', but are rather 'interpretations' or 'applications' of Christ's will which ensnare our deeds under human jurisdiction, while Bonhoeffer holds there should be 'no interpretation or application' in following Christ, 'only obedience or disobedience'.[27] However, bearing in mind the genealogy of the terms *Gestalt* and *Gestaltung* in Bonhoeffer's work, particularly his preference for the term *Gestalt* in avoiding the apparent domestication of Christ in liberal Protestantism, there are good grounds to argue that approaching reflective discernment as a reflection on how best to instantiate Christ's *Gestalt* can bring us some way towards sustaining 'simple obedience' in reflection.

Because *Gestalt* involves an openness, in that a *Gestalt* cannot be 'completed' or exhausted by a reductive division into components, we can contend that to reflect on how to enact Christ's *Gestaltung* preserves a certain 'otherness', a sense that the deed arrived at cannot be wholly enclosed or 'fitted' into 'a classification system I have at hand'.[28] Insofar as deeds arrived at in this fashion therefore may not fully cohere transparently with an agent's own assessment of a situation, there is a sense in which we can hold that these deeds are not decided upon *by* the

---

25. Regenbogen and Meyer, *Wörterbuch*, 260–1.
26. DBWE6, 93.
27. Ibid., 378–9.
28. DBWE12, 301.

agent, but 'proceed from the *Gestalt* of Christ'. Nonetheless, we are faced with a straightforward critical problem with this, in that it is not clear how deeds decided upon (by an agent) as Christ's *Gestaltung* of the world are *genuinely* Christ's, for being reflectively arrived at there is still a sense in which these deeds would be chosen by an agent. In other words, it is unclear how a reflective *Gestaltung* convincingly sustains the volitional unity of 'simple obedience'. This section offers a promising line of enquiry for understanding how practical discernment might be commensurable with simplicity as 'simple obedience' with the broadness of the term *Gestaltung* over against 'unreflective doing', but has made only limited gains as yet, for establishing any deeds which are reflectively arrived as instantiating Christ's will is deeply challenging.

Focusing on our second practical locus of 'purity of heart', however, promises to shed some light on this issue. Bonhoeffer holds in *Discipleship* that the 'agent centeredness' of practical reflection is based on evaluating how to proceed according to autonomous criteria for action (or the 'knowledge of good and evil'), which in being rooted in the self dictates that deeds reflectively arrived 'belong' to the agent. In *Discipleship* Bonhoeffer thus presents 'purity of heart' as a disposition in which the disciples unreflectively act without 'knowing good and evil'. In *Ethics*, however, he gestures towards modes of *reflection* in which an agent does not know good and evil, and so, by turning our attention to our second objective of understanding how reflection can retain 'purity of heart', promises to shed light on our issue with reflective *Gestaltung*, that is, the belongingness to Christ of deeds discerned reflectively.

6.2 'Not knowing good and evil' and the reflective

In this section we shall look more closely at Bonhoeffer's stance towards reflection in *Ethics*, with a view to exploring how reflection can retain 'purity of heart'. In what follows, we shall demonstrate that Bonhoeffer's attitude to reflection is two-sided – exhibiting positive and negative facets – and this is based on his view of conscience.

6.2.1 Reflection and the 'content' of conscience

Reflection in the practical sphere involves a split between the 'I' as agent, and his or her options or intended actions, which are reflected on in evaluating how to proceed. We have seen in Chapter 2 that this 'split' therefore involves a 'twoness' (agent and ends), and our task in this discussion is to ask if this 'twoness' (like that met with 'I and myself' in Chapter 5) can be approached in a more neutral sense than it is in *Discipleship*, where it is connected with being *zweifältig* and so on. In 'God's Love and the Disintegration of the World', Bonhoeffer employs one of the problematic *zwei*- words we met in *Discipleship*, *Entzweiung* ('disunion'). But, here *Entzweiung* has two different, yet connected, referents, only one of which is directly linked with reflection. First, *Entzweiung* refers to a primordial 'disunion' arising from the Fall, and not reflection per se. Secondly, however, Bonhoeffer connects this primordial *Entzweiung* with the 'disunion' involved in reflection itself, between an 'I' and its object or objects (or between agent and intended action).[29] This distinction is important, for ascertaining exactly why some reflection is seen as symptomatic of the primordial *Entzweiung* of the Fall will provide an important preliminary step to understanding how Bonhoeffer proceeds to approach other modes of reflection positively. The first task is to outline why Bonhoeffer connects *Entzweiung*, as the 'split' or 'disunion' inherent in the process of reflection itself, as symptomatic of the primordial *Entzweiung* of the Fall.

To elucidate the different uses of *Entzweiung*, the drafts of the manuscript, 'History and the Good' need to be examined. Each begins with a programmatic statement summing up the preceding chapters and outlining the key elements of *Ethics*. Bonhoeffer gives three refutations of the ethical thought he wants to challenge, thinking he describes as 'dominated by the abstract notion of an isolated individual who, wielding an absolute criterion of what is good in and of itself, chooses continually and exclusively between ... good and ... evil.'[30] He goes on to critique in turn the isolated individual, the possibility of having an absolute criterion of the good, and finally the idea that good and evil 'manifest themselves in history in their pure form'.[31] The second point of refutation points us to Bonhoeffer's more negative stance towards reflection. When reflection impinges on the ethical domain, through being used to discern 'an absolute criterion of what is good in and of itself', he considers it highly problematic. His main line of reasoning is that seeing oneself as being in possession of an 'absolute criterion' does not enable ethical conduct, but actually obstructs right behaviour. He contends that if one is able to arrive at what is 'absolutely good', then the criterion for this will serve as the key orientation for action and thus override ethical demands presented by concrete circumstances, outside of what is considered absolutely good according to this criterion.

Bonhoeffer fleshes this out with an example from one of the best-known points of ethical discussion in Western philosophy: Kant's famous assertion that when sheltering a friend from a murderer, if the murderer comes to the door and asks after the friend, it is right to tell the truth and let the murderer know the potential victim is inside. Kant's reasoning is that the maxim of the action of lying could not be made a universal law, and thus it is not 'good in itself' or 'absolutely'. It is rather only a relative good, good on the basis of achieving a further end, namely the protection of the friend. Bonhoeffer calls Kant's position a 'grotesque conclusion',[32] and this example shows why he sees possession of an 'absolute criterion' of the good as obstructing responsibility.[33]

---

29. Compare DBW6, 302 with 310 for examples of the two uses of the *Entzweiung*.
30. DBWE6, 247.
31. Ibid.
32. Ibid., 278.
33. It should be pointed out that this is neither a fair nor accurate portrayal of Kant's own position. See Immanuel Kant, *Practical Philosophy*, trans. and ed. Mary J. Gregor, Cambridge: Cambridge University Press, 1999, 612–13.

It might well be asked what this has to do with reflection per se. Bonhoeffer does, at a certain point of his discussion, link human reflection with being orientated by an 'absolute criterion' in a discussion of conscience, and his understanding of conscience is multifaceted. He acknowledges that 'it can never be advisable to act against one's conscience', for conscience is 'an authority the defiance of which is extremely inadvisable'.[34] This is based on what he calls the 'form' side to the conscience, meaning its conditioning or structuring impulses, and he locates this 'form' in the furthest reaches of human subjectivity: 'beyond one's own will and reason'.[35] In fallen humanity, this form is a primordial 'disunion' [*Entzweiung*] and is seen as intrinsically conditioning 'human existence' as a drive for 'unity with itself'.[36] We shall see shortly why Bonhoeffer holds that it is 'extremely inadvisable' to defy conscience, but we need first to examine his understanding of the Fall.

Before the Fall, Bonhoeffer considers humanity to have been 'in unity',[37] and he considers the knowledge of good and evil to be the seat of a primordial disunion in fallen humanity, showing itself in the human drive to ground one's goodness through one's own measure or standard: before God, other human beings and oneself. He claims that the Fall throws human beings into a state of ethical autonomy, where they possess within themselves a measuring stick for good and evil. This constitutes disunion, because insofar as the 'I' is in possession of a yardstick for measuring its own good, it is separated from true solidarity with other human beings. More deeply, insofar as the 'I' carries at the centre of its own being an 'absolute criterion' for the good, it is '*sicut deus*', bearing an absolute within itself and not in an appropriately humble and reverent posture before the Creator. Conscience is presented as a corollary of this, for Bonhoeffer sees it as an urge for unity, welling up from deep within oneself, calling one back to proper fellowship with God, others and oneself. That is, he sees it 'formally' as making an entirely legitimate demand, reminding oneself that one is in a state of *Entzweiung*, and driving oneself to put this right. Conscience is thus 'the call of human existence for unity with itself'; and the inherent legitimacy of this call is why he considers it 'extremely inadvisable' to defy it.[38]

However, what Bonhoeffer calls the 'content' side to the conscience is more ambiguous. However legitimate the call back to unity is, an autonomous human being is unable to achieve the unity for which the formal conscience yearns. The content of the conscience – the ways (actions) by which human beings seek to fulfil the demand for unity – aims to rectify the disunion by aligning one's conduct to an absolute criterion of the good. The 'I' seeks thereby to 'justify itself' before God, others and oneself by adhering to an autonomous ersatz pseudo-union, aligning with what is considered 'good', as a firm basis by which to relate to God, others

---

34. DBWE6, 279.
35. Ibid.
36. Ibid.
37. Ibid.; see DBWE3, 127.
38. DBWE6, 279.

and oneself. He writes, the 'I' 'which fails to find any grounding in its contingent individuality, traces itself back to a general law of the good and seeks unity by conforming to this law'.³⁹ An 'absolute criterion', then, seems to promise unity through its apparent universality. In aligning itself with 'a general law of the good', the fallen human being seems right with God, others and itself on that basis, and so the content of conscience is seen as tending towards alignment to an absolute good, with the promise of restoring unity.

This differentiation of form and content demonstrates the two-sidedness of Bonhoeffer's position on conscience. As regards form, the conscience makes an appropriate and valid demand for unity arising from the *Entzweiung* of the Fall, but as regards content, it is inhibited by the means at its disposal to fulfil this demand and so can only perpetuate the disunion by seeking to ground unity through an autonomous measure, when it is autonomy which is precisely at issue with the formal disunity itself. When this two-sidedness to conscience is grasped, Bonhoeffer's negative attitude to reflection in ethical decision-making can be better understood. In the manuscript 'God's Love and the Disintegration of the World', he explicitly links human self-reflection with the content side to the conscience. He argues that it is through *reflection* that human beings seek to establish an absolute criterion for the good and try to align themselves to it. He writes, 'in the voice of their conscience' humans 'call themselves back ... to the good', and this 'good' is sought through reflection: 'Knowing good and evil in *Entzweiung* with the origin, human beings enter into reflection.'⁴⁰ Reflection is condemned by Bonhoeffer insofar as it is seen as a seeking after an 'absolute good', which is grounded in human autonomy and provides an apparently stable point of self-justification.

On one level, Bonhoeffer's comments on reflection here are quite straightforward, as he takes a negative stance towards applying reflection in service of the deeper and more fundamental issue rooted in the 'form' of the conscience. However, on another level, there seems to be an implication that there is something more problematic inherent in the nature of reflection per se, as something which draws apart or differentiates. Indeed, this calls to mind the opening lines of *Act and Being* with which we are now familiar, where reflection is described in terms of 'I and myself' moving 'apart'.⁴¹ In this way, reflection is not merely something applied in service of a deeper and more fundamental disunion arising from the Fall, but as intrinsically fostering disunion, as a process that differentiates the subject from its object or objects. As Bonhoeffer states, 'Seeking self-knowledge is the never-ending attempt of human beings to overcome their disunion with themselves through thought, and, through unceasing self-differentiation, to find unity with themselves.'⁴² This obviously places human beings in a problematic state. The only means of establishing the unity demanded by the 'form' of the

39. Ibid.
40. DBW6, 310 (my translation).
41. DBWE2, 33.
42. DBWE6, 308.

conscience are essentially autonomous and thus perpetuate the disunion, further differentiating the 'I' from God, others and itself through reflection, which is an inherently 'dis-unifying' activity. In this sense, we can understand Bonhoeffer's statements that, with the application of reflective self-knowledge, 'everything is pulled into the process of *Entzweiung*'. He goes on to describe the differentiations that arise through human reflection, through seeking to align oneself with an 'absolute criterion', and his list of differentiated opposites involves many of the best-known terms of ethical philosophy. Everything 'splits apart', he says, 'is and ought, life and law, knowing and doing, idea and reality, reason and instinct, duty and inclination, intention and benefit, necessity and freedom', and the 'universal and the concrete'.[43] In all of these, reflection – as that which separates – is operative insofar as 'I and myself draw apart' and establish dichotomies, such as how I am and how I ought to be, or between my inclinations and my duty, and so on. As it stands, then, Bonhoeffer seems to see *Entzweiung* as a primordial disunion arising from the Fall and yet also as something pertaining to reflection per se, as an inherently separative process within consciousness.

6.2.2 Reflection on the basis of Christ's reconciliation

Notwithstanding the clear criticisms of reflection in the practical domain outlined in the previous subsection, there are points in *Ethics* where reflection is presented as morally neutral in and of itself, and even positively encouraged. Outlining how and why this is the case in this subsection will move this discussion towards elucidating how reflection can retain 'purity of heart'. In 'God's Love and the Disintegration of the World', Bonhoeffer discusses those who, 'in knowing Jesus … no longer know their own good',[44] meaning no longer living with the internal measure of an 'absolute criterion' of the good. He sees this occurring on the basis of 'the overcoming of the *Entzweiung*' through Jesus Christ, viewing Jesus' salvific 'reconciliation' as rectifying the primordial disunion of the 'form' side of the conscience. This means that the demand for unity with oneself, signalled by the prompts of the conscience, is superseded and supplanted by the person of Christ, who is now the central pivot of unity for the 'I'. He writes, 'Jesus Christ now occupies the very same space in [human beings] that had previously been occupied' by the 'knowledge of good and evil',[45] and 'blessed' are they who 'are freed from the union of their own knowledge of good and evil to be in unity with Jesus Christ'.[46]

This leaves the question of how this reconciliation affects the 'content' of the conscience. Bonhoeffer envisages both the 'form' and 'content' of the conscience to be superseded by the reconciliation of Jesus, for the content refers to the

43. Ibid.
44. Ibid., 318.
45. Ibid., 325.
46. Ibid., 330–1.

substantive matter of how the conscience attempts to fulfil the primordial demands of its 'formal' nature. This significantly reconfigures the place of reflection in Bonhoeffer's thinking. If the primordial *Entzweiung* is superseded, then the reflective process of 'moving part' of the agent from intended action or actions is on a very different footing, and the process of separation no longer perpetuates the fundamental disunion.

To elucidate this different footing of reflection, we must return to 'God's Love', where Bonhoeffer describes modes of reflective practical discernment which are based on the new ground of the reconciliation accomplished in Jesus, which, rather than seeking to align an agent to an 'absolute good', seek to discern the 'will of God'. Bonhoeffer writes of 'a searching for the will of God that is certainly legitimate and necessary' and claims that 'intellect, observation, and experience must work together in this discernment'.[47] The 'moving apart' of reflection is no longer inherently problematic, for this 'separating' activity must be at work, such as when Bonhoeffer states 'the will of God may lie deeply hidden among many competing possibilities'.[48] That is, possible ends or actions 'move apart' from the reflecting agent, who is thus not absorbed in the performance of a deed, as with 'unreflective doing'. Because this discernment is not seeking to establish an absolute good and align oneself to it, Bonhoeffer presents the separating process of reflection as something which can and should be put into service in Christian life.

6.2.3 Critical issue with 'reflective discernment' in Ethics

Thus far, attention has been given to the more negative and positive sides to reflection in Bonhoeffer's *Ethics*, with the positive side being reflection on the basis of Christ's reconciliation as a searching after the will of God. But, there is a pressing problem with this, in that Bonhoeffer's discussion does not convincingly establish how the knowledge of God's will gained through reflective discernment is effectively differentiated from an 'absolute good'. That is, having reflectively discerned God's will, the question remains of how that which is gained is not then borne autonomously (having an 'independent status'[49]), and how it does not therefore function as a good to which one must align oneself.

Although Bonhoeffer presupposes that knowing the will of God is different from knowing good and evil (having a measure of the 'absolute good'), there are numerous instances where he describes the knowledge of the will of God in ways which seem markedly similar to precisely the sort of 'knowing of good and evil' or an 'absolute good' which he is criticizing. Put differently, he seems to presuppose a form of 'principledness' which can serve as an orientating basis for ethical reflection without positing an 'absolute good', although he does not discuss directly what such a principledness might be or consist in. For example, he frequently uses

---

47. Ibid., 321, trans. altered.
48. Ibid.
49. Ibid., 328.

the terms 'necessary' and 'necessity' to describe the nature of God's will in concrete situations. That is, the awareness of the will of God that is reflectively discerned is presented as pointing to deeds which are 'necessary'. This obviously cannot be arrived at with a principle used to discern something like the 'good in itself', and yet it is still described as leading to deeds which are 'necessary'. Yet, Bonhoeffer's own example of a paradigmatic knowing of an 'absolute good' is Kant's categorical imperative, which is by Kant's definition based on the 'demands of necessity and universality' regarding practical reason, for the categorical imperative is said to describe the 'form' of the moral law, as an a priori 'objective principle of action'. To quote Guyer, Kant 'premises that a moral law must be necessary'.[50]

Bonhoeffer obviously has a different understanding of necessity in view than that involved in the categorical imperative. He states that the 'point is not to apply a principle' but 'to discern what is necessary or "commanded" [*Gebotenes*] in a given situation'. Green suggests that Bonhoeffer's writing of the word *Gebotenes*, meaning 'what is commanded' in quotation marks, 'indicates that he wanted it understood both in its everyday meaning of "what is appropriate" and also meaning God's "commandment"'.[51] This dual reference to *Gebotenes* elucidates the question of 'necessary' deeds. We are not dealing with the principled necessity of the categorical imperative, but something closer to a sense of *having* to act – in response to a demand arising from concrete circumstances – the need for a particular, contextual, responsible action, necessitated by a demand for taking responsibility for other human beings in light of those circumstances. This action is also 'appropriate' in the sense of 'fitting' for those specific circumstances, which for Bonhoeffer also implies a sense of being 'commanded' by God. Bonhoeffer obviously does not consider this classification of deeds as 'necessary' or 'appropriate', as irredeemably subjective and merely contextual, but without outlining how Christ offers a form of 'principledness', outlining a critically robust way of defining how deeds can be 'necessary' is a significant challenge which he does not achieve in the extant manuscripts.

Nonetheless, Bonhoeffer frequently uses the terms 'necessary' and 'necessity' in the *Ethics* manuscripts to refer to the knowledge of God's will, claiming it is our task is to do what 'is objectively necessary [*Notwendige*]'.[52] Being unable to ascertain how this can be principled, the level of subjective and contextual particularity is further problematic in that Bonhoeffer has, earlier in *Ethics*, critiqued what he terms 'casuistry', a seeking after the 'good' which gets 'caught up in the enterprise of taking up and elaborating all conceivable contents in order to say ... for every conceivable case what is good'.[53] We could turn Bonhoeffer's critique back onto himself here and ask how positing certain circumstances as necessarily requiring certain actions does not merely render all ethical orientation dependent on

50. Paul Guyer, *Kant*, London: Routledge, 2006, 177.
51. Green, in DBWE6, 221–2, n14.
52. DBWE6, 224–5; cf. discussions of *necessitas* in DBWE8, 240.
53. DBWE6, 99f.

specific circumstances, and how this allows us to discern an overarching ethical orientation without descending into casuistry.

6.4 Summing up

This chapter can now close with some important gains having been made. The first objective of understanding how reflection can sustain 'simple obedience' has progressed somewhat, as utilizing Bonhoeffer's descriptions of *Gestaltung*, we can envisage practical discernment as reflecting on how to enact Christ's *Gestaltung* of the world. This offers a valuable alternative to the apparent exclusivity of *un*-reflective 'simple obedience' in *Discipleship*. This constitutes a movement towards wisdom, in its potential commensurability with 'simple obedience', and this movement has developed further through analysing the semantic background to the term *Gestaltung*, showing us how an 'openness' or 'otherness' to the term suggests that reflecting on Christ's *Gestalt* need not ensnare Christ in human structures of understanding. Nonetheless, although these gains are important and will be developed in the subsequent chapters, the steps made here towards wisdom are still limited, in that it is difficult to establish how exactly this reflective *Gestaltung* can be seen as leading to deeds grounded on 'Christ alone' and not the reflective deliberations of the disciple as agent, for in reflecting 'within' *Gestaltung* it still seems that the deeds arrived at would be chosen by the agent.

We saw above that agent-centredness seems to be rooted in a more fundamental issue related to 'purity of heart', for Bonhoeffer presents agent-centredness as connected to the bearing of autonomous criteria. Bonhoeffer provides a framework (based on his understanding of the Fall and conscience) which moves us closer, again, towards 'wisdom' by offering an alternative approach to criteriological reflection with seeking after the will of God. But, these gains are again limited, for it remains unclear how the reflectively discerned knowledge of God's will effectively differs from knowing an 'absolute good'. This problem is also intensified in that Bonhoeffer presents the paradigm of bearing a criterion for action – an 'absolute good' – with Kant's 'categorical imperative' and yet utilizes terminology which seems directly reminiscent of Kant's own work, namely, language of necessity. In Chapter 7, then, we shall examine certain pertinent aspects of Kant's 'categorical imperative' in order to ascertain thereby why it is so problematic for Bonhoeffer, with a view to applying our findings to outlining a mode of reflection that can avoid the problems of an 'absolute good', and which builds on the foregoing discussion surrounding *Gestaltung*, by asking how discerning how to proceed by reflecting on the *Gestalt* of Christ can involve the deeply contextual necessity to which Bonhoeffer points, thus bringing us more effectively to 'wisdom', by sustaining both 'simple obedience' and 'purity of heart'.

Chapter 7

THE 'TRANSCENDENTAL UNITY OF APPERCEPTION' AND THE 'CATEGORICAL IMPERATIVE' IN THE 'FLOW OF LIFE'

The previous chapters presented two avenues for further enquiry, which – in different ways – are related to Bonhoeffer's inheritance of elements from the philosophy of Immanuel Kant (1724–1804). We closed Chapter 5 recognizing that Bonhoeffer brings us towards wisdom in *Act and Being* by offering two modes of self-reflection which maintain the subject–'object' singularity of the *actus directus* in an *actus reflectus*, while also concluding that these modes of self-reflection involve a residual sense of fragmentation. Yet, in the 'transcendental attempt', Bonhoeffer has pointed us to a conceptuality which promises to avoid this fragmentation by preserving a hiddenness to the self-reflecting subject: the 'transcendental unity of apperception'. Our first concern in this chapter therefore is to examine this conceptuality more closely.

Bringing our second (practical) concern into view, Chapter 6 ascertained that Bonhoeffer brought us closer to wisdom in *Ethics*, first by enabling us to approach discernment as reflecting on how to enact Christ's *Gestaltung* of the world, and pointing us towards understanding how this can be Christ-centred, through approaching discernment as reflectively seeking God's will rather than aligning oneself to an 'absolute good'. Yet, it remains unclear how a reflectively discerned knowledge of God's will does not merely present a self-legitimizing point of autonomous ethical security like an 'absolute good'. Because Bonhoeffer presents Kant's categorical imperative as the paradigmatic example of 'absolute good', we shall examine Kant's 'categorical imperative' more closely in this chapter,[1] to discern why it is so problematic for Bonhoeffer, with a view to understanding how practical discernment can proceed without self-legitimizing criteria in the following chapters.

---

1. It is worth noting that Bonhoeffer's clear differentiation between Kant and German idealism does not seem to endure into *Ethics*, where he is more critical of Kant, much less inattentive to Kant's own writing, and at points fudges the distinction of Kant from idealism which he makes prominent as early as *Sanctorum Communio* (DBWE1, 45, n5); see for example, DBWE6, 175–80.

7.1 The transcendental unity of apperception

7.1.1 A basic aim of the first Critique[2]

Kant's *Critique of Pure Reason* (1781 and 1787) is widely (if not universally) acknowledged as one of the most important works in Western philosophy. One of the various overarching aims of the *Critique* provides important background for understanding the pertinent elements of the book for this chapter. This aim arises from Kant's attempt to steer a path between two prevalent philosophical outlooks of his milieu, towards both of which he was antithetical: 'dogmatism' and 'scepticism'. Dogmatism refers to the overstepping of proper rational bounds by certain rationalist philosophers, particularly Spinoza and Leibniz, who for Kant, engage in an improper use of 'pure reason without an antecedent critique of its own capacity'.[3] Therefore, Kant wants to analyse – by way of an 'antecedent critique' – the proper manner in which 'pure reason' can be employed, to establish precisely what it can and cannot achieve. Dogmatism is famously condemned by Kant for arrogating to itself 'the proud name of an ontology',[4] which can be understood as allowing reason to make claims to domains where it cannot rationally demonstrate any legitimate jurisdiction.

The second prevalent outlook Kant criticizes shows his *Critique* is not restricted to pure reason alone. A letter he wrote in 1771 includes an early working title for the *Critique* which demonstrates a twofold concern underlying the book, for he says he is working on a book to be called *The Bounds of Sensibility and of Reason*.[5] His evaluation of 'scepticism', then, seeks to demarcate not the bounds of reason, but sensibility. Kant's main protagonist of a sceptical outlook is David Hume (1711–76).[6] Hume is seen as guilty of an antithetical error to dogmatism; not making room for the demands of conceptual, rational cognition, in the shape of necessity and universality. Hume's empirical, experience-orientated approach produces an outlook whereby he argues that necessary and universal laws cannot be deduced to pertain in reality. This leads him to question the fundamental tenets of traditional metaphysics, such as the law that 'every event has some cause'. Hume saw no way to hold that a law encountered in experience can confidently be said to apply universally and necessarily, that is, apart from the 'finite range of prior cases'

---

2. Speaking of the 'First', 'Second', and 'Third' *Critiques* is a common way of referring to the *Critiques* of '*Pure Reason*', '*Practical Reason*' and '*the Power of Judgement*' respectively.

3. Janz, *Desire*, 128, n9.

4. CpR, 358.

5. Paul Guyer, in 'Introduction' to Guyer (ed.), *The Cambridge Companion to Kant's Critique of Pure Reason*, Cambridge: Cambridge University Press, 2010, 3.

6. Kant also has Cartesian and Pyrrhonian scepticism in mind, Guyer, *Kant*, 11f.

given to experience.⁷ That is, just because every event in *our* experience has some cause, we cannot know that this is necessarily and universally the case.

This is the so-called 'Humean problem', and it is a prime example of the scepticism Kant seeks to counter,⁸ the view that 'universal and necessary principles' are 'nothing but contingent and incomplete generalities'. Yet, at the same time, he wishes to refute the 'dogmatism' which he sees as guilty of 'flying off into ungrounded metaphysics'.⁹ In this way, Kant claims to be conducting a 'metaphysics of metaphysics', that is, an enquiry into the possibility of an enquiry into the nature of reality *as such*.¹⁰ Understanding this twofold aim of the *Critique of Pure Reason* is the most basic requirement for understanding the elements of it which this chapter will now focus on.

7.1.2 *The transcendental unity of apperception*

Having been led to examine the 'transcendental unity of apperception' by the previous chapters, the first task is to situate it within the purview of the *Critique*'s aims. It arises first in a section of the *Critique* called 'the Transcendental Deduction'. This section is considered by Guyer to be 'the centrepiece of Kant's response to Humean scepticism'.¹¹ Here, Kant seeks to establish the 'categories', which are 'pure concepts of the understanding [*Verstand*]',¹² as a necessary feature of our spatio-temporal experience. These refer to the basic classes of determinable features of objects perceived in sensible intuition. In cognizing an object, Kant holds that the mass of data which impinges on the senses is spontaneously ordered by the intellect, according to classificatory properties which are ultimately reducible to one of a framework of possible properties which are structural coordinates intrinsically rooted in the *Verstand*. The categorial ordering of intuition is, for Kant, a necessary feature of experience, by means of which we organize the sheer affectivity of intuited perceptions. In the Transcendental Deduction, he seeks to show that the categories are the condition of the possibility of experience, and so the categories 'apply to all our experience, bar none'.¹³

Kant's attempt to explain where the 'pure concepts' of *Verstand* originate leads him to posit the transcendental unity of apperception as something that unifies our experience of an object, providing a necessary and universal base level of subjectivity from which he can go on to argue that the categories must necessarily apply to all experience. This substratum is defined as a 'unity of consciousness that

---

7. Ibid., 12–13.
8. That is, by outlining synthetic a priori knowledge, which cannot be discussed directly within the scope of this chapter.
9. Guyer, *Kant*, 49.
10. See Janz, *Desire*, 125–6.
11. Guyer, *Kant*, 71.
12. CpR, 271.
13. Guyer, *Kant*, 83.

precedes all data of the intuitions' and as an 'unchanging consciousness' (A107) of the 'numerical identity' (A113) of 'oneself in all one's various experiences'.[14] Guyer defines 'the basic idea' of 'transcendental apperception' as the notion that 'at any time I have any experience I can also know that I have the experience, and that knowing *that* is equivalent to knowing that experience belongs to the same self that has all my other experiences'.[15] Guyer goes on to present Kant's use of transcendental apperception in the Deduction as an attempt to argue that it 'somehow entails the necessary application of the categories … to all of our experiences without exception'. Insofar as cognizing an object involves ascribing to it certain features which can be found to originate in the conceptual ordering of the categories, this in turn depends on the continuity underlying cognition.[16] As Kant describes it, this fundamental subjective ground is 'a necessary condition of the possibility of all representations' (A116), for without it, the categorial ordering of experience would not be possible.[17] In knowing all our representations must pertain to the same unified subject, Kant therefore holds that this active and spontaneous base level of subjectivity presents them as distinctively 'mine'.

Kant's 'transcendental unity of apperception' is contrasted to the 'empirical I' which is known a posteriori through self-representation. To bring out the difference in the way the 'transcendental I' and the 'empirical I' are each conceived or known, it is necessary to examine two aspects of Kant's use of the noun *Vorstellung* (representation).[18] First, within his use of the term *Vorstellung*, we can denote an understanding of representation which relates 'immediately to the object and is single' (A 320/B 377), a representation of intuited data presented to oneself, usually through the activity of the five senses. This representation therefore always pertains to objects, items with data to be ordered as properties. With the classificatory activity of *Verstand*, however, we encounter an understanding of representation at work in Kant which relates to objects 'mediately by means of a feature which several things may have in common' (CPR A 320/B 377).[19] This refers to the representation of the properties themselves, which will of course be shared by other objects, namely, *concepts*. While the former mode of representation is always 'singular', conceptual *Vorstellung* is 'universal', in that concepts represent properties common to many objects, as certain concepts can be seen to apply to all objects under its jurisdiction universally.[20]

---

14. CpR, 232, 235.
15. Guyer, *Kant*, 84.
16. Ibid., 85.
17. CpR, 237.
18. Our discussion is primarily focused on *Vorstellung* as 'objective perception', where the subdivision into intuition and concept pertains (CpR, 398–9); see 'representation', *A Kant Dictionary*, ed. Howard Caygill, Malden, MA: Blackwell, 2004, 321.
19. CpR, 398–9.
20. See Guyer, *Kant*, 53–4.

These two aspects to *Vorstellung* point to an important difference between the transcendental and empirical 'I', which shows how the former answers to one of the challenges bequeathed to Kant by Hume. With the 'empirical I' we are dealing with one's a posteriori knowledge of oneself. Although this can involve sensory intuition (such as looking at one's image in a mirror), Kant maintains that we know ourselves primarily through our inner states, through how we spontaneously react to life in momentary self-awareness. Kant distinguishes between 'outer' and 'inner sense', and holds that with the former 'we represent to ourselves objects as outside us' (A22/B37) through sensibility, and with the latter, the 'I' 'intuits itself or its inner state' not as an object but as the 'determinate form in which alone the intuition of inner states is possible' (A23/B37).[21] He considers the 'empirical I' as 'consciousness of oneself in accordance with the determinations of our states in internal perception' and argues that – as 'merely empirical' – this consciousness of oneself is 'forever variable' (A107).[22] Calling to mind the two aspects to *Vorstellung* outlined above, the 'empirical I' is fundamentally intuitable (albeit primarily through 'inner', not 'outer' sense). This means, for Kant, that it is ultimately only grasped transiently, resistant to being 'pinned-down' at any level beyond the different percepts in which it is encountered. So one is unable to make necessary and universal stipulations about the 'empirical I', because it is always perceived only in particular experiences and does not offer anything necessarily and universally pertaining to all experience. This mode of knowing the self is similar to Hume's, which considers any attempt to locate a fundamentally unified notion of the self as inevitably concluding we 'are nothing but a bundle or collection of different perceptions, which succeed each other with an inconceivable rapidity, and are in a perpetual flux and movement.'[23] This is Hume's well-known 'bundle theory' of the self, his view that the 'I' cannot be grasped at all apart from a mere 'bundle' of different perceptions.

Kant's taking Hume to task on the bundle theory is demonstrated in his discussion of the 'paradox of self-knowledge', a subsidiary discussion of the Transcendental Deduction. As our primary way of representing ourselves to ourselves is through affects, Kant comes across a paradox in that he holds that the 'I' that thinks 'is active and spontaneous'.[24] This activity and spontaneity of the 'I' is demonstrated by the spontaneous synthesizing of representations as pertaining to the same subject. The 'paradox of self-knowledge', then, is that, on the one hand, the 'I' is active, yet seems to perceive itself passively, in 'inner sense' on the other. Kant's way of dealing with this is interesting for the purposes of this chapter, for it offers an epistemological differentiation pertaining to self-representation. Kant answers to this apparent paradox by separating the way transcendental and

21. CpR, 174.
22. Ibid., 232.
23. David Hume, *A Treatise Of Human Nature*, Oxford: Clarendon Press, 2007, 165.
24. Jill Vance Buroker, *Kant's Critique of Pure Reason*, Cambridge: Cambridge University Press, 2006, 131–2.

empirical self-awareness are represented to the self, which aligns with the two different forms of *Vorstellung* outlined above. As regards affects, he considers these to be intuited, and as such – given the analysis of his *Critique* – not the 'thing-in-itself' (here: the 'I'). But with the transcendental unity of apperception, he writes, 'I am conscious of myself not as I appear to myself ... but only *that* I am' and this can be represented only by 'thinking' (B157).[25] He therefore holds that the transcendental unity of apperception is not cognized, because 'it does not have the least predicate of intuition' (B278).[26] The unified experience of the 'I' which precedes all representation has no affective data; it is 'pure' of characteristics which can be perceived by inner (or outer) sense. It is, therefore, something we can only *conceive* via conceptual representation, as a necessary and universal condition of self-consciousness, but which cannot be *known* or cognized. By delineating this necessary and universal aspect to the 'I', Kant challenges Hume's bundle theory, and thus the transcendental unity of apperception forms part of his broader response to the Humean problem.

7.1.3 'Original' and 'pure' apperception

The foregoing analysis has provided a backdrop against which two different aspects to the transcendental unity of apperception can be brought into relief, and outlining these will show how the Kantian 'transcendental I' can inform this enquiry. On the one hand, the unity of the 'I' is experienced in the flow of life, and on the other, it is represented to oneself conceptually. Although Guyer has shown that Kant himself uses the terms 'original' and 'pure' apperception interchangeably,[27] we will classify the first aspect (the unity of the 'I' experienced in the flow of life) as 'original apperception', and the second (its conceptual representation) as 'pure apperception'.

Transcendental apperception in the flow of life is a basic facet of experience in that one is consciously aware of oneself as a unified 'I', and Kant holds that this facet pertains to all experience. Julian Werth gives a helpful description of this, in speaking of the self-consciousness of the 'transcendental I' as 'a base *awareness* of one's own existence as a thinking thing distinct from its particular mental states'.[28] This means we have an original awareness of ourselves as the subject of our experiences and not only as a particular subject which emerges relatively disconnectedly 'in' different experiences. This points to what Kant describes as the fact 'we are *conscious* ... of the thoroughgoing identity of ourselves with regard

---

25. CpR, 259.
26. Ibid., 328.
27. See Paul Guyer, *Kant and the Claims of Knowledge*, Cambridge: Cambridge University Press, 1987, 83–4.
28. Julian Werth, 'The Paralogisms of Pure Reason', in Guyer (ed.), *The Cambridge Companion to Kant's Critique of Pure Reason*, 210–44 (212).

to all representations that can ever belong to our consciousness' (A116).²⁹ This is something given 'in' or 'to' 'consciousness' (A107) in the flow of life, a feature of experience itself. We can therefore call this feature of 'transcendental apperception' 'original', in the sense it *originally* pertains as a 'base awareness' or dimension of 'consciousness' in life, without necessarily being conceptually represented by thinking.³⁰

If, however, we enquire into this 'original' apperception, Kant holds that it can only be represented conceptually, as a matter of what he terms 'the *pure* understanding' (A119).³¹ This shows that the representation of original apperception is via conceptual *Vorstellung*, which is always universal or general and not particular. In Kant's epistemology, concepts can only yield knowledge by being related to appearances. The fact that we are conscious 'of the thoroughgoing identity of ourselves with regard to all representations that can ever belong to our consciousness' (A116)³² is not something that can be intuited; it has no content, there is no material that goes with it that can be perceived, and therefore it cannot be cognized. He says we 'do not have yet another self-intuition' beyond this thoroughgoing identity of ourselves which would enable us 'to determine' that of which 'we are only conscious' (B158n).³³ This 'thoroughgoing identity' is therefore described by Werth as 'completely indeterminate, and thus inadequate for knowledge'.³⁴

In this way, there is a certain sense that the transcendental unity of apperception shares some characteristics of the Kantian *noumena*. This word derives from the Greek *nous*, meaning 'pure intellect'.³⁵ The *noumena*, such as the famous '*Dingen-an-sich*', are unknowable as they have no possible content. Yet, they are *conceivable*, or *thinkable*, being purely conceptual notions about which nothing further can be predicated beyond being limits. As Kant writes, the *ding-an-sich* is a 'problematic' concept the 'objective reality of which can in no way be cognised' (B310).³⁶ In this sense, Guyer calls the thinking of *noumena* as 'entirely negative', and Kant describes them as 'entirely ... empty' (B298).³⁷

The purely conceptual conceivability of the *noumena* is shared by 'pure apperception' as something with no intuitable data to be classified by the categories. We are thus offered here a thinkable limit of the 'I', as a negative limit only, about which nothing further can be predicated. This 'I' is a mere condition of thinking, about which we can reason that it is necessary and universal, but which cannot

---

29. CpR, 237.
30. Werth, 'Paralogisms', 212.
31. CpR, 238 (my emphasis).
32. Ibid., 237.
33. Ibid., 260.
34. Werth, 'Paralogisms', 215–16.
35. Guyer, *Kant*, 29.
36. CpR, 362.
37. Guyer, *Kant*, 136; CpR, 356.

be cognized itself. Kant states: 'Through this I ... which thinks, nothing further is represented than a transcendental subject of thoughts = X' (A346/B404).[38] The key point is that Kant presents us with both the 'original' occurrence of this awareness *in* consciousness *and* the 'purely' conceptual representation *of* it *to* consciousness. Kant points out that

> it must seem strange that the condition under which I think in general, and which is therefore merely a property of my subject (i.e. 'original' apperception as experienced in the flow of life), is at the same time to be valid for everything that thinks, and that on an *empirical-seeming proposition* we can presume to ground an apodictic and universal judgement, namely that everything that thinks is constituted as the claim self-consciousness asserts of me. (A346/B404)[39]

That is, with 'original apperception' we have an 'empirical-seeming' feature of consciousness, for it pertains in concrete experience, and yet it can only be represented in the universal terms of 'pure' conceptuality.

7.1.4 'Pure' apperception interrupting 'the flow of life'

To bring this discussion back into view of our concern with subjective 'hiddenness', this analysis offers us two different options for self-representation, or, to use the terminology we adopted in Chapter 2, the 'I' 'mirroring itself to itself'. These two options pertain to Kant's differentiation of the 'empirical I' from the 'transcendental I'. First, the 'I' can represent oneself to oneself with intuitable data, which threatens to lead ultimately, as we have seen, to a Humean-style 'bundle theory' of the self. Kant holds that this mode of self-representation will lead us to 'turn in a constant circle' (A346/B404),[40] because every representation of ourselves will always be undergirded by an execution of the act of thought by a unified-I, which in turn also needs to be represented and so on. Secondly, however, the 'I' can represent itself to itself as 'pure' apperception, a condition of thinking. This option is – as we have seen – promising for our purposes in that the 'I' is not entirely given over to the self-reflective gaze, but is held to be 'entirely empty'. This can be approached as constituting a form of 'hiddenness', because we cannot state anything *about* the 'I', and it is not known or cognized, but is a boundary *to* the knowable, a preservation of a dimension of subjectivity as insurmountable to the self-reflective gaze. But, although a 'pure' representation of the transcendental unity of apperception offers a coordinate for self-reflection which preserves hiddenness, its status as 'entirely empty' renders it dubious for our purposes. This is because this hiddenness necessitates conceiving of the 'I' as non-temporal and abstract. To conceive of the 'I' as a nothing more than a necessary condition of subjectivity 'interrupts', 'breaks'

38. CpR, 414.
39. Ibid.
40. Ibid.

or 'ruptures' the 'I' we represent to ourselves from the 'I' in which we experience life in the concrete.

However, we can close this section by noting an important finding, which will configure our cognitively orientated discussions in the following chapters. Although Kant holds that the transcendental unity of apperception is 'completely empty', he also maintains that it is genuinely experienced in the flow of life, or something which is 'empirical-*seeming*'. This presents us with a task for the foregoing chapters, and ultimately for understanding how self-reflection can preserve subjective 'hiddenness' in a way more fitting for our purposes, through preserving its concrete situatedness. We shall seek therefore to understand the unity of the 'I' as a subjective hiddenness not entirely given over to the self-reflective gaze, yet without considering reflection on it as 'hidden' through the restriction to pure conceptuality. That is, we will be seeking to discover how the unreflective 'I' can be represented as temporally situated and concrete, yet while preserving its 'hiddenness'. Kant has given us a valuable pointer to this end, in his holding that the unity of the 'I' is given *to* consciousness in temporal and concrete experience, although as yet we have no means of reflecting on this unified 'I' while preserving its hiddenness.

7.2 *The categorical imperative*

7.2.1 *Aims of the* Groundwork of a Metaphysic of Morals *and the* Critique of Practical Reason

There are two aims of the key works of Kant's practical philosophy which are important for this enquiry, which provide important background for what follows. The *Groundwork of the Metaphysics of Morals* (1785) was intended to provide a preliminary basis for another subsequent work, which Kant expected to involve a 'metaphysic of morals', or rather, a work focused on the 'demands of necessity and universality' regarding *practical* reason. To quote H. J. Paton, The *Groundwork* aims to 'lay the *foundations* for such a metaphysics of morals'.[41] What this involves most basically is a kind of ground-clearing exercise, whereby the various components which make up the 'determining grounds' of action are separated out and defined, so that the purely intellectual or 'metaphysical' elements can be accurately discerned. For Kant, this involves delineating the appetites and motives which are empirically orientated, to those which are 'higher' in the sense of originating not empirically, but rather reflecting the demand for the necessity and universality of pure reason.

A stated aim of the *Critique of Practical Reason* (1788), by contrast, is 'merely to show that there is *pure practical reason*',[42] which refers to demands *for* necessity

---

41. H. J. Paton, in GMMb, 15 (original emphasis).
42. CprR, 139.

and universality in practical reasoning. He is not embarking on a *critique* of 'pure practical reason', he states, rather that he wants to show that its demands exist. A 'critique' (*Kritik*), for Kant, is a 'critical examination' of a faculty 'that sets out its powers and limits, and in particular establishes the legitimacy of any *a priori* concepts and principles' that 'structure [that] relevant domain'.[43] Kant is not critiquing '*pure* practical reason', but practical reason itself, not interrogating demands for necessity and universality, but rather the 'impure' demands that are 'empirically conditioned'.[44] These are impure in the sense of not deriving solely from rationality, such as desires with a bodily or emotional orientation. Therefore, Kant claims his second *Critique* stands in 'precisely the opposite relation from what could be said of pure reason in speculative use'.[45] While the first *Critique* was concerned to delimit the bounds of 'pure reason' in the speculative domain, the second *Critique* is concerned with delimiting the bounds of what Kant calls the 'empirically conditioned use' of reason. Because of this, Heiner F. Klemme claims the argumentative aims of the first *Critique* are 'inverted' in the second.[46] With these basic aims in view, we can briefly summarize the points that are germane for this study, involving a central element of both the *Groundwork* and the second *Critique*: the 'categorical imperative'.

7.2.2 *The categorical imperative*

In order to bring out the aspects of the categorical imperative *ad rem* to our concerns, there is some background to it that should be discussed. Kant famously opens the *Groundwork* by claiming, 'It is impossible to conceive anything at all in the world, or even out of it, which can be taken as good without qualification, except a *good will*.'[47] If something is good without any qualification, it means it is good purely and solely on its own merits and not on account of standing in any kind of relation with (being qualified by) any other thing. The difference between an unqualified and qualified good can be described with the example of someone performing a deed considered good *because* it brought pleasure to other people, or someone performing a deed considered good in and of itself regardless of the consequences. The first evaluation of good is a *qualified* good; so if the deed backfired and did not have the desired effect, it would cease to be good. The second deed, however, in being evaluated as an *unqualified* good, remains good regardless

---

43. Andrews Reath, 'Introduction' to Andrews Reath and Jens Timmermann (eds), *A Critical Guide to Kant's Critique of Practical Reason*, Cambridge: Cambridge University Press, 2010, 1.
44. CprR, 148.
45. Ibid., 148–9.
46. Heiner F. Klemme, 'The Origin and Aim of Kant's Critique of Practical Reason', in Reath and Timmermann (eds), *A Critical Guide to Kant's Critique of Practical Reason*, 11–30 (29).
47. GMMb, 59.

of context or circumstances. It is hard to imagine concrete events which can be given the solid, philosophical evaluation of 'good' in this way, for circumstances are always open to interpretation and consequences often too complicated to provide a definite conclusion. So, because he wishes to explore this second, unqualified way of evaluating human actions, Kant seeks the good in volition, rather than in the actions themselves, stating 'a good will is not good because of what it effects or accomplishes'.[48] Paton paraphrases this by saying, 'a good will alone is good *in all circumstances*' and in this sense is 'absolute'.[49] That is, it is good absolutely, meaning without any conditions to qualify it as such, but in and of itself.

The difference between a qualified and an unqualified or 'absolute good' can be elucidated further by highlighting Kant's terminology of 'maxims' or 'subjective' and 'objective' 'principles of action', which will lead us to the 'categorical imperative' itself. A maxim is a principle on which a rational agent acts, a 'principle manifested in actions which are in fact performed'.[50] The point is not that an agent is seen as having distilled a discursive principle, or maxim, before performing a deed – obviously that would not be a realistic representation of most human action – but that any action *can* be understood and described by using this concept. A maxim is thus seen as iterating the 'determining ground of the will', and a *subjective* principle of action demarcates the principle on which the volition of an agent is indeed acting. An 'objective principle of action', however, is objective in the sense of offering a transparent (rationally verifiable) criterion of rectitude which would apply regardless of circumstance or perspective – in short, something which offers an unqualified good, which need not be qualified by situational conditions. For this reason, Kant states that an objective maxim is a principle on which 'every rational agent *would necessarily act* if reason had full control' over his or her actions. For Kant, this means such a principle is one on which we '*ought* to act'.[51]

Examining the concept of an objective principle of action more closely will enable us to focus on the categorical imperative, and in doing so, we should outline some further terminology from the Analytic of the second *Critique*. There, Kant states, 'the will is thought of as independent of empirical conditions' when '*determined by the mere form of the law*', which, according to Andrews Reath, means such law 'provides a ground of choice through its form rather than its matter'.[52] This form and matter distinction can be understood through the language of qualification from the opening of the *Groundwork*. The 'matter' of a maxim is the qualification by which it might be evaluated as good. To return to our previous example, in an action considered good for bringing other people pleasure, the 'matter' is the desired end of pleasure-giving. A 'ground of choice' determined through its form,

---

48. Ibid., 60.
49. Paton, in GMMb, 16.
50. Ibid., 20.
51. Paton, in GMMb, 20.
52. CprR, 164; Andrews Reath, 'Formal Principles and the Form of a Law', in Reath and Timmermann (eds), *A Critical Guide to Kant's Critique of Practical Reason*, 31–54 (32).

however, would not have a condition or qualification by which to evaluate its goodness. So, Kant seeks to delineate the 'form' of the law, an *a priori* 'objective principle of action', which would pertain necessarily for a perfectly rational agent. That is, to quote Guyer, 'he premises that a moral law must be necessary ... then concludes that only a moral principle that is entirely formal and makes no reference to any object of desire ['material'] can satisfy that requirement'.[53]

This formal, moral law is expressed in the human domain as the 'categorical imperative'. The word 'categorical' indicates it 'can be recognised in, or derived from, the purely rational "categories" which for Kant can be found in the ... practical *intellect* alone'.[54] The categorical imperative is formulated in five different ways in the *Groundwork*,[55] but for our purposes, we need only specify the first formulation, usually referred to as 'the formula of universal law'. It states: 'I ought never to act except in such a way that *I can also will that my maxim should become a universal law*'.[56] Paton paraphrases this as, 'a man is morally good ... as seeking to obey a law valid for *all* men and to follow an objective standard not determined by his own desires'.[57] That is, Kant sees the demand of pure practical reason on our actions as offering a way to measure the worth of an action according to the standard with which we envisage the permissibility of the corresponding maxim as a universal law which can be applied to all people in all circumstances.

Importantly for our purposes, the categorical imperative gives the shape, or 'form' of an action which aligns with what an agent would *necessarily* do if he or she were perfectly rational. The term 'imperative' applies only in the human domain. For Kant, the demands of 'pure practical reason' for necessity and universality are only formulated as an 'imperative' to human beings, because human beings are imperfectly rational agents. A perfectly rational agent would always act in accordance with the law, but for us, the law is formulated as an 'obligation or command to obey'.[58] As Guyer notes, 'we human beings are not perfectly rational, and thus although we recognise the unconditional validity of the moral law, it also appears as a constraint to us.'[59] In Kant's language, the way in which objective principles seem to constrain the will is spoken of as *necessitating* the will. That is, with a 'wholly rational agent' objective principles *necessarily* delineate the way that agent would behave, but for human beings these principles *necessitate* how they should behave, in the sense of compel or command, and hence are expressed as imperatives.[60]

53. Guyer, *Kant*, 77.
54. Janz, *Command*, 90 (my emphasis).
55. See GMMa, 73, 79, 82–5.
56. GMMb, 67.
57. Paton, in GMMb, 22.
58. H. J. Paton, *The Categorical Imperative*, London: Hutchinson, 1947, 128.
59. Guyer, *Kant*, 179.
60. Paton, in GMMb, 26.

We might well ask what it is that interferes with human rationality and renders it imperfect. The answer is that Kant holds that our wills are not always able to act in a way that is unconditioned by the desire to achieve an empirically orientated end, because of natural desires to fulfil subjective wants, like bodily or emotional satisfaction. These are called by Kant the 'inclinations', including, for example, basic desires for physical nourishment, and emotional needs for friendship, love and, ultimately, happiness.[61] The inclinations cause us to 'struggle against unruly impulses and desires' as these are 'human conditions' in which we act.[62] That is, our maxims will inevitably usually be 'material', in the sense of being qualified by a certain 'matter', the 'subjective' or 'relative' ends, whose value 'is relative and conditioned', as opposed to being 'formal' and having only 'objective ends', and therefore being of 'absolute and unconditional value'.[63] Choosing to act in accordance with the demand of pure practical reason for necessity and universality, over against the inclinations, is for Kant to act from *duty* (*Pflicht*).[64] This means that under human conditions of imperfect rationality, 'a good will is manifested in acting *for the sake of duty*'.[65] To act for the sake of duty is to choose one's course of action solely on the degree to which this action conforms with the form of the law and to not be influenced in any way by a certain 'matter' or desired end. That is, 'action done from duty has its moral worth, not from the results it attains or seeks to attain, but from a formal principle or maxim – the principle of doing one's duty whatever that may be'.[66] Having outlined the fundamental tenets of the 'categorical imperative' for the purposes of this discussion, and having drawn out how it is considered 'absolute' and 'necessary', we can now point to two facets of it, which will connect this section to the previous, insofar as the issue presented to us is closely related to the issue of Section 7.1.4, for this aspect of Kant's philosophy also threatens to involve abstraction 'interrupting' the flow of life.

7.2.3 'Pure practical reason' and the imperative 'in concreto'

This subsection differentiates the concrete situatedness of the demands of the 'categorical imperative' from its relatedness to 'pure practical reason'. That the categorical imperative is an outcome of 'pure practical reason' is indicated first by the term 'categorical', as we have seen, pointing to the rootedness of this imperative in pure intellect. 'Pure reason' is concerned with establishing universality, as we have seen, and the 'categorical imperative' serves as the arrival or presence of a universal 'moral law' in the human domain. The form of this law is universal in the sense of being 'valid for *all* men' and calling us 'to follow an objective standard

---

61. CprR, 224.
62. GMMb, 18.
63. Ibid., 31–2.
64. GMMa, 53; CprR, 172.
65. Paton, in GMMb, 18.
66. Ibid., 20.

not determined by [our] own desires,'[67] as is aptly demonstrated by the 'formula of universal law'. In being aligned to the 'form' of the law, the categorical imperative points us to a priori objective principles of action, which are rationally verifiable and therefore transparent to an agent. In this way, the 'categorical imperative' is an outcome of 'pure practical reason'.

However, common misunderstandings of Kant's practical philosophy often centre on overemphasizing the *categorical* nature of the imperative,[68] over against its status as an *imperative* which emerges in lived decision-making. That is, as we have seen, the categorical imperative is not synonymous with the 'form' of the law, because it surfaces or emerges in the human domain, and as such necessitates a response from imperfectly rational creatures. This questions those who condemn the imperative as exhibiting an 'empty formalism', because Kant does not hold that the 'form of the law' merely impinges abstractly on life, but that human beings are faced with concrete decisions which carry a sense of 'absoluteness', and it is in grounding that 'absoluteness' as genuinely principled – or genuinely 'good absolutely' – that he grounds the imperative on 'pure practical reason'. This means the categorical imperative is not held by Kant to involve formulations like the formula of universal law somehow arriving in consciousness as formulae, but that within 'the flow of life' – faced with real decisions – the conviction emerges that things 'ought' or 'ought not' to be a certain way. This can be seen, for example, in his comment that human beings are *conscious* of the fact that their wills have a determining ground other than the apparently endless conditions and qualifications of circumstantial considerations, as a fact of life, saying this is 'plain … to everyone' and 'is seen quite easily and without hesitation by the most common understanding'.[69] Paton makes a similar point in saying that 'the ordinary good man does not formulate the moral principle in abstraction'.[70] For this reason, Kant argues that 'the concept of an empirically unconditioned causality' has 'a *real application* which is exhibited *in concreto*'.[71]

The 'categorical imperative' can thus be seen to pertain in concrete situatedness, while also being grounded philosophically in 'pure practical reason'. Further indications of this point are given by Kant's discussion of 'moral endowments' in *The Metaphysics of Morals* (1797). He describes these 'endowments' as lying 'at the basis of morality' and as 'natural predispositions of the mind (*praedispositio*) for being affected by concepts of duty'. He argues that we are conscious of these endowments, and therefore we can claim they pertain in 'the flow of life'. The pertinent endowment for this discussion is what he terms 'moral feeling', which

---

67. Ibid., 22.
68. See Caygill, 'Categorical Imperative', in *Dictionary*, which discusses construals of Kant's practical philosophy as an 'empty formalist moral philosophy', and a 'glorification of the Prussian virtue of disinterested obedience' (65).
69. CPrR, 169.
70. Paton, in GMMb, 22–3.
71. CprR, 173.

he describes as 'the susceptibility to feel pleasure or displeasure merely from being aware that our actions are consistent with or contrary to the law of duty', and 'every human being (as a moral being)' has this endowment 'in him originally'.[72] This suggests that, quite apart from philosophically grounding this endowment as rationally verifiable, there is – in life – an original emergence of this consciousness *in concreto*, which calls human beings to perform certain actions without having engaged in any philosophical grounding of the rationale behind those actions as and when the demand announces itself.

7.2.4 'Pure practical reason' interrupting 'the flow of life'

The differentiation made in the previous subsection presents two pertinent points. First, accounting for the 'absoluteness' of the categorical imperative by grounding it on pure practical reason entails that it is fundamentally understood *abstractly*; as necessary and universal, apart from the considerations of concrete circumstances, and as valid for all human beings in all places. This brings us some way towards achieving the second objective of this chapter, to understand the notion of an 'absolute good' more deeply. Some progress has been made here, in that by grounding the 'absoluteness' of the categorical imperative abstractly, we render it rationally verifiable – transparent to the agent – and this presents the self-legitimizing and autonomously validating sense of ethical security that Bonhoeffer consistently wants to avoid.

However, this discussion has offered a second advance which is not merely negative. This is because Kant holds that an 'absoluteness' (in imperatives) emerges '*in concreto*' and thus impinges 'on' or pertains 'in' genuinely concrete situations and real-life decision-making. This opens up the possibility of examining how an 'absoluteness' emerges in life itself but does not necessarily involve the validation and legitimization given by grounding it abstractly in 'pure practical reason'. A task for the following chapters, then, includes an exploration of how to articulate this 'absoluteness' as a basic and 'original' human endowment; as a sense that things ought to or ought not to be a certain way that surfaces in concrete decision-making in 'the flow of life'. In short, the task is to seek a concrete 'absoluteness' or 'necessity' firmly grounded in life itself.

7.3 Summing up

This discussion of certain aspects of Kant's philosophy has presented a twofold direction to pursue in the subsequent chapters, both of which are centred on maintaining concretion in the flow of life in both cases. On the one hand, insofar as the 'unity' of the 'I' is experienced in the flow of life, we shall enquire into how it can be reflected on *as* something experienced, maintaining its situatedness in

---

72. Kant, 'Metaphysics', in *Practical Philosophy*, 528.

concrete life thereby, while yet preserving its 'hiddenness'. On the other, we are led to investigate how concrete 'absoluteness' can orientate practical discernment, without involving a self-validating and self-legitimizing sense of ethical security.

The basic concern underlying these two directions is centred on maintaining or preserving the concrete flow of life over against the non-temporal and abstract nature of 'pure reason'. For this reason, this book will now embark on investigating the work of a thinker consistently concerned with describing and articulating lived-experience in a manner faithful to its authentic character in life itself, and yet importantly orientated by insights of a fundamentally Kantian nature, involving specifically both the 'hiddenness' of the 'I' from self-reflection and the 'absoluteness' of concrete imperatives: Wilhelm Dilthey.

Chapter 8

ARTICULATING THE 'ORIGINAL TOGETHERNESS' OF LIFE: WILHELM DILTHEY IN RELATION TO DIETRICH BONHOEFFER

The findings of Chapter 7 combine to present a desideratum for this juncture of the book: to preserve or maintain the 'hiddenness' of the 'I' and the 'absoluteness' of ethical demands in the 'flow of life' – human lived-experience in temporal, concrete reality. This chapter takes some important preliminary steps to embark on attaining this desideratum, through drawing extensively on Wilhelm Dilthey, who argues that centralizing of 'pure reason' as lying 'behind life', 'truncates' or even 'mutilates' our understanding of 'lived-experience' (*Erlebnis*).[1] This chapter shows that this is not an outright denial of Kant's findings, but rather a methodological shift which is intended to complement the Kantian endeavour. Dilthey claims that human 'lived-experience' is fundamentally unified 'in' or 'to' the consciousness of a concrete subject as it is undergone, and so he seeks to 'articulate' or 'describe' this life in what he terms its 'original togetherness'.[2] Before demonstrating exactly how Dilthey will facilitate responses to the specific issues involved in articulating subjective 'hiddenness' and an 'absolute good' directly, more detail is required to show how Dilthey is a promising interlocutor for this book's aims. Moreover, it is necessary to delineate how this project draws on Dilthey to elucidate Bonhoeffer's theology and how this engagement with Dilthey is to be situated in relation to the work of commentators who have previously explored the Bonhoeffer–Dilthey relationship themselves.

8.1 Wilhelm Dilthey in overview

8.1.1 Dilthey's life and intellectual milieu

Wilhelm Dilthey (1833–1911) completed his doctorate at the Friedrich-Wilhelms-Universität in Berlin in 1864 and worked at the same university from 1882 after he was invited to occupy the prestigious chair of philosophy, which he held until

---

1. SWI, 49, 79, 490; GSV, 5.
2. Rudolf A. Makkreel and Fritjof Rodi, in SWIII, 2.

1905.³ Dilthey's output is vast, and he is rightly considered a polymath,⁴ having made significant contributions not only to philosophy, but also to literary theory and hermeneutics, art theory and aesthetics, history, psychology and pedagogy. The best way to approach his vast body of work is to grasp his philosophical raison d'être: to establish an epistemological foundation for the human sciences, or *Geisteswissenschaften*. This has been called the 'one enduring theme' holding all his writings together.⁵ Dilthey describes the *Geisteswissenschaften* as 'the sciences of man, of history, and of society',⁶ and they would mostly be grouped under the rubric 'arts and humanities' in the contemporary English-speaking world. Dilthey's understanding of his task is shown by the description of certain of his works as constituting 'the Critique of Historical Reason' (*Kritik der Geschichtlichen Vernunft*).⁷ This points to a basic Kantian orientation to Dilthey's work, involving the Kantian sense of the word 'critique' we met in Chapter 7, meaning a 'critical examination' of something 'that sets out its powers and limits'.⁸ In Dilthey's view, Kant's first *Critique* had established the veracity, and parameters, of the mode of knowing involved in the natural sciences, but a corresponding endeavour for the human sciences was needed.⁹ Dilthey in no way wants to subtract from Kant's achievement; he considers that the first *Critique* presents a highly appropriate and effective epistemology for the *Naturwissenschaften*. Rather, Dilthey seeks to *complement* this with his own 'Critique of Historical Reason', to find an equally valid and appropriate approach for the human sciences.¹⁰

Rudolf A. Makkreel describes Dilthey's undertaking as a consideration of 'the limits within which it is possible to form a system of the human sciences and to what extent their procedures and methods can be distinguished from those of the natural sciences'.¹¹ While Dilthey thus exhibits a broadly Kantian orientation, there are other key streams of influence which should be highlighted here. Herbart A. Hodges outlines two of these, 'romanticism' and 'British empiricism'.¹² By romanticism, Hodges means those thinkers who provide an anthropological orientation to Dilthey's work. In Goethe, for example, we read of the 'sciences of man' as the 'highest rung' in his 'ladder of sciences', and in Novalis, of an anthropology which is the basis of all the 'studies of human life'.¹³ Friedrich

---

3. Ilse Nina Bulhof, *Wilhelm Dilthey*, The Hague: M. Nijhoff Publishers, 1980, 10.
4. H. P. Rickman, *Wilhelm Dilthey, Pioneer of The Human Studies*, Berkeley: University of California Press, 1979, 166.
5. H. A. Hodges, *The Philosophy of Wilhelm Dilthey*, London: Routledge & Paul, 1952, xiii.
6. SWII, 56.
7. SWIII, 213ff.
8. Reath, 'Introduction', 1.
9. Hodges, *Philosophy*, xvi–xvii.
10. Ibid.
11. Makkreel, in SWIII, 1.
12. Hodges, *Philosophy*, 6f.
13. Ibid., 7.

Schleiermacher is seen by Hodges as the key influence on Dilthey from this 'romantic' strand, being Dilthey's 'philosophical guide',[14] and he outlines two central points where this is most apparent. First, Schleiermacher's *Dialectic* showed 'how every man is a vehicle, unique and irreplaceable'.[15] Secondly, Schleiermacher's hermeneutic theory, a critical elucidation of the process of understanding and interpreting written texts, was seen by Dilthey as an important precursor to his own *Critique*. That is, Dilthey saw in Schleiermacher an invaluable attempt at a 'philosophical analysis of the conditions which made understanding possible'.[16] The understanding of written texts was, for Dilthey, a form of understanding utterly central to the human sciences, as will be seen in what follows.

However, Hodges points also to an element of Schleiermacher's hermeneutic theory with which Dilthey was uncomfortable. Highlighting this element will point towards the influence of British empiricism in Dilthey's work.[17] Various of Dilthey's works show he was deeply affected by Schleiermacher's hermeneutics regarding the 'reconstruction' (*nachbilden/nachkonstruktionen*) of a creative moment which gives birth to a text. Schleiermacher's confidence in his own method here famously went so far as to claim 'he knew an author better than he knew himself', a statement frequently reproduced by Dilthey.[18] However, Hodges argues that Dilthey also found Schleiermacher's attempts to 'go behind the outer form of a text', to this creative moment, or 'general determination' (*Keimentschluss*)[19] more ambiguous. This 'reconstruction' of a creative moment, in Schleiermacher's scheme, entailed for Dilthey a going 'behind' the concrete situatedness of the author to an 'understanding of man not in his social and historical situation, but in some timeless principle which he embodies'.[20] The move to an individual essence behind social-historical life was for Dilthey unsatisfactory, because he considered it to reduce history to nothing more than 'the mere shadow of a timeless dialectic'.[21]

This shows Dilthey is concerned with the worldly, notwithstanding his deep affection for the romantic tradition, and the high regard in which he holds British empiricism bears this out, from where he singles out J. S. Mill in particular. British empiricists tend to share in common a great respect for (inductive) methods of empirical investigation and the conclusions of the natural sciences. Mill sought to extend these methods of empirical investigation into areas which Dilthey would later classify as 'human sciences'. In fact, Dilthey took the term *Geisteswissenschaften* from the German translation of J. S. Mill's *System of Logic*,

---

14. Ibid., 9.
15. Ibid., 10.
16. Ibid., 13.
17. Ibid., 16f. (this strand is connected by Hodges to Dilthey's reading of the French 'positivist' Auguste Comte).
18. See for example, SWIII, 238.
19. Hodges, *Philosophy*, 13.
20. Ibid.
21. Ibid.

where the word was used to translate Mill's 'moral sciences'.[22] Dilthey ultimately condemned Mill's 'borrowing [of] principles and methods from the natural sciences', describing it as 'mutilation of historical reality', for reasons which will become clear later.[23] Nonetheless, we find that Dilthey was impressed with Mill's deep-rooted recognition that the 'human mind lives and works in the physical world' in contrast to the tendency in nineteenth-century German philosophy to 'run-off into metaphysical speculation'.[24] Dilthey's desire to maintain an empirical orientation, without reducing the richness of empirical reality into scientific laws, is shown paradigmatically in his clarion call to investigate the empirical without subscribing to empiricism: '*Empirie, nicht Empirismus*'.[25]

These influences on Dilthey converge to present his life and work in broad overview. The general standpoint is Kantian in aim, seeking a prior scrutiny of the manner of knowing appropriate to the *Geisteswissenschaften*. It bears traces of romanticism, particularly Schleiermacher and some of his contemporaries, who shared 'a lively sense of the depth and movement of the mind's life', and the uniquely particular status of human subjects.[26] Yet, he is also informed by the worldly rooted nature of British empiricism, seeking to emulate its 'proper respect for scientific knowledge' and its aim of avoiding ultimate explanations for natural phenomena which are super-sensible. This last concern of course resonates with desideratum articulated at the outset of this chapter, and Dilthey articulates his concern for the concrete situatedness of life with a paradigmatically Diltheyan statement to which we shall return: 'behind life thought cannot go.' The next task is to define the basic terminology of Dilthey's philosophy, demonstrating Dilthey's appositeness for this book's purposes in more detail.

8.1.2 Basic terminology of Dilthey's philosophy

8.1.2.1 Erlebnis Dilthey writes: 'there are two great tendencies' which 'come to play in all scientific (*wissenschaftlich*) endeavours'.[27] The first is exhibited in natural science, which seeks to establish 'uniformities' in the physical world, uniformities he considers to be known through 'abstract comprehension'.[28] The second 'great tendency that determines scientific work' is that of the *Geisteswissenschaften*, and this involves the study of what he calls *Erlebnis*, a term all English translators of Dilthey have rendered as 'lived-experience'. *Erlebnis*, the foundational ground of the *Geisteswissenschaften*, is arguably the most important conceptuality of Dilthey's

---

22. Makkreel and Rodi, in SWI, 9–10; Rudolf A. Makkreel, *Dilthey: Philosopher of the Human Sciences*, Princeton: Princeton University Press, 1975, 36.
23. SWI, 49.
24. Hodges, *Philosophy*, 18.
25. SWI, 8.
26. Hodges, *Philosophy*, 23.
27. SWIII, 104.
28. Ibid.

8. Articulating the 'Original Togetherness' of Life

philosophical oeuvre, being the enduringly central point of orientation for his epistemology. He states that the human sciences are 'founded' on the 'coexistence and sequence of lived experiences' (*Erlebnisse*) and 'grounded *in* lived experience' (*im Erleben ... begründet*).²⁹ Dilthey presents the 'task of the human sciences' to be the examination of the 'human-historical-social world' which we *experience in life*, which he describes therefore as an examination which must proceed 'without losing sight' of the 'original togetherness' of 'concrete ... ordinary life'.³⁰

Erlebnis points most fundamentally to the unified, integrated and cohesive nature of human experience as it is actually undergone in life. Dilthey maintains that an effective understanding of life, such as that which sciences like literature or history must involve, should seek to reproduce the way in which experience proceeds in the life of concrete subjects, where a complex intertwining of manifold factors exhibits a unitary 'togetherness'. To break this 'togetherness' down by reductive analysis, for Dilthey, 'truncates' it, so that its authentic character is lost, a distinct and particular character which can only be preserved by taking *Erlebnis* as an irreducible 'unity' in and of itself. On the most basic level, as derived from the verb *leben*, we can see Dilthey seeking to highlight the vitality and 'livedness' of human experience, something that is *humanly* undergone and applicable thereby to the *human* sciences, not something to be analysed like the objects of natural science. The word *Erlebnis* itself developed late in the evolution of the German language, being a nominal form of *erleben*, which arose around the mid-nineteenth century.³¹ An early English translation of one of Dilthey's works explains that 'the past participle "lived" indicates the peculiar, quasi-objective status of this experience [which is *erlebt*], grammatically an object of living, [yet] really identified with it'.³²

This is unavoidably somewhat cryptic at this point, but elucidation can be given by differentiating the word from *Erfahrung*, commonly translated into English as just 'experience', without the qualifier 'lived'. *Erfahrung* is Kant's word for experience, and Dilthey's opting for *Erlebnis* shows that he questions a philosophizing about experience that analytically breaks down components, elements and structural conditions, which are then ordered and understood through taxonomical, classificatory activity. Again, he does not deny the rectitude of the findings of this analytical approach, but rather argues that it will not suffice for the *Geisteswissenschaften*. Being concerned with the human, he seeks to accommodate experience as it is lived, and therefore *Erlebnis* refers to experience as it actually *is* for a lived subject. This means it is approached as 'ultimate',³³ something which cannot be understood effectively if considered to be undergirded or structured

---

29. SWIII, 24, 140 (my emphasis).
30. SWII, 23.
31. Makkreel and Rodi, in SWV, 20.
32. Stephen A. Emery and William T. Emery, in *The Essence of Philosophy* by Wilhelm Dilthey, Chapel Hill: University of North Carolina Press, 1954, x.
33. Makkreel, *Philosopher*, 8.

by conditions which are not given explicitly to *Erlebnis* itself, nor composed as an aggregate of different impressions which can be broken down and delineated. As Makkreel puts it, to approach experience as *Erfahrung* is to consider 'experience as a conceptual ordering of inert sensations', whereas to approach it as *Erlebnis*, is to hold that '*qua* consciousness there is nothing more ultimate behind it'.[34]

Further indications that *Erlebnis* is primarily to be defined in terms of the 'original togetherness' of life, can be seen by highlighting its genealogy in Dilthey's work. It comes to the fore in Dilthey's writings during the 1890s and emerges particularly in his work on aesthetics, particularly with regard to literary aesthetics, or poetics. The editors of the English critical edition of some of Dilthey's aesthetic works point out that the term *Erlebnis* became more prominent in his *The Imagination of the Poet: Elements for a Poetics* (*Die Einbildungskraft des Dichters: Bausteine für eine Poetik* hereafter: *Bausteine*).[35] They suggest the literature of Goethe instigated Dilthey's use of the term; 'a good number of concepts through which Dilthey' had previously 'tried to express the fullness and vitality of concrete human experience are derived from Goethe', including '*Lebensbezug* (life-relation), [and] *Lebensgefühl* (feeling of life)'. Although *Erlebnis* is not 'of Goethean origin', they write, it 'epitomises' the latter's '*holistic* approach'.[36] Again, as holistic, Dilthey's concern with *Erlebnis* is based on his desire to express the 'original togetherness' of human life. More attention will be given to this term, and its close relatedness to unreflective experience, in Chapter 9.

8.1.2.2 A 'descriptive' method *Erlebnis* serves for Dilthey as the foundational bed of the *Geisteswissenschaften*, and in his overall methodological standpoint of a 'descriptive approach'[37] we discern *how* he considers the foundation of *Erlebnis* is (or should be) studied in the human sciences while preserving its 'original togetherness'. To break experience down into constituent elements and conditions, in Dilthey's view, *explains* experience, in the sense of providing the grounds which account for the why and how of things occurring. This understanding underlies his classification of natural science as 'explanatory' (*erklärende*),[38] in which he argues that things are explained by way of what he calls 'heuristic constructions', such as 'force, atom and molecule'.[39] The word 'heuristic' indicates that Dilthey considers the explanatory grounds of that which we experience arrived at by natural science are essentially constructions of the human intellect. This does not mean he thinks they do not correspond to the real as genuinely external to the intellect, but that he wants to highlight that focusing only on explanatory grounds which are not

34. Ibid.
35. The *Bausteine* is published in GSVI and SWV, comments by Makkreel and Rodi, in SWV, 15.
36. Makkreel and Rodi, in SWV, 20 (my emphasis).
37. SWI, 84.
38. Ibid., 198–9.
39. Ibid.

present 'to' or 'in' *Erlebnis* inevitably detracts from the richness of experience itself, in that aspects of experience are 'supplanted' by 'adding thought'.[40] He stipulates that the natural sciences seek 'hypothetical causal grounds' for the interrelation of matters arising in experience and posits 'systematic connections' not given to *Erlebnis* itself and which therefore go 'behind' lived-experience, to *explain* it.[41]

His alternative approach is to 'describe' (*beschreiben*) or 'articulate' (*artikulieren*) *Erlebnis* as something 'ultimate', seeking to reproduce its authentic character faithfully, not ground it or explain it, for he maintains that our primary knowledge of the 'human-historical-social world' is rooted in life.[42] He says his descriptive method involves 'no hypothetical assumptions (*Annahmen*) that impute (*unterlegen*) something to what is given (*Gegebenen*)'.[43] An example of this can be given by picturing someone reading a book of poems. The natural scientist sees the book as a chemically constructed physical object, apprehended through the senses, perhaps invoking inner impressions due to human capacities for language comprehension and emotional reflexes to stimuli, which 'explains' the scene of someone reading a book of poems. Someone seeking to understand the scene in the manner of Dilthey, however, would seek only to 'describe' the scene as it is undergone. This involves not 'grounding' the scene on 'heuristic constructions', like the chemical formulae of the components of the paper and ink, or inferred properties of humanity like language comprehension and emotional reflexes. Rather, Dilthey would seek to articulate as accurately as possible the actual experience of the person reading the poems, not explaining why the impressions are given as they are, but articulating their specific character. Insofar as these impressions will be deeply personal, we can already discern that Dilthey's descriptive method involves understanding human beings as concrete subjects, each with individual and unique life-trajectories of their own.

8.1.2.3 *Verstehen* So Dilthey seeks to preserve the 'original togetherness' of life, through describing *Erlebnis* and not explaining it. For the most part (and pertinently for us), we can surmise that *Erlebnis* is broadly unreflective, in that experience as it is undergone in life mostly involves simply attending to the present moment and not reflecting on one's self or one's tasks. With his descriptive method, Dilthey points to how he seeks to incorporate reflective activity with *Erlebnis*, while preserving the integrated and cohesive character of the latter, a character lost by the analytical, reductive philosophical reflection on experience as *Erfahrung*. The place of the reflective in Dilthey's philosophy is of course important, for, as scholarly disciplines, the *Geisteswissenschaften* are intrinsically reflective. Relatively late in his writings, then, he extended his call for a 'descriptive method'

---

40. SWIII, 191–2.
41. This means inductive inference primarily; see Hodges, *Philosophy*, 203.
42. SWIII, 23.
43. Ibid., 140.

by outlining an approach to reflective understanding, which he calls *Verstehen*, a term which begins to feature highly in his work from around 1895.[44]

Dilthey considers the human sciences to be 'an articulation' of 'the general structures of historical life',[45] and as such he seeks to outline how they involve 'conceptual cognition' (*Erkenntnis*) without making recourse to the Kantian understanding (*Verstand*), which, as we have seen, involves 'pure concepts' rooted in the intellect which Dilthey considers explanatory. His task therefore is to ask how concepts can work as 'general structures' without these generalities being 'split' from life and 'subsisting' in themselves as pure intellection.[46] The human sciences, for Dilthey, strive to 'attain ... objectively valid conceptual cognition of the interconnectedness of lived experiences in the human-historical-social world'.[47] He iterates this further by claiming that the 'original togetherness' of *Erlebnis* can be brought into a reflective *understanding* of life as *Verstehen* rather than *Verstand*: 'connectedness' is actually given 'in *Erlebnis, and* in reflective understanding (*Verstehen*)'.[48] He thus seeks to demarcate how reflecting on life while preserving its intrinsic connectedness involves a categorial analysis of sorts, but he seeks to differentiate his categories of *Verstehen* from those of the Kantian *Verstand*.[49] He calls his categories '*life*-categories' and claims these 'are not applied to life *a priori*' but 'lie in the very nature of life'.[50] These categories are intended to describe the form or pattern of cognitive, emotive and volitional processes as they occur in lived-experience itself, 'processes which we observe in our ourselves and that make themselves known to us in distinguishing, connecting, relating, ordering'.[51]

The primary 'life-category' is Dilthey's category of 'meaning' (*Bedeutung*).[52] Reflection as it most commonly occurs in lived-experience, says Dilthey, is primarily an attempt to establish the meaning of things. This category is very broad, and the term 'meaning' is applied by him in various different contexts, becoming crucially important in some of his best-known works in textual hermeneutics.[53] In order to stay focused on the objectives of this book, I will concentrate on meaning as it applies to self-reflective understanding, or self-reflection (*Selbstbesinnung*). In this connection, Dilthey argues that the category of *Bedeutung* 'provides the

---

44. Makkreel, *Philosopher*, 251, 255–6.

45. Makkreel and Rodi, in SWIII, 1.

46. One could argue that a mathematician engaging in geometry undergoes an *Erlebnis* of pure intellection, but Dilthey would argue that even in this example, the mathematician is concretely situated in ways which colour the experience itself.

47. SWIII, 23.

48. Ibid., 235 (my emphasis).

49. Makkreel, *Philosopher*, 223.

50. SWIII, 252.

51. SWII, 59.

52. Ibid., 252ff.

53. See 'The Rise of Hermeneutics', in SWIV.

relation that determines and articulates the apprehension of the course of a life'.[54] As someone looks back over his or her life, certain events are related as meaningful to the whole of that life, and the sense of the whole in turn imparts meaning to the parts (aspects being reflected on).[55] This basic mode of self-reflection which Dilthey detects in the common human 'recollection' of a 'life-course' constitutes the most basic example of the category of 'meaning'.[56] It also extends beyond a single life to become almost a *Grundkategorie* of the *Geisteswissenschaften*, for he argues that determining meaning in our own lives serves as the basis enabling us 'grasp and explicate simultaneous and successive life-courses in history'.[57]

In order to examine more closely what *Bedeutung* involves for Dilthey, we must bear in mind that, to preserve the 'original togetherness' of life, this category cannot be rooted in any kind of framework 'external' to, 'outside' of, or 'behind' life itself. Taking the part–whole determination of meaning outlined above, this requires that no 'part' of life – say a particular event – is considered meaningful through being situated in relation to an 'external' reference. To give an example, let us consider someone believing that a past event is particularly meaningful for him or her, because he or she were led to value the concept of justice. If in this example, justice is being seen as an 'exterior' principle, which makes this particular event seem meaningful to the subject simply because he or she is committed to a world view that considers justice supremely important, it does not sufficiently capture the inherent 'connectedness' Dilthey is seeking to articulate. Justice in this instance (as something 'outside' life) is what is allowing the meaning of the 'part' to be determined, rather than the 'whole'. An alternative example which *does* show what Dilthey is trying to do can be seen if that same person were, say, a human rights campaigner or a high court judge. Then the 'part' is deemed 'meaningful', in that the meaning itself is clearly something which can only be ascertained in reference to the 'whole'. The frame of reference which facilitates the determination of the meaning of a 'part' is therefore the 'whole' life-course, unavoidably embedded in concrete particularity.

Before moving on to the final subsection, it is worth pointing out why this way of determining meaning as a 'life-category' becomes so central for Dilthey's work, which will situate this discussion in relation to one of the best-known aspects of his philosophy. The determination of meaning outlined above presents a self-reflective instance of what in textual hermeneutics is called the 'hermeneutic circle'. He calls this circularity an 'insoluble riddle', namely, that we 'must understand the whole from the parts', yet 'it is the whole that imparts meaning and that accordingly assigns the part its place'.[58] He is clear that he by no means wants to avoid this circularity and thereby lose sight of concrete reality. He claims

54. SWIII, 95.
55. Ibid.
56. Ibid.
57. Ibid.
58. Ibid., 281.

there 'would be a simply escape from this circle' if something 'unconditioned' were to 'set the standard for contemplating and apprehending history'.[59] Thus, we can now approximately situate his textual hermeneutics in relation to his fundamental epistemological concern to preserve the 'original togetherness' of concrete life, in that the manner in which texts are understood in circularity embeds meaning in its context.

8.1.3 Dilthey and neo-Kantianism

The most salient aspects of Dilthey's background having been covered, it is necessary also briefly to situate Dilthey in relation to neo-Kantianism before commencing a detailed examination of his work. Neo-Kantianism was highly influential during Dilthey's lifetime, but he was invariably deeply critical of it. It is beyond this book's scope to undertake a detailed discussion of neo-Kantianism, but as something central to understanding Dilthey's work and its congruence with Bonhoeffer's, some basic facets of it need to be touched upon.

Neo-Kantianism had two different centres of influence, Marburg and Baden. Dilthey's criticisms of neo-Kantian thinking are primarily concerned with the Baden School, specifically Wilhelm Windelband (1848–1915) and Heinrich Rickert (1863–1937). The first point to bear in mind is that, despite its name, neo-Kantianism takes an ambivalent attitude to 'classical' or 'orthodox' Kantianism. Neo-Kantianism is not an attempt to perpetuate the philosophical *oeuvre* of Immanuel Kant himself, but to employ some of his insights in a different undertaking, as shown in Windelband's claim, for example, that to 'understand Kant is to go beyond Kant'. Indeed, it is worth asking if at least some neo-Kantians would be more accurately described under a different name, and the secondary literature acknowledges some apparently more accurate alternatives, such as 'neo-idealism'[60] or 'neo-Fichteanism'.[61] In fact, it is not uncommon to come across statements like Fritz Kaufmann's comment that neo-Kantianism 'bordered on anti-Kantianism'.[62] The relationship between Kant's writings and the neo-Kantians is aptly described by Martin Heidegger as exhibiting a 'radical one-sidedness'.[63] Insofar as Kant's first *Critique* is two-sided in its approach to human cognition as

---

59. Ibid.
60. Ludwig Stein quoted in Thomas E. Willey, *Back to Kant*, Detroit: Wayne State University Press, 1978, 37.
61. Makkreel, *Philosopher*, 224; Rudolf A. Makkreel and Sebastian Luft, 'Introduction', in Rudolf A. Makkreel and Sebastian Luft (eds), *Neo-Kantianism and Contemporary Philosophy*, Bloomington: Indiana University Press, 2010, 1–21 (1–2).
62. Kaufmann quoted by Simon Fisher, in *Revelatory Positivism?*, Oxford: Oxford University Press, 1988, 21.
63. Quoted by Claude Piché, 'Heidegger and the Neo-Kantian Reading of Kant', in Tom Rockmore (ed.), *Heidegger, German Idealism & Neo-Kantianism*, Amherst, NY: Humanity Books, 2000, 179–207 (179–80).

involving both intuition (*Anschauung*) and intellect (*Verstand*),⁶⁴ neo-Kantianism can be considered as *one*-sided in its attempt to construct a philosophical system on the intellect alone (hence 'neo-idealism'). Simon Fisher calls this refusal a 'purification' of Kantian epistemology, which minimizes 'the importance of empirical intuition'.⁶⁵ This 'one-sidedness' is certainly apparent in *Kants Theorie der Erfahrung* (1871) by the key Marburg figure, Herman Cohen. This work sets out to refute the Kantian view of experience as 'union [*Verbindung*] between intuition and thought',⁶⁶ by arguing that what is experienced is fundamentally dependent on the formal rules of mathematics which undergird both intuition and the understanding.

Cohen attempts to base the inductive reasoning of the natural sciences on the formal rules of mathematics, as the condition of their possibility, showing how he considered his philosophy to be transcendental. The transcendental method involves finding the conditions of the possibility of something, and for Cohen, this is applied to natural science in seeking after the 'necessary *a priori* conditions' which underlie the natural scientific endeavour.⁶⁷ This aspect of Marburg neo-Kantianism influenced the Baden philosophers, whose work will be discussed in the following chapters. Windelband, for example, held that the natural sciences are aimed at uncovering universal laws, but the human sciences (which Rickert termed *Kulturwissenschaften*)⁶⁸ are aimed at understanding only particulars, and as such should be limited to describing particulars, being 'idiographic' rather than 'nomothetic'.⁶⁹ Prima facie, this seems to resonate with Dilthey's work, but we shall see in the following chapters that he criticizes Windelband and Rickert on various fronts, perhaps most decisively through his 'life-categories', which, he argues, present overarching generalities or patterns of lived-experience with a certain lawfulness (*Geseztlichkeit*) of their own, embedded or inhering only 'in' concrete life, and thus with a lawfulness of a different order to what Windelband calls the 'nomothetic' (universal) lawfulness of the natural sciences.

Before we extend this preliminary overview of Dilthey's life and work to elucidate the specific tasks ahead of us, it is necessary to clarify how this book will draw on Dilthey in relation to Bonhoeffer, and how this is to be situated in relation to existing interpretations of the Dilthey's influence on Bonhoeffer's writings.

64. Fisher, *Positivism?*, 44.
65. Ibid.
66. Ibid., 37.
67. Sebastian Luft, 'Reconstruction and Reduction: Natorp and Husserl on Method and the Question of Subjectivity', in Makkreel and Luft (eds), *Neo-Kantianism and Contemporary Philosophy*, 59–91 (63).
68. Theodore Plantinga, *Historical Understanding in the Thought of Wilhelm Dilthey*, Toronto: University of Toronto Press, 1980, 42.
69. See Makkreel, *Philosopher*, 218–20.

8.2 Scholarship on Dilthey's relation to Bonhoeffer

8.2.1 References to Dilthey in Bonhoeffer's work

Before examining the Bonhoefferian commentators who have studied Dilthey's influence, a brief outline of the main loci of Dilthey references in Bonhoeffer's writing is required. The earliest reference to Dilthey in Bonhoeffer's writing is in a 1925 student essay, 'On the Historical and Pneumatological Interpretation of Scripture',[70] but the first substantial cluster occurs in *Act and Being*. In four of these, Bonhoeffer directly references Dilthey himself, and in another, he makes a Diltheyan-seeming observation, which is acknowledged as such by the editors of the critical edition.[71] Overall, these references suggest that Dilthey is a thinker to whom Bonhoeffer takes recourse to because he wants to hold the wholeness or integrity of human life in unity. For example, he mentions 'the movement of decision-making existence, that Dilthey calls the "totality of life"', calling to mind his own concern with the unity of the 'empirical total I', which we discussed in Chapter 5.[72] Moreover, in a footnote, Bonhoeffer praises an essay by Dilthey as being of 'decisive significance'[73] for overcoming 'the whole idealistic theory of knowledge' with 'a philosophy of life shaped by history'.[74] To discuss this essay in detail would divert this chapter from its purposes, but it should be acknowledged that 'a philosophy of life shaped by history' points to an understanding of life as concretely situated and unified, in opposition to the idealist privileging of speculation. Moreover, Bonhoeffer references Dilthey in using terminology about 'explaining' and 'understanding' in a discussion of the ungraspability of 'act'. He states that as 'something taking place in consciousness [*Bewußt-Seiendes*], the act is a temporal, psychic event', but warns the act 'can never be "explained" but only "understood"'.[75] This seems to adhere to the basic, Diltheyan injunction against 'explaining' concrete ('temporal') events (as interrupting the 'flow of life'), but the exact meaning of the reference to *Verstehen* here is oblique and is considered by Boomgaarden to belie a misunderstanding.[76] Nonetheless, in broad terms, Bonhoeffer's reservation about explaining 'act', when it is 'a temporal psychic event', like the other references discussed here, indicates again that Dilthey's concern for articulating the integrated and cohesive nature of human life is something broadly congruent with Bonhoeffer's own intentions.

---

70. DBWE9, 285–99, cites Dilthey's *The Rise of Hermeneutics* in the bibliography, with Diltheyan thinking clearly perceptible in the text itself.
71. DBWE2, 29, 55, 72, 127–8, and indirectly 46 (see n29).
72. Ibid., 72.
73. This essay is 'Beiträge zur Lösung der Frage vom Ursprung unseres Glaubens an die Realität der Aussenwelt und seinem Recht', in GSV, 90ff.
74. DBWE2, 55, n26 (footnote by Bonhoeffer).
75. Ibid., 29.
76. Boomgaarden, *Verständnis*, 57–8.

The most extensive cluster of references to Dilthey in Bonhoeffer's work is in the prison literature. In Tegel, Bonhoeffer engages with Dilthey in a much more thoroughgoing way than he had hitherto, and as we shall see, he begins a trajectory that may have developed into a full-scale, theological appropriation of Dilthey's work. Feil concludes that 'only in prison' did Bonhoeffer 'intensively study' Dilthey's work and that the references before then are 'only scattered'.[77] The following subsection will examine Feil's understanding of the Tegel references more closely, but there are already good grounds to point out that the abovementioned Dilthey references in *Act and Being* are connected with a shared concern of Bonhoeffer's and Dilthey's to preserve the unity or 'totality' of life, and this concern resurfaces frequently in Tegel, such as when Bonhoeffer discusses the ἄνθρωπος τέλειος (whole man) as one who is not 'split or torn apart', and interprets Mt. 5:17 as an admonition to 'be whole [τέλειος], as your heavenly Father is whole', as opposed to being one who is 'double-minded' (ἀνήρ δίψυχος).[78] This gives a pointer in that, although the direct references to Dilthey before Tegel are 'scattered', there is a broad congruence in seeking to preserve what Dilthey calls the 'original togetherness' of 'the psychophysical life unit' (*Lebenseinheit*),[79] and Bonhoeffer, the ἄνθρωπος τέλειος.

8.2.2 Interpretations of Dilthey's influence on Bonhoeffer

We saw in Chapter 3 that Feil's work on Bonhoeffer is seminal, and here we shall focus on the fact he was one of the first to unearth the engagement of Bonhoeffer with Dilthey in Tegel. Feil shows that Bonhoeffer draws on Dilthey rather suddenly, from early 1944, and that many of the best-known motifs of the highly creative months that followed are related to conceptualities in Dilthey's writing. For example, Bonhoeffer's reading of Dilthey's essay '*Von deutscher Dichtung und Musik*' is seen by Feil to offer direct correspondences with Bonhoeffer's understandings of 'worldliness', 'metaphysics as religious metaphysics' and 'inwardness', corresponding point-by-point (or 'proof texted') in the letters being written while Bonhoeffer read the essay.[80] He goes on to highlight the importance of Bonhoeffer's reading of Dilthey's *Weltanschauung und Analyse des Menschen seit Renaissance und Reformation*, claiming this was instrumental in Bonhoeffer's supposition of an impending 'completely religionless time'.[81] Feil therefore concludes that 'Bonhoeffer's train of thought ... shows how much he had immersed himself in Dilthey's historical assessment of the course of modern intellectual history'.[82]

---

77. Feil, *Bonhoeffer*, 178.
78. DBWE8, 278.
79. SWIII, 108; GSVII, 86.
80. Feil, *Bonhoeffer*, 179.
81. Ibid., 180–1.
82. Ibid.

In drawing attention to the influence of Dilthey on the prison letters, Feil offers a convincing thesis and a highly important contribution to the field. The direct correspondences of terminology and concepts, not to mention Bonhoeffer's own comment that after reading Dilthey's *Das Erlebnis und die Dichtung* caused him to 'regret his own ignorance'[83] of Dilthey's work, make the case for the Dilthey influence on the prison writings to appear incontrovertible. It should be reiterated that Feil is concerned with direct, forensic 'proof texting' of Diltheyan conceptualities in Bonhoeffer's work. This approach is also seen in Christian Gremmels, who simultaneously with Feil, discovered the marked points of contact between the development of Bonhoeffer's ideas and his reading of Dilthey in Tegel. Gremmels interrelates various conceptualities between each thinker, drawing particularly on Dilthey's *Weltanschauungen* essay and Bonhoeffer's understanding of 'coming of age' and 'autonomy'.[84] Like Feil, then, he also points to various instances of 'verbatim agreement' between expressions in Bonhoeffer's letters and Dilthey's essay.[85]

A concentration on historical veracity and direct 'proof texting' in Feil and Gremmels is also seen in Wüstenberg, whose *Theology of Life* is the most extensive study of the Dilthey influence on Bonhoeffer to date.[86] Because Wüstenberg's overarching concern is the Tegel theology, he is focused particularly on the notion of 'religion' as it is found throughout Bonhoeffer's writing. He observes that Bonhoeffer's earliest work is initially relatively positive about religion, and then moves to a deeply critical view of religion, under the influence of Karl Barth and dialectical theology around 1924/5.[87] Wüstenberg builds on a suggestion initially made by Feil that Bonhoeffer went on later to switch from a 'systematic-theological' understanding of religion to a 'historical' view.[88] The systematic view is Barth's, seeing religion as an unwarranted and idolatrous seeking after God.[89] The 'historical' view is close to Dilthey's, who, as regards metaphysics particularly, sees humanity progressing, or 'growing-up' into maturity, so religion has much less control over, say science, or social organization.[90] Wüstenberg argues that Bonhoeffer allows both these understandings of religion to stand side-by-side throughout his writings from the early 1930s until Tegel, stating that 'historical

---

83. Ibid., 179; see DBWE8, 285.
84. Christian Gremmels, *Mündige Welt und Planung*, Marburg/Lahn: N.p., 1970, 14–15 (my translation).
85. Ralph K. Wüstenberg, *A Theology of Life*, Grand Rapids, MI: Eerdmans, 1998, 70.
86. Ralph K. Wüstenberg, *Eine Theologie Des Lebens,* Leipzig: Evang. Verl.-Anst., 2006.
87. Wüstenberg, *Life*, 31f.
88. Feil quoted in ibid., 91.
89. For a full discussion of Barth's view on religion, see Greggs, *Religion*, 15–38.
90. It must be noted Dilthey does not predict a religionless time and argues that *Religiosität* 'is especially central' for understanding 'the objectification and organisation of the human spirit' (SWIII, 284–5).

and systematic-theological considerations stand next to each other everywhere in Bonhoeffer's treatment of religion, occasionally complementing each other'.[91]

Where Wüstenberg departs from Feil is with his view that a decisive shift occurs in Tegel, when Bonhoeffer *fuses* the two approaches to religion together. He claims that Bonhoeffer joins Dilthey's understanding of humanity's outgrowing of certain religious dependencies to Barth's critique of religion as something inherently idolatrous and theologically problematic, supposing that both point to a future where belief in Christ will be entirely 'this worldly' and liberated from religious encumbrances. Wüstenberg concludes therefore that 'Bonhoeffer's understanding of religion in Tegel radicalises [the Barthian] critique with systematic recourse to Wilhelm Dilthey'.[92]

Wüstenberg's study is seminal in developing the understanding of the Dilthey influence, and it is rightly understood as a crucial secondary work on Bonhoeffer. Wüstenberg's analysis is also particularly impressive for moving beyond just straightforward 'proof texting', through showing that Dilthey's 'historical' view of religion was present in Bonhoeffer's thinking from quite early on, and more substantially, through his suggestion that the Tegel theology should be understood as a 'theology of life' (*Theologie des Lebens*). This title is a direct analogy with the term 'philosophy of life' (*Lebensphilosophie*), a classification of a group of philosophers which many hold to include Dilthey.[93] This seems to point towards a sense of broad congruence between Bonhoeffer and Dilthey. To call Bonhoeffer's thinking a 'theology of life' actually predates Wüstenberg, originating in the work of Hans-Jürgen Abromeit (1991). Abromeit also cites Dilthey as being instrumental on Bonhoeffer in Tegel, but argues for Bonhoeffer's 'life-theology' being rooted in *Ethics*, such as in Bonhoeffer's exposition of Christ as, what Abromeit describes as, 'life *par excellence*' (*Leben schlechthin*).[94] Abromeit does not give sustained attention to this idea, being focused in his monograph on the concept of 'mystery' (*Geheimnis*), nor does he connect this centrality of 'life' exclusively with Dilthey, mentioning Nietzsche as similarly instrumental. But, he gives some pointers which suggest that his view of the relatedness of *Lebensphilosophie* (and thereby Dilthey) to Bonhoeffer is highly significant to this study. For example, he points to a shared 'emphasis on the "livingness" (*Lebendigkeit*) and concreteness of life', and importantly, claims his 'analogy between *Lebensphilosophie* and Bonhoeffer's *Lebenstheologie*' is based on 'the shared basis of each in the interdependence of *Erlebnis* und *Verstehen*', a feature of Dilthey's thinking which will be central to Chapter 9.

---

91. Wüstenberg, *Life*, 93.

92. Wüstenberg also considers the 'scattered' references of the early 1930s to be much more important than Feil, ibid., 74; 186–7.

93. A difficult term to define accurately, it not taken by Wilhelm Dilthey himself, and applied in very different ways to thinkers as diverse as Nietzsche, Simmel, Bergsen, Spengler, among others; see Regenbogen and Meyer, 'Lebensphilosophi', in *Wörterbuch*, 374–5.

94. Abromeit, *Geheimnis*, 117.

Bearing in mind that Abromeit touches closely on interpreting the Dilthey influence in a way that corresponds with this book, it is instructive that Wüstenberg criticizes Abromeit, on the ground that the passages of *Ethics* in question do not feature any historically verified Dilthey references.[95] In seeking to understand Wüstenberg's criticism of Abromeit more deeply, there are good grounds for suggesting that certain elements of Wüstenberg's interpretation of both Dilthey and Bonhoeffer perhaps restrain the possibility of his fully appreciating the congruence in shared concerns between each thinker. First, Wüstenberg consistently presents Kant as an *alternative* to Dilthey, at times sounding almost like an *either/or* choice, implying that Bonhoeffer's appropriation of Dilthey was actually a turning away from the Kantian elements of *Sanctorum Communio* and *Act and Being*. This inhibits the disclosure of the shared concern of Dilthey and Bonhoeffer to preserve the 'totality of life', as seen, for example, in Wüstenberg's discussion of Bonhoeffer's reading of William James at Union Theological Seminary. Wüstenberg draws our attention to Bonhoeffer's comment that for James, 'questions such as the Kantian question of knowledge are "nonsense"', and he connects this assertion with Dilthey's adage that 'no real blood runs in the knowing subject of Kant, Locke and Hume'.[96] This is instructive, because Dilthey's adage is not an outright dismissal of Kant alone, but questions also Locke and Hume, showing how the issue for Dilthey is that the 'original togetherness' of life is threatened by *both* a Humean/Lockean approach to the empirical 'I', *and* Kant's transcendental 'I'. This mirrors (in a theological transposition) Bonhoeffer's issue with maintaining the continuity of the 'empirical total I' and the Barthian 'heavenly double', and the congruence between Dilthey and Bonhoeffer with this shared concern for 'original togetherness' is much harder to discern if Dilthey is set up as an either/or to Kant alone.

Moreover, Wüstenberg also omits to distinguish Kant from neo-Kantianism, when this distinction is made clearly enough in Bonhoeffer's own writing.[97] For example, he describes Bonhoeffer's discussion of philosophy at his inaugural lecture in Berlin, as 'neo-Kantianism', due to Bonhoeffer's assertion that 'only one philosophy' recognizes the ability of self-limitation to human *ratio* as 'the essence of Kantian philosophy', when this 'essence' of self-limitation in Kant is not actually *neo*-Kantian. Again, this limits the degree to which Dilthey and Bonhoeffer's shared concern for unity is perceptible, because the writings of Bonhoeffer's where Kant is highly praised often exhibit Bonhoeffer's concern for the 'totality of life', as we have seen in *Act and Being*, where Kant is called the 'protestant epistemologist

---

95. Ralph K. Wüstenberg, *Bonhoeffer and Beyond*, Frankfurt am Main: Peter Lang, 2008, 32f.

96. Wüstenberg, *Life*, 6; SWII, 9.

97. See DBWE2, 47–8, where Bonhoeffer claims neo-Kantianism 'follows the path of Fichte', before drawing a sharp distinction between 'genuine transcendentalism' and the Marburg neo-Kantian Paul Natorp, who he says offers a level of 'speculation' which sees him 'approach Hegel'.

par excellence' in the section where Bonhoeffer raises concerns about the 'continuity' of the subject in the 'transcendental attempt'. By confusing Kant with neo-Kantianism, Wüstenberg interprets Bonhoeffer's criticism of Barth's 'neo-Kantian eggshells' in Tegel as a recanting of Bonhoeffer's earlier praise of Kant. But, pointedly for us, these earlier works feature Bonhoeffer's concern for the 'totality of life', which endures into the prison letters with the ἄνθρωπος τέλειος, and which is broadly congruent with Dilthey's concern for 'original togetherness'.

Before summing up this chapter, there is a final commentator who has highlighted Dilthey's relation to Bonhoeffer's thinking to be discussed: Michael DeJonge. DeJonge draws on what he considers Diltheyan aspects of Bonhoeffer's work to delineate what he calls the different 'thought forms' of Bonhoeffer and Barth. He argues that Bonhoeffer and Barth each exhibit a different approach 'to thinking about parts and wholes', claiming that Barth stands in the 'Kantian tradition' which is 'combinatory' in 'joining parts into wholes', whereas Bonhoeffer follows 'Dilthey and the hermeneutic tradition' in interpreting individual parts in terms of the 'whole'. DeJonge focuses on Christology, arguing that Barth's dialectic presents 'parts' (such as the divine and human natures of Christ) 'in an effort to point to revelation as that which alone synthesises those parts into a whole'. In contrast, he claims Bonhoeffer starts with Christ as the 'whole' (the person of Christ) and 'proceeds hermeneutically, [in] unpacking definitions of God and humanity from the logically prior person'.[98] DeJonge's work is important for this discussion in that, in contrast to Feil, Gremmels and Wüstenberg, he does not engage in specific 'proof texting', but, like Abromeit, points to a broad shared 'thought-form' between Bonhoeffer and Dilthey. However, DeJonge's analysis is not without problems. First, Dilthey's part–whole relationship is more deeply reciprocal than he suggests. Secondly and more pressingly, in view of our analysis which highlights a shared concern in preserving the 'original togetherness' of life 'behind which thought cannot go', to consider either Bonhoeffer or Dilthey has fundamentally orientated by a 'logically prior' unity, rather than a unity cohering in the 'flow of life', is questionable. Indeed, even with Christology, Bonhoeffer states the 'unity' of Christ 'lies in the midst of history'.[99] For this reason, in what follows this study will seek unity 'in the midst of history' within the purview of its own concern for the integrating the unreflective and reflective problematic in Bonhoeffer's account of human subjectivity.

8.3 Summing up

This chapter has given a preliminary overview of Dilthey's work and delineated some basic concepts for understanding it. Of key importance is his concern for maintaining the 'original togetherness' of concrete 'lived-experience', which we

---

98. DeJonge, *Formation*, 98–100.
99. DBWE6, 82.

shall see (as *Erlebnis*) is closely related to the unreflective. Moreover, by discussing 'reflective understanding' (*Verstehen*), an important pointer for the following chapters has been gained. That is, Dilthey's express desire to integrate reflection (as *Verstehen*) with the unreflective (as *Erlebnis*), further establishing that he is a highly promising interlocutor for this project.

Moreover, that Dilthey's concern for maintaining 'original togetherness' is broadly shared by Bonhoeffer has been established, with recourse to references to Dilthey in *Act and Being*, which are connected to the concern for the ἄνθρωπος τέλειος in Tegel. By working primarily from a shared *concern*, rather than a historical influence, this book can be demarcated as offering a different emphasis to the work of Feil, Gremmels and the historical focus of Wüstenberg. Moreover, this book will extend Wüstenberg's, Abromeit's and DeJonge's pointers towards a deeper Diltheyan thought-form in Bonhoeffer's theology, but with a specific investigation into their shared concern for preserving the 'original togetherness' of life in relation to the unreflective and reflective. The efficacy of this approach will be made apparent through conducting a close reading of Dilthey on his own terms, so this will be the next undertaking.

Chapter 9

THE UNREFLECTIVE 'I' AND REFLECTIVE SELF-UNDERSTANDING IN DILTHEY

Having shown that Dilthey is a promising interlocutor for this book, we shall now investigate his approach to the unreflective 'I' and reflective self-understanding, with a view to uncovering how his concern for 'original togetherness' bears fruit applicable specifically to the cognitive side of our problematic: maintaining both the subject–'object' singularity and the 'hiddenness' of the unreflective 'I' in self-reflection. Our study of *Act and Being* highlighted the preservation of a subjective 'hiddenness' in 'genuine transcendentalism', and having examined relevant aspects of Kant's first *Critique* to enquire into this 'hiddenness' more deeply, we ascertained that our task is to articulate the unity of the 'I' in the flow of life. Now, we can bring Dilthey's interlocution with Kant on precisely this issue into discussion and examine how the former's concern for 'original togetherness' develops into his understanding of a concrete and temporal unreflective 'I'.

The previous chapter also pointed to Dilthey's work on reflective understanding or *Verstehen*, and on the relatedness of *Verstehen* to self-reflection through determining the meaning of the 'parts' of one's life in relation to the 'whole'. This chapter will extend our understanding of these aspects of Dilthey's work, drawing further on the critical engagement between Dilthey and neo-Kantianism, focusing particularly on the distinctive way in which Dilthey considers that 'meaning' (*Bedeutung*) is determined in self-reflection. Finally, we have seen that Dilthey not only promises to articulate unreflective and reflective subjectivity in a way highly apposite for this book, but also seeks to *coordinate* them, which has direct bearing on our fundamental problematic.

9.1 Dilthey's unreflective 'I'

9.1.1 'Reflexive awareness' and Erlebnis

This subsection discusses two closely interrelated elements from Dilthey's philosophy: 'reflexive awareness' (*Innewerden*) and *Erlebnis*. We group these two together here as pertaining to the '*unreflective-I*', rather than using a term which crops up often in the secondary literature, '*pre*-reflective',[1] because these elements are not merely preliminary stages to be superseded or cancelled out by reflection, but stand as primary and central points of orientation for Dilthey's understanding of life. The first element, *Innewerden*, was intended by Dilthey to play a key part in a subsequent volume to his first major work, the *Introduction to the Human Sciences* (*Einleitung in die Geisteswissenschaften*, hereafter: *Einleitung*) (1883).[2] His drafts for this subsequent volume includes material which is highly pertinent for our purposes, particularly a subsection called 'Foundations of Knowledge'.

'Foundations of Knowledge' begins with two principles which need to be outlined before turning to *Innewerden* itself. The first is what Dilthey calls 'the principle of phenomenality'.[3] This arises in his description of consciousness, which he claims he cannot define, but only 'exhibit [what it denotes] as an ultimate datum incapable of further analysis'.[4] The principle of phenomenality is: 'Everything is a fact of consciousness, and accordingly is subject to the conditions of consciousness.'[5] By this, he means that everything in conscious experience, which is itself taken as an 'ultimate datum' as it stands, is simply 'there' for consciousness. We have learned that phenomena are things Kant defines by breaking down conscious experience into constituent elements and conditions. Dilthey's principle of phenomenality, in contrast, is intended to draw a line under the straightforward emergence of things in conscious experience, taken as an 'ultimate datum' as it stands. These things are taken as they are in a unitary fashion, as simple 'facts of consciousness'.[6]

These 'facts of consciousness' are differentiated more specifically from Kantian phenomena in that Dilthey does not separate inner and outer perception. They therefore partake of a broad range of experiences, as demonstrated by his definition of the 'second main principle' of his analysis: 'Facts of consciousness – including perceptions, memories, objects and representations of them, and finally concepts' are 'contained in the totality of psychic life'.[7] These examples make clear that he has in mind any and every thing that arises in conscious awareness.[8] His second principle states that each type of fact of consciousness is to be located in the same unified whole of conscious awareness. This means that things which are very different in terms of their background constituents for Kant, such as thinking about a problem of algebraic geometry and the feeling of romantic desire, are for Dilthey both maintained as objects of philosophical reflection *while* being enmeshed in the same unified 'manifold web' of lived consciousness. For Dilthey,

---

1. For example, Jacob Owensby, *Dilthey and the Narrative of History*, Ithaca, NY: Cornell University Press, 1994, 87.
2. GSI/SWI.
3. SWI, 247.
4. Ibid., 246.
5. Ibid., 60.
6. Ibid.
7. Ibid., 263–4.
8. Ibid., 248.

these two different facts of consciousness *can* of course be explicated accurately by philosophical reflection in the analytic, Kantian manner. But, he wishes to work with every fact of consciousness without analysing its constitutive causes and conditions precisely to preserve a sense of the overarching unity in which these facts are actually apprehended in life. As he puts it in his later work, *The Formation of the Historical World in the Human Sciences* (*Der Aufbau der Geschichtlichen Welt in Den Geisteswissenschaften* hereafter: *Aufbau*) (1910),[9] 'Representations, judgements, feelings, desires, acts of will are always interwoven in … the empirical given in psychic life.'[10]

Dilthey's approach to consciousness as an 'ultimate datum' enables him to ground the human sciences epistemologically in unreflective lived-experience. This is because he considers the 'ultimate datum' of consciousness to be a basic, foundational level of certainty for his wider endeavours. He states that this 'knowing (*Wissen*)' is 'unshakeable'.[11] Dilthey thus seeks to outline a point of immediate certainty, working from the way in which a fact of consciousness is understood by him to be indubitably certain for the apprehending subject. Although a subject may of course doubt that *what* is being apprehended is accurate, the fact it is *being apprehended* in that particular way is unquestionable. As Makkreel puts it, this is Dilthey's 'indubitable experiential starting point'.[12] Every fact of consciousness is taken as it is apprehended in consciousness, a basic mode of awareness which Dilthey calls in the *Aufbau*, 'objective apprehension'.[13] This use of the word 'objective' is meant to point to the indubitable certainty ('objectivity') involved in simply taking the apprehension of facts of consciousness as the 'ultimate datum' of what we experience.

The mode in which facts of consciousness arise in objective apprehension is called by Dilthey 'being-there-for-me' (*da-für-mich-sein*).[14] Something is 'there-for-me' which I apprehend; it is simply *there*, and not accounted for, or grounded by me.[15] Here, we encounter *Innewerden*, which is the simple awareness with which a conscious subject apprehends something as 'there-for-me'. With this, Dilthey is pointing to the fact that this awareness necessarily involves reference to a subject; there is no conscious experience without someone being conscious *of* experience, self-awareness is in this case *reflex*-ive in the sense of being a reflex action arising spontaneously with the apprehension of something which

9. GSVII/SWIII.
10. SWIII, 45.
11. SWI, 248.
12. Makkreel, *Philosopher*, 58.
13. SWIII, 45ff.
14. Ibid., 47. For a discussion of the resonances between 'being there for me' and the 'pro me' of Bonhoeffer's Christology lectures, see my 'Wilhelm Dilthey and Bonhoeffer's Christology lectures of 1933', in Adam C. Clark, Michael G. Mawson and Clifford J. Green (eds), *Ontology and Ethics*, Eugene, OR: Pickwick Publications, 2013, 57–71.
15. See SWI, 249.

is 'there-for-me'. He calls this 'self-possession of a fact of consciousness' and claims that 'in most cases an *Innewerden* that the object given is there for me is connected with the emergence of the object'.[16] This means, for example, there would be no reflexive awareness of, say, the view from a window when someone is gazing through that window, staring into space, and thinking intensely about a remembered incident from the past (although there would be a reflexive awareness of the remembered incident). Dilthey gives the example of someone being so engrossed in a theatrical play, they lose all sense of being in a theatre. In examples like these, the view out the window or the stage lights and the fellow audience members in the theatre are 'there', but not 'there' for a 'me'. The self-awareness of the conscious subject in the encounter with the object has become so remote as to be imperceptible on the level of conscious experience itself.

With *Innewerden*, we see that Dilthey understands the unreflective 'I' to exhibit important analogous similarities with what this book is terming subject–object singularity. For Dilthey, when the conscious subject is apprehending something 'there-for-me', the apprehensive act is singularly 'unitsed' with the fact of consciousness being apprehended. Self-consciousness is necessarily involved, but this self-consciousness is a reflex action and not thematized in itself as a discrete element of the experience. He says, 'I do not need to become conscious of my consciousness, nor do I need to feel myself feeling; I know about consciousness from its very occurrence', and in *Innewerden* one is focused 'simply' on 'a fact of consciousness'.[17] Dilthey is pointing to the straightforward mode of everyday conscious awareness, in which thoughts are thought, memories remembered and percepts perceived without our focusing at all on the fact that we are engaging in acts of thinking, remembering or perceiving. What we 'see' is only the content of the apprehension, but not the act of seeing.

Given that conscious experience is taken as an 'ultimate datum', this means that *Innewerden* constitutes a point where Dilthey holds that the subject–object and act–content distinctions do not apply: 'Reflexive awareness precedes all the reflective distinctions between subject and object, [and] act and content.'[18] In reflecting *on* an experience of *Innewerden*, the subject is able to delineate between act and content, but *in* the experience itself, these distinctions do not apply. Because consciousness is his 'ultimate datum', *Innewerden* presents an ultimate moment of act–content unity, which he calls a 'unified knowing' (*In-eins-wissen*), since 'what is conscious and what consciousness is about are *united* in our self'.[19]

Innewerden is closely related to *Erlebnis*, in that both share this 'unified knowing' which is reminiscent of subject–object singularity. *Innewerden* is Dilthey's preferred conceptuality for unreflective consciousness in the early 1880s, but he later thematizes *Erlebnis* as a key technical term around 1894, in

16. Ibid., 249, 247.
17. Ibid., 250.
18. Makkreel and Rodi, in SWI, 26; see SWI, 332.
19. Ibid., 331 (my emphasis).

his *Ideas for a Descriptive and Analytic Psychology* (*Ideen über eine beschreibende und zergliedernde Psychologie*, hereafter: *Ideen*) (1894). There, he describes a 'unit of experience' as that 'in which the entire mind or psyche (*Gemüt*) cooperate and in which totality is given'. He also says of *Erlebnis* that 'its connectedness, both in terms of itself and in relation to the whole of psychic life, belongs to immediate experience'.[20] This suggests that an *Erlebnis* is a 'unit of experience' involving a complex interweaving of many facts of consciousness, which interplay in apprehending something and are thus 'given' in a unitary fashion. Due to the sheer volume of Dilthey's writings, their disciplinary range, and the number of years over which he worked, it is often hard to pin him down on the precise interrelationships between meanings of terms. With the exception of Makkreel, *Erlebnis* is described in the secondary literature in ways which could just as well be applied to *Innewerden*. For example, it is described by Emery and Emery as any 'act' that 'is conscious, but distinguished from the object to which it is directed, and not itself the object of any other act'.[21] Klubeck and Weinbaum say that it is an 'act' which is 'inherently conscious (*bewusst*), but we are not conscious of it'.[22] For Makkreel, however, '*Innewerden* is what is possessed in *Erlebnis*', and he claims that it designates 'the intimate mode in which we appropriate *Erlebnis*'.[23] This suggests that *Innewerden* is a particular appropriation of *Erlebnis*, in which a lived-experience is particularly focused on a specific object or content which is 'there-for-me'.

Overall, *Erlebnis* appears to provide Dilthey with a broader alternative to *Innewerden*, which in its sense of a complex intersection of interwoven, multifaceted elements given in a cohesive whole can encompass more than his descriptions of *Innewerden*, which involve reflexive awareness of just *one* particular fact of consciousness. The key point for present purposes is that both these characteristic modes of experience of Dilthey's unreflective 'I' bear strong resemblances to the subject–object singularity we discussed in Chapter 4. In the *Aufbau*, he writes, 'the consciousness of an *Erlebnis* is one with its nature, its being-there-for-me and what in it is there for me are one.'[24] In this subsection, we have highlighted the centrality of the unreflective to Dilthey as a realm of 'indubitable certainty' underlying the *Geisteswissenschaften*, and have drawn a parallel with what we term 'subject–object singularity'. Now we can explore how this unreflective 'I' is situated in the concrete 'flow of life' without undermining its 'hiddenness', thus advancing us beyond the point where we left our discussion of Kant in Chapter 7.

20. GSV, 172, trans. Makkreel, *Philosopher*, 142–3.
21. Emery and Emery, *Essence*, x.
22. William Klubeck and Martin Weinbaum (eds), *Dilthey's Philosophy of Existence*, New York: Bookman Associates, 1957, 74.
23. Makkreel, *Philosopher*, 147, 283.
24. SWIII, 160, 46.

9.1.2 A concrete and temporal apperception

We shall first examine the way Dilthey presents his unreflective 'I' as an alternative to the Kantian 'transcendental unity of apperception' before showing how his unreflective 'I' is concrete and temporal. The first task is to show how *Innewerden* and *Erlebnis* involve characteristics which make his unreflective 'I' an alternative to Kant's 'transcendental I', or put more pertinently, how he preserves the 'hiddenness' of his unreflective 'I'. It should be apparent from the previous subsection that there is 'hiddenness' to Dilthey's unreflective 'I', in that the bearer of the act with which one is aware of a fact of consciousness is not directly beheld *by* consciousness. This mirrors the basic characteristic of the transcendental unity of apperception as a 'primitive fact of consciousness'[25] called in Chapter 7, 'original apperception'. The original execution of the act of apprehension 'in' or 'pertaining to' *Erlebnis* itself is not beheld, for in *Erlebnis*, we are conscious only of objects that are 'there-for-me', but not the acts of apprehension by which we apprehend those objects, and seeking to apprehend those acts themselves would necessitate a further apprehensive act which would then need to be apprehended and so on ad infinitum.

Dilthey seeks to offer an alternative to the 'transcendental I', first by discussing the differentiation of subject and object as applied to the self, or rather, the 'I' viewing 'myself' as object. He sees 'only two possibilities' for philosophy here. The first is to represent one's subjectivity to oneself in a way which, as he puts it, 'mental activity can apprehend itself by becoming its own object and then recognising the identity of this object with the apprehending subject'.[26] He connects this route of enquiry with what he calls 'abstract philosophy', and he mentions Fichte as one who 'made the resultant subject-object the core of his entire philosophy'.[27] Given Dilthey's safeguarding of the imperceptibility of the act of conscious awareness mentioned in the previous subsection, it comes as no surprise when he opts for a second option, saying 'self-consciousness is an immediate *Innewerden*, which is followed by a gradual unfolding of a self-image by means of object representation'.[28] This 'gradual unfolding' will prove important later in this chapter, but here it suffices to point out that Dilthey preserves the distinction between the original execution of the act of apprehension, from the content 'seen' by apprehending oneself, and therefore does not posit an absolute identity between 'I and myself'.

For Dilthey, 'Kant <correctly grasped> the two true sources of explanation', meaning 'the differentiation between the subject *qua* subject and *qua* object'.[29] Dilthey wants to maintain this distinction, and he goes on to discuss the 'unity of apperception' as a necessary facet to a philosophical understanding of experience, provided that the latter term is approached as *Erfahrung*. He acknowledges that

---

25. Buroker, *Critique*, 131–2.
26. SWI, 333.
27. Ibid.
28. Ibid.
29. Ibid. Angle brackets are used by the editors of the English critical edition to indicate inclusions made for the sake of clarity.

the 'empirical consciousness that accompanies different representations' cannot provide 'self-consciousness' as such, merely a disconnected array of representations. That is, there is nothing in the mere representation of things in consciousness which provides the connectedness between representations of *self*-consciousness, namely, the awareness that each of these representations is '*mine*'. He comments that this sense of a unified 'I' as an 'a priori activity' is 'expressed in the "I think" that can accompany all my representations', and he says this is 'the core of [Kant's] critique of reason'.[30] In view of Dilthey's concern for 'original togetherness', he will obviously need to ground self-consciousness differently. Yet, we have seen that he wants to preserve what he calls 'the differentiation between the subject *qua* subject and *qua* object', presumably to avoid both a Fichtean 'absolute identity' and a Humean-style 'bundle theory'. His response is highly instructive for this book, because he does so in a way which preserves the hiddenness of the 'I' ['*qua* subject'], yet situates it concretely in the 'flow of life'.

Dilthey sets about this by holding that there is an 'apperception of *Erlebnis*',[31] which functions as subject-centred, spontaneous 'unity'. He works from his basic position that 'what we call "ours" receives its stamp' from the 'reflexive awareness of feeling, longing, and states of will'.[32] He claims that with *Innewerden*, there is given an unmistakably unified, conscious subject. He claims that acknowledging this unity is unavoidable, for without it, there would be merely 'momentary images that follow one another ... without any connection between them'. He claims that 'through the unity of consciousness all acts of waking life are connected with one another' and uses the metaphor of 'pearls on a string' to describe their succession.[33] But, while wishing to avoid a bundle theory, he does not want to abstract the 'string' or the 'I' from the acts of apprehension themselves, but ground it *in* those acts, with the 'me' of the 'there-for-me'.

Dilthey goes about this by arguing that 'inner relations are developed through reproductive processes, particularly when past moments are reproduced from the vantage of the present'.[34] With this, he means that when objects are apprehended, insofar as such objects include desires, feelings and states of will, the nature of their apprehension is inseparable from the life-trajectory of the apprehending subject. This can be seen particularly in the way someone's desires are clearly influenced by that person's life history, as in the way people respond emotionally to different life circumstances. The 'reproductive processes' refer to the way desires, particularly, tend to reproduce themselves through establishing ongoing habits, and the 'inner relations' are the way in which each instance of objective apprehension is interwoven into a complex whole which points backward, particularly, in that the way one apprehends facts of consciousness is necessarily

30. Ibid., 334–5 (my parentheses).
31. SWII, 88–9.
32. SWI, 340.
33. Ibid., 343.
34. Ibid.

configured by prior personal experience. Of course, this is obviously perceptible in memory, the act of apprehending a fact of consciousness which is a remnant of past experience of which one is still consciously aware, and which one thinks about, or feels, in present conscious experience. But the key point is that although these reproductive processes are seen as thematizable if reflected on, they are not actually *beheld* in unreflective *Innewerden* or *Erlebnis*. In this sense, the unified life history of an individual is, for Dilthey, spontaneously present to unreflective, direct consciousness, but not explicitly beheld.

From this, we can appreciate why Dilthey states 'The fact of self-consciousness does indeed presuppose that every psychic process, every psychic fact, every representation, is connected with every other in a real unity', and this 'real unity' is something he claims is a 'presupposition' of his understanding of human subjectivity.[35] He is cautious in making this move, saying he wants to keep his 'insight ... within its critical limits', in the sense, he goes on, that we 'do not possess an immediate reflexive awareness of a unified self', but we are 'compelled to assume it in order to explain what we are reflexively aware of'.[36] That is, the reproductive processes at work in *Innewerden* and *Erlebnis* do not themselves posit a unified self, because each one 'unit of *Erlebnis*' is only momentary and particular, and cannot be extended to provide a robust level of conceptually grounded unity which we can apply to all experience bar none, like Kant. But, from the perspective of his descriptive approach, Dilthey feels we are 'compelled to assume' this 'unity', due to the characteristic nature of the reproductive processes themselves.

Dilthey's grounding of a unified 'I' on this basis is considered by Makkreel to be a prime example of the 'quasi-transcendental features'[37] of his philosophy. This indicates that it will prove helpful in being applied to the problem of maintaining the 'hiddenness' of the 'I', or 'original apperception', of the 'transcendental I'. The remainder of this subsection will point to the ways in which Dilthey's 'quasi-transcendental I' avoids rendering this 'I' as abstract and non-temporal, and thus offers a highly promising alternative to the Kantian 'transcendental I' for a latter application to Bonhoeffer's work.

These points are almost self-evident from the foregoing discussion. To show how his 'quasi-transcendental I' is concrete, Dilthey says he wants to lift the Kantian 'transcendental unity of apperception' out of the purely 'intellectual' realm and situate it only in reference to the 'totality of psychic life'. 'Assuming' a subject-centred unity on the grounds of the reproductive processes at work in direct consciousness does not represent this unity purely conceptually. That this unified 'I' is concrete is suggested with the claim that, rather than an 'I think', Dilthey posits an 'I think-feel-will',[38] meaning his unified 'I' is not rooted in the intellect or understanding, but is seen as equally rooted in all the activities of conscious

---

35. Ibid., 348–9.
36. Ibid.
37. Makkreel and Rodi, in SWI, 34.
38. Ibid., 30.

experience.[39] Staying situated in 'concrete lived experience' does not permit him to abstract different faculties of consciousness out from each other, and therefore each is 'included' at the base level of the 'I' he presupposes from the reproductive processes at work in consciousness.

That Dilthey's unified 'I' is temporal is demonstrated by his conviction that acts of apprehension are always configured by prior experience. The 'inner relations' which he connects between the different apprehensions of facts of consciousness are precisely temporal relations. Here it is worth mentioning that he has parted with the Kantian notion of time as the ideal form of inner perception.[40] Because he considers the objects of inner perception to have an 'indubitable reality' in 'objective awareness', it would severely impinge on his analysis to work from this level of supposed immediately given certainty, if he also maintained the Kantian position on time. He maintains that the description of consciousness must involve an articulation of the fact that moments of conscious awareness feature some kind of intersection of past, present and future. It is simply unsustainable to work from consciousness as an 'ultimate datum' and not include temporality as embedded in that matrix of experience. He claims, 'the present is filled with the past and carries the future within itself.'[41] This is partly because many facts of consciousness must involve reference to a temporal continuum, like those discussed above, such as memories and 'states of will'. It is also partly because even straightforward, sensory perception would, in a Diltheyan approach, very often require that same reference, in that we perceive things in a way conditioned by prior experience. Moreover, Dilthey's analysis of consciousness maintains that, just as the present cannot be entirely abstracted from the past and future, neither can the past or future be abstracted from the present. That is, we are only consciously aware of the past or the future (with, say, memories or intended actions) in the present. His understanding of the temporal situatedness of human consciousness is two-sided, then, between holding on the one hand that 'reflexive awareness of the advance of the present implicitly distinguishes between past, present and future' while on the other hand maintaining that 'the past and future' cannot be facts of consciousness 'in isolation from the present'.[42]

So Dilthey's unreflective 'I' exhibits first a subject–object (or act–content) singularity in which the 'I' apprehends only the object and not its own act of apprehension. Secondly, it exhibits a certain hiddenness of the 'I' *qua* subject, through maintaining that there is an apperception 'of' or 'in' *Erlebnis* which is unthematized and not beheld directly. Thirdly, this 'quasi-transcendental' unreflective 'I' is concrete and temporal, which is highly promising for us, as an alternative to the conceptually represented 'pure apperception' of Kant's first

---

39. Ibid., 299.
40. Makkreel and Rodi, in SWI, 27–8.
41. SWIII, 252.
42. Makkreel and Rodi, in SWI, 27–8.

Critique. To see how these elements can bear fruit for integrating the unreflective and reflective, the reflective itself must now be examined.

9.2 Reflective self-understanding in Dilthey

9.2.1 From 'reflex to reflection'

As Dilthey's thinking develops from the *Einleitung* of the early 1880s, self-reflection grows in prominence in his work. His mature perspective is most fully expressed in his last major work, the *Aufbau* (1910), on which we shall focus in this subsection. The general movement from the *Einleitung* to the *Aufbau* is aptly described by Makkreel's description of Dilthey undergoing a move 'from reflex to reflection'[43] from the 1890s onward. During this decade, Dilthey gives more attention to human reflective understanding, and an important milestone of this turn is provided by his essay, *Contributions to the Study of Individuality* (*Beiträge zum Studium der Individualität*, hereafter: *Beiträge*) (1894–5).[44] This piece involves extended discussions with Windelband and Rickert, and because the disagreements underpinning the *Contributions* essay led Dilthey to demarcate a form of human reflective understanding appropriate to the *Geisteswissenschaften*, we will examine this discussion here.

The disagreement in question began with a lecture of Windelband's, given in 1894, which 'marked the opening of a long controversy' with Dilthey.[45] Windelband took issue with Dilthey assigning a foundational level to psychology for his epistemology of the *Geisteswissenschaften*. Because Dilthey maintains the 'ultimate datum' of consciousness as a realm of indubitable certainty, he grounds epistemology on psychology, over and above say, mathematical axioms or the Cartesian *cogito*. Windelband questions the validity of Dilthey's approach, for he considers that indubitable certainty can only be achieved by positing laws, which must apply in all circumstances without exception, whereas a descriptive psychology like Dilthey's cannot find conditions which must necessarily pertain outside the circumstances being described. For this reason, he says psychology should be approached as a natural science, saying that properly conceived 'according to its procedure or method, [it] is from beginning to end a *Naturwissenschaft*'.[46] He thus presents a view of psychology as aiming at universal and necessarily pertaining laws, like those of the then dominant forms of natural science, such as mechanistic physics.

Rickert added to Windelband's criticism, arguing that psychology deals with 'a natural system of inner causality' which parallels the natural world from which

---

43. Makkreel, *Philosopher*, 206.
44. GSV/SWII.
45. Makkreel, *Philosopher*, 218.
46. Ibid., 218, n14.

natural science abstracts laws of physical causality, arguing that psychological phenomena are undergirded by causes and can thus be explained.[47] For Windelband and Rickert, then, psychology should be lawfully explanatory, as opposed to Dilthey's claim that it should be descriptive. This differentiation has many ramifications across various aspects of Dilthey's work, but the important point here is that Rickert argues that Dilthey's ('descriptive') presentation of a subject-centred unity will always disintegrate into a 'bundle' of perceptions under analysis. He therefore argues that a unified 'I' can only be established through pure epistemology. He writes, 'Because concept-formation in psychology refers exclusively to the *content* of psychical life, the logical unity of consciousness can never become its object.' And thus, '*no* empirical science concerns itself with this form [i.e. logical unity] which properly belongs to the *logical* presupposition of every empirical enquiry' (*Empirie*).[48] This wording seems almost polemically aimed at Dilthey, whom we have seen famously opened his *Einleitung* by declaring his concern for '*Empirie, nicht Empirismus*'.[49]

Dilthey's *Beiträge* responds by arguing that the neo-Kantian construal of psychology as a *Naturwissenschaft* is a consequence of their 'divorcing' outer from inner perception. He claims that the Baden philosophers see the content or subject matter of psychology to be only 'inner perception' (and thus relatively unorganized or 'unlawful'). However, there is actually a certain lawfulness in this subject matter, but it is a lawfulness which cannot be extracted from it.[50] He begins his response with a discussion of 'outer or sensory perception' and 'inner perception'. The former is defined as involving 'impressions received' by 'sense' which are 'combined into a whole that is distinct from the self'. This means straightforward perceiving of empirical externalities which combine into a sense of an exterior world which is separate from the subject. He then specifies that outer *experience* arises when 'that complex of processes by which discursive thought brings one or several outer perceptions into a nexus of intelligibility that expands our cognition of the external world'. By this, he is showing how outer perception is organized into a comprehensive and reliable picture of reality by way of the intellect, which is accounted for by the Kantian *Verstand*. Inner perception, by contrast, is seen as arising when 'we turn our attention' to the 'inner processes or states' of psychic life or internal affects. Dilthey then seeks to show how inner perception can be seen as 'organized' into something constituting 'inner *experience*' [*Erfahrung*] in a way similar to the organization of 'outer perception' by the intellect, claiming there is a 'nexus of intelligibility' at work in our own internal comprehension of ourselves.[51]

Dilthey's way of describing 'inner experience' is important for this discussion, because it shows him seeking to establish a form of reflection which does not

---

47. Ibid., 220. Dilthey defines the natural sciences in terms of 'cause' (*Ursache*).
48. Quoted by Makkreel, ibid., 220–1, n16 (my emphasis and parenthesis).
49. SWI, 1.
50. See Makkreel, *Philosopher*, 221.
51. SWII, 215f.

involve separating the organizing activity of the intellect from the content of (inner) perception. He brings Kant in directly at this point and mentions that he 'was the first to create a special name' for uncovering the 'discursive thought processes that coordinate' perceptions, namely, 'transcendental' philosophy.[52] He claims to be seeking to establish another class of 'transcendental reflection' other than the Kantian model by providing counterparts to the purely discursive forms of *Verstand*. So Dilthey takes issue with Rickert's critique on the ground that there is a concrete counterpart to the Kantian *Verstand* which is operative in psychic experience and not something that can be distilled into pure categories apart from psychic states. This means that abstracting and distilling laws like those in Newtonian mechanics, for example, cannot take place in psychology, for this inner lawfulness pertains only in the particularities which instantiate it. Here, there is an important move in Dilthey's development towards a distinctive form of 'transcendental reflection', a way of reflecting on consciousness in which the 'original togetherness' of conscious experience is effectively maintained.

9.2.2 Reflective self-understanding

We have seen that Dilthey's concept of *Verstehen* serves as a concrete counterpart to the Kantian *Verstand* for the *Geisteswissenschaften*. *Verstehen* begins to feature highly in Dilthey's work in his papers which follow the *Beiträge*, whereas it has no specific or technical reference in the earlier works.[53] There are good grounds, therefore, to approach it as developing out of the 'transcendental reflection' he seeks to outline in the *Beiträge*. *Verstehen* most basically involves a way of reflectively understanding life which stays within the critical limits of Dilthey's philosophy, seeking to work only in a way which does not break down the original togetherness of lived-experience.[54]

It has also been mentioned that Dilthey's 'life-categories' (of *Verstehen*) are held not to be 'applied to life *a priori*' but to 'lie in the very nature of life'.[55] This was demonstrated with his primary 'life-category' of 'meaning' (*Bedeutung*) and the example he gives of someone seeking to understand the 'parts' of life in reference only to the 'whole', and thus not positing criteria of meaning which in anyway subsist 'outside' or 'behind' life. We discerned that he considers self-reflection (*Selbstbesinnung*) to function as a basic activity of attributing 'meaning' which undergirds the more specialized attributions of meaning in the *Geisteswissenschaften*. Before bringing out how he coordinates self-reflective understanding (*Verstehen*) with unreflective *Erlebnis*, it is necessary to concentrate here on a peculiarity to the determination of meaning in *self*-reflection, which differentiates it from other determinations of meaning.

52. Ibid.
53. Makkreel, *Philosopher*, 251.
54. Ibid., 255–6.
55. SWIII, 252.

Dilthey maintains that the parts–whole circle in self-reflection is unique, because the whole of life is not complete for a self-reflecting subject. This means that an event might seem meaningful to a self-reflecting subject now, but could be superseded by other events which may reconfigure this apparent meaningfulness, or fresh information could come to light regarding some previously insignificant detail, leading one to determine that detail as meaningful after all. Self-reflective understanding is thus considered by Dilthey to be open-ended, because 'life' is 'never completely consummated'.[56] He claims that 'only in the hour of death could one ascertain the relation between whole and parts' with any sort of finality.[57] As life itself is lived, the determination of meaning is provisional, but this incompleteness in no way underplays the importance of self-reflective understanding for Dilthey. On the contrary, he considers it supremely important, because he wants to articulate his categories from their *embeddedness* in life itself, from the way they arise in the conscious experience of the living subject, and the open-endedness of reflective self-understanding is an authentic characteristic of life. Moreover, the level of everyday experience, in which his 'life-categories' emerge, only differs from a 'complete' whole by degree. In literary criticism, for example, determining meaning is always relatively open-ended, such as with a classic play or a poem, as something always subject to different interpretations of its meaning in relation to different contexts.

Nonetheless, the pointedly 'open-ended' nature of one's own life-course, for Dilthey, means that determining meaning in self-reflection is markedly circular; the part is understood in relation to the whole, which in turn modifies the understanding of the part, and so on. He sees this as progressive circular movement between two poles (whole and part) and describes these two poles in a way which will prove important in the discussions of the final section of this chapter: as determinate and indeterminate (*bestimmt-unbestimmt*).[58] The meaning of the 'parts' of a life-course can be 'determined' only in relation to an 'indeterminate' (open-ended) whole, in that individual events from one's past can be relatively final (determinate), but their significance is always open to modification. This moving between the determinate and indeterminate is what gives rise to understanding meaning, which 'always hovers between these two modes of consideration'.[59] This same pattern is seen to be important for allowing him to 'overcome the limitations of spatial coordination and rational subordination that characterise the natural sciences and metaphysical systems respectively'.[60] This determinate–indeterminate relation also allows us to discern the difference between two key terms of Dilthey's, 'sense' and 'meaning', which will also prove important in the discussions to follow. To the indeterminate pole pertains 'sense' (*Sinn*), which as regards self-reflection is the sense one has of one's whole life, a vague, undetermined and unthematized impression of that

---

56. Ibid., 253 (translation altered).
57. Ibid.
58. Ibid., 254–5; GS VII, 220.
59. SWIII, 253.
60. Makkreel, *Philosopher*, 381.

whole. At the determinate pole pertains 'meaning' (*Bedeutung*), which can only be determined, or 'understood', in relation to the indeterminate whole.[61] Now we can turn to the aspect of his thinking most pertinent for our concerns: his attempts to coordinate both the unreflective centre (*Innerwerden/Erlebnis*) and reflective self-understanding (*Verstehen/Bedeutung*) in an account of human subjectivity as integrated and cohesive.

9.3 Coordinating the unreflective and reflective

Thus far it has been ascertained that, on the one hand, Dilthey avoids positing an 'absolute identity' between the 'I' as bearer of acts of apprehension and the 'myself' as content of acts of apprehension. Yet, on the other hand, he values the process of reflecting on oneself as 'content' in the determination of meaning. Now we shall investigate how Dilthey coordinates these two aspects of his philosophy, with two forms of continuity between the lived-experience of the 'I' as subject, or bearer of the act, and self-reflective understanding of 'myself' as object, or content of the act. Dilthey's continuity works in two directions, which we class as an 'explicative' and 'implicative' continuity respectively, using terms found in his work, albeit reappropriating them here specifically as titles of these forms of continuity.[62] As Makkreel notes, these terms come from the Latin root verb, *plicare*, meaning 'to fold', and explication 'folds out or opens up', while implication 'folds in or draws together'.[63] In what follows, we shall see how Dilthey considers the unreflective 'I' (subject/act) to be *explicated* or *unfolded* by way of reflective self-understanding, and reflective self-understanding to be *implicated* or *drawn together* 'in' unreflective *Erlebnis*.

9.3.1 An explicative continuity

Dilthey's explicative continuity works from the determination of meaning as a 'hovering' between the determinate parts of life and the indeterminate sense of the whole. In the initial description given above, both poles are reflective (beholding the 'whole' of life and the 'part' involves apprehending 'myself' as content). At some points in his writings, however, Dilthey also describes a hovering between the determinate parts of life (reflective content) and an indeterminate sense given unreflectively in *Erlebnis*. *Erlebnis* has been described as providing 'an immediate sense which needs to be explicated',[64] and he outlines one way in which this explication can proceed through determining the meaning of a 'part' of life as the explication of a 'whole' *Erlebnis*. In this, the determinate pole is reflective (the 'part'

---

61. SWIII, 254–5.
62. See GSVI, 316.
63. Makkreel, *Philosopher*, 378.
64. Ibid., 255–6.

of life) and the indeterminate pole is unreflective (the 'whole' *Erlebnis*). He maintains that an indeterminate sense of the significance of what is occurring is spontaneously given to unreflective experience in direct consciousness, but this is not thematized or objectified in momentary awareness itself; the subject is merely caught up in the manifold of intertwined elements which present themselves as a unified impression. He then shows how, in reflecting on 'parts' of life (such as particular places or relationships and so on), we can determine their meaning as partially explicating the unified whole of a certain unreflective *Erlebnis*. So, on the one hand, there is a discrete part beheld self-reflectively. On the other, there is the memory of a whole *Erlebnis*, a happening of direct consciousness which imparted an indeterminate sense (*Sinn*) of its significance during its original unreflective occurrence. To determine the meaning of the discrete part, he holds that we understand it as explicating the whole, a partial unfolding of that original sense which was spontaneously 'given' or 'present' but not objectified or thematized in process. An example of what this involves could be someone concluding that a past event (or 'part' of life), such as the death of a friend, is having ongoing meaning in their life, not because of (or in relation to) its ramifications on the whole of their life, but in terms of its particular relationship to a specific moment of reflexive apprehension, such as seeing someone who looks very similar to that friend in a particularly poignant setting and undergoing a complex emotive reaction, which is itself given as unitary whole as it is lived. That is, a retrospective look at that unit of experience will allow one to delineate the various factors involved, but the *Erlebnis* simply *happens*, with an immediate, indeterminate sense, in which all the factors cohere in a unitary togetherness, and which is subsequently explicated as the person who underwent this experience determines how the relationship with the deceased friend is meaningful for him or her. In this case, meaning is determined through bringing an unreflective 'whole' moment (seeing a strong likeness to the deceased in someone else) and reflecting on a discrete 'part' (the person's relationship with the deceased).

With this explicative continuity, Dilthey presents us with a coordination of unreflective and reflective consciousness, and to establish how this brings us closer to fulfilling our main objective we must ask whether this explicative mode of self-reflection fulfils our two cognitive requirements of maintaining the unreflective subject–object singularity and the 'hiddenness' of the 'I'. With the first of these, we can state that, in certain circumstances, this explicative continuity could maintain the subject–object singularity of the original *Erlebnis*. An example can be given by amplifying the instance given above: if someone determining the meaning of their relationship with a deceased friend through seeing it as explication of an *Erlebnis* of seeing a strong likeness to the deceased in another somehow maintained the singular directedness to the deceased friend of the original unreflective *Erlebnis* in reflecting on it. This is unavoidably rather cryptic at this point, but we can conclude that maintaining subject–object singularity in the reflective seems to be an implication of Dilthey's explicative continuity, which will require further exploration when this continuity is applied to the Bonhoefferian problematic in the final chapter.

The problem which is more pressing from our discussions of *Act and Being* and Kant's 'transcendental unity of apperception' is how reflective self-understanding can preserve the 'hiddenness' of the unreflective 'I'. Here, Dilthey offers us a solid advance. In this explicative continuity, the 'I' is brought into reflection in the determination of meaning, but – crucially – it is preserved as hidden in this reflective activity. This is because in the imparting of the original sense in direct consciousness, the 'I' is not delineated as a discrete element of the experience; the sense itself is inextricably bound up with the memory of a moment in which the 'I' is present but not thematized as a segregated component; it does not 'see' itself, but is merely caught up in the multifaceted impression of the original *Erlebnis*. If we were to focus in on the 'I' of that memory as a discrete element, the sense itself would be lost, because that sense is imparted precisely 'in' the dynamics of the original occurrence; the sense itself depends on the unique interpenetration of the diverse elements at play in those circumstances. In this way, the sense depends on the 'I' being preserved as hidden. Using the example given above, to gaze only on the 'myself' of the original *Erlebnis* would cause the focus of that *Erlebnis* (the person with a likeness to the deceased) – and the manifold elements enmeshed in that moment (the factors which combined to make it a poignant setting) – to be displaced by a concentration on oneself. By displacing the integral elements involved in the interplay of the impressions which characterized the original *Erlebnis*, the sense of that moment would be lost. By self-reflectively determining the meaning of a 'part' of life as an explication of this original occurrence, however, the 'I' is present 'in' this self-reflective process – but precisely as embedded as 'hidden' in the 'sense' of the original whole.

9.3.2 An implicative continuity

In order to examine Dilthey's second form of continuity between the unreflective and reflective, we must outline a concept of his philosophy which gained prominence around the time of his turn 'from reflex to reflection': the 'acquired psychic nexus' (*erworbener seelischer Zusammenhang*).[65] This concept is designed by Dilthey to describe the way in which some experiences undergone by a subject are incorporated or assimilated into structural conditions of consciousness which are 'carried through' life, although the 'I' is not consciously aware of them in the given moment. In every *Erlebnis*, claims Dilthey, the 'I' is structured, or conditioned, by prior experience, and this has some measure of influence on *Erlebnis* itself. The 'acquired psychic nexus' is his term for this 'structure' of consciousness, which has been described as an 'apperceptive framework'.[66] Makkreel notes that the word *erworben* is meant to point to the fact that 'the nexus or structuring of our experience is not abstract or inferred, but concretely "possessed" through the individual's life history'.[67] This means that, although we can discern an acquired psychic nexus at work in lived-experience, configuring our acts of apprehension

---

65. GSVI, 90–102.
66. Makkreel and Rodi, in SWII, xxii.
67. Makkreel, *Philosopher*, 98.

in consequence of past experience, it is not arrived at through inference, but can be articulated by description. Moreover, it is not abstract, because the nexus is inseparable from the concrete circumstances in which it can be discerned. Dilthey's acquired nexus challenges the approach to apperception of Johann Friedrich Herbart (1776–1841). Herbart had also pointed to an accumulative aspect to apperception, in which 'ordinary perception' was seen as involving seeing 'present givens' in terms of an 'apperceptive mass' of 'representations accumulated through past experience'.[68] Dilthey contends that, although apperception is configured by past experience, this is not a matter of simple accumulation. Rather, it is more than the 'sum' of experiences, something 'taking shape' (*sich gestalten*)[69] through the complex interactions between the myriad of different factors efficacious in the development of a human life-unit.

Development is described by Dilthey as 'simultaneous' with 'the concept of something "taking shape"' (*sich gestalten*).[70] We see the acquisition of the psychic nexus is then not just accumulative, but formed in a certain way according to the particular circumstances and tensions at work in life. It has been described as 'more than just a storage capacity' but as something that 'functions selectively to weed out what is inessential for our life'.[71] In his essay, *Life and Cognition* (1892–3),[72] Dilthey states that 'life itself forces us to distinguish between what matters, what is decisive and primordially powerful in life, and what can be dispensed with without loss to our present fullness of life'.[73] It is clear that this process of 'distinguishing' between the inessential and essential will involve at least a measure of self-reflection. This is also alluded to when he states that 'the meaning' of 'life inheres in what is essential',[74] for he understands meaning to be presented through reflective determination. He states that 'each life-unit comes to terms with itself by delineating a spectrum of interests from a central point to more peripheral interests on all sides'.[75] This refers to the way an individual makes choices, according to what he or she considers essential in his or her own self-understanding, and this process must involve self-reflection.

In this way, Dilthey presents a continuity between the unreflective 'I', to which pertains the acquired psychic nexus, and the reflective 'I', which influences the configuration of the acquired psychic nexus. When he claims that 'each life-unit comes to terms with itself', with its 'core' drives, this involves a measure of self-reflection, a 'coming to terms' with oneself, which has some accumulative effect

---

68. Edwin G. Boring, *A History of Experimental Psychology*, New York: Appleton-Century-Crofts, 1950, 256f.
69. SWIII, 252.
70. Ibid.
71. Makkreel and Rodi, in SWII, xxii.
72. GSXIX.
73. SWII, 101–2.
74. Ibid., 102.
75. Ibid.

on the acquired psychic nexus. This continuity is implicative, because the acquired psychic nexus 'folds in' or 'gathers together' various factors, including reflective understanding. That is, to some degree, the self as content or object is *implicated in* the way we apprehend objects unreflectively. Dilthey gives us an example of what he has in mind, in a discussion of a tension existing in a man who is considerably ambitious, but has to overcome his shyness to engage in public speaking.[76] He describes him self-reflectively acknowledging the challenge (the need to overcome shyness) and reflectively discerning what constructive steps are required to surmount it. Having made progress, Dilthey says this person's subsequent experience of public speaking will be permanently altered without any ongoing, explicitly thematized concentration on himself (self-reflection) every time he speaks in public. Rather, his experience is altered, and the 'fruits' of that self-reflection are thus 'lived-through' unreflectively; the past is 'implicated in' the present.

As above, establishing how the self-reflection which 'feeds into' the unreflective (acquired psychic nexus) maintains subject–object singularity threatens to seem rather oblique without an extended discussion of concrete examples which is beyond the scope of this chapter. Therefore, this question will be tackled in Chapter 12, and the focus here will be on examining how Dilthey's implicative continuity responds to the more pressing problem of preserving the 'hiddenness' of the unreflective 'I' in self-reflection. It should be recalled here first that his concrete and temporal unreflective 'I' is delineated through what he terms 'reproductive processes' between momentary acts of awareness, in which apprehensions in direct consciousness interplay with previously experienced moments, leading him to claim that we must presuppose a unified 'I' even in the transitory apprehensions of unreflective awareness. This description of 'reproductive processes' can also be seen to develop into the more complex view of past experiences configuring unreflective present moments of the acquired psychic nexus, for again, Dilthey argues that the past is effective 'in' unreflective experience, changing the way we experience things. This constitutes a form of hiddenness, in that the unity of the 'I' is not apprehended directly itself, but considered to pertain there unperceived. Returning to his example, the ambitious man does not 'see' himself as the same 'I' who embarked on self-analysis to overcome shyness, but the effects of this self-analysis are 'present' in the lived-experience of public speaking, without being brought explicitly before consciousness.

9.4 Summing up

This chapter can now close with two significant advances being made in seeking to integrate unreflective and reflective consciousness with Dilthey's explicative and implicative continuities. Building on Dilthey's unreflective 'I' as concretely and temporally situated in the flow of life, and his approach to reflective self-

---

76. GSV, 232.

understanding which preserves the 'original togetherness' of lived-experience by avoiding abstract categories, he is able to show us how moving from the consciousness of the unreflective 'I' to reflection on 'myself' and back need not involve a fragmentation or rupture in self-consciousness. In reflecting on 'parts' of life as explicating a 'whole' *Erlebnis*, the unreflective 'I' remains 'hidden' through preserving the 'sense' of the original *Erlebnis*, yet the 'I' as 'myself' is reflectively beheld, and so the 'I and myself' are properly differentiated but deeply interconnected. Moreover, Dilthey's concrete and temporal unreflective 'I' is configured or structured by the self-reflection 'implicated in' it, and so again, there is genuine continuity between the two, without unreflective 'hiddenness' being undermined. This book's final chapter will apply these two forms of continuity directly to the cognitive side of the Bonhoefferian problematic. But before proceeding with this, the investigation of Dilthey will continue by returning to the practical side of our enquiry.

Chapter 10

UNREFLECTIVE AND REFLECTIVE AGENCY IN DILTHEY

Having shown that Dilthey's concern to maintain the 'original togetherness' of concrete 'lived-experience' develops into forms of continuity between unreflective and reflective consciousness which bear directly on the cognitive side of this book's concerns, this chapter asks whether the same is true of the practical side. The challenge here is one of seeking to retain the volitional oneness of unreflective agency, and its non-autonomous (non-criteriological) nature, in reflective discernment of how to proceed. Our examination of *Ethics* presented unanswered questions for the second objective to maintain a non-criteriological orientation in reflective discernment, for it was left unclear how a reflectively gleaned knowledge of God's will effectively differ from knowing an 'absolute good'. Kant's practical philosophy involves the conviction that ethical demands arise 'absolutely' in the 'flow of life', and this opens up the possibility of investigating how to construe this 'absoluteness' without abstracting grounds or criteria for it. Bearing in mind the fruitfulness of Dilthey's philosophy for the discussions of the previous chapter, he is again put to work here to shed light on this issue.

10.1 Unreflective and reflective consciousness in feeling and willing

10.1.1 The Kantian background

We have met Dilthey's 'quasi-transcendental' alternative to the Kantian 'I-think'; a foundational point of unity described as an 'I-think-feel-will'.[1] In this section, we shall examine how the 'act–content unity' of the unreflective-I in *Erlebnis*, and the 'moving apart' of this unity in reflection, can be applied to feeling and willing, thus outlining the basic parameters of Dilthey's approach to unreflective and reflective agency. However, when we follow his extension of the 'I-think' into an 'I-think-feel-will', we encounter significant complexities in understanding how the terms 'act' and 'content' apply to feeling and/or willing. This is more complex than in the previous chapter, for he sees 'acts' of feeling sometimes to have 'contents' of willing, and so the act–content unity/split between unreflective and reflective in his philosophy

---

1. SWI, 30.

can pertain in the domain of either feeling or willing, or involve both. In order to explain this, it is necessary to situate his position in relation to the philosophical forebears he draws on in determining his approach. After this, the ground will be clear to outline his understandings of unreflective and reflective agency. Beforehand, Kant's differentiation of three 'faculties of mind' will be outlined, based on different understandings of an 'object' (or content) for each. Then we will highlight how the work of Brentano challenges Kant, which will be shown to influence some aspects of Dilthey's approach. The mature Dilthey can then be situated between Kant and Brentano, in that he acknowledges feeling and willing *can* share contents or objects (like Brentano) but still maintains that there are irreducibly differentiated acts and contents specific to each (which is closer to Kant).

Dilthey states 'We are willing-feeling-cognising beings',[2] and this reflects his tripartite approach to consciousness. This division is derived in important ways from Kant's understanding of three 'faculties', which are outlined most fully in the first introduction to the *Critique of the Power of Judgment* (1790). There, Kant writes 'We can trace all faculties of the human mind back to these three: the faculty of cognition [*Erkenntnis*], the faculty of feeling of pleasure and displeasure (or "taste"), and the faculty of desire' [*Begehrungsvermögen*].[3] Kant presents these faculties as irreducible, because there is 'always a great difference' in the way each represents its objects. He argues that representations belonging to cognition are 'related merely to the object', meaning that in cognizing objects we seek to understand what they are and focus on the objects themselves. He goes on to show this is different from situations where the subject is 'considered as at the same time the cause of the reality of [an] object'.[4] This refers to representations of the faculty of desiring, meaning objects of desire are those we seek to bring about: desired ends. As regards the 'faculty of feeling pleasure and displeasure' or 'taste', the representations of objects are different again, being described as related 'merely to the subject' and 'considered merely as grounds for preserving their own existence in it and to this extent in relation to the feeling of pleasure'.[5] So Kant claims this faculty is not concerned with the properties of the object itself, but rather with how the object feels to the subject. Guyer states, 'The doctrine that the feeling of pleasure or displeasure reflects the relation of an object to the subject rather than the properties of the object by itself is one of Kant's most entrenched views.'[6]

Kant differentiates these faculties further by claiming that in a judgement arising from the faculty of feeling pleasure or displeasure, a judgement of 'taste' regarding whether or not 'something is beautiful' or pleasing, the 'satisfaction that determines [this] judgement' is 'without any interest'.[7] He defines interest in terms

2. SWII, 6.
3. CpJ, 11.
4. Ibid.
5. Ibid.
6. Ibid., 359, n5.
7. Ibid., 90.

of a 'satisfaction that we combine with the representation of the existence of an object', meaning we are satisfied by the object's existence or possible existence and so want to ensure its continued existence, or to bring it about, through our own causality. Therefore, interest is something pertaining to the objects of the faculty of desire, 'either as its determining ground or else as necessarily interconnected as its determining ground'.[8] In the judgement of a thing's beauty, however, Kant states that 'one does not want to know whether there is anything that is or that could be at stake ... in the existence of the thing, but rather how we judge it in mere contemplation'.[9] He amplifies this in a footnote which states that one can make a judgement about an object of satisfaction which 'can be entirely disinterested yet still very interesting', which means that in some cases satisfaction does not arise on account of the 'representation of the existence of an object', but actually 'produces' such an interest. This sort of judgement is what he calls a 'pure moral judgement', which means a judgement solely grounded in accordance with the 'moral law' and not on subjective inclinations.

This last point is only a subsidiary remark in the third *Critique*, but we will revisit it in the following chapter, so let us note here that it points to a link between the practical and aesthetic spheres. A 'pure moral judgement', in Kant's view, shares a characteristic with an aesthetic judgement in that it is subjectively disinterested, meaning there is no drive to cause or maintain the existence of the object coming from the inclinations (and we have seen that overriding the inclinations is closely linked to the 'absoluteness' of moral demands). However, a moral judgement differs from an aesthetic judgement, because it involves a drive to cause or maintain the existence of the object, a drive to perform an action which corresponds to the moral law. With a purely aesthetic judgement, however, we are 'indifferent with regard to the existence of an object', and this judgement is therefore described as 'merely contemplative'.[10]

Kant's three faculties thus differentiate three irreducible human activities on the basis of the different ways the subject or agent relates to objects in each sphere. To point forward to Brentano, we can point out that there might be potential confusion in the Kantian scheme, insofar as *feelings* like yearning, or longing, for example, can be confused with *desires* for a particular end. This confusion would centre in the 'inclinations': drives to fulfil a qualified or mediate good, to which we 'feel' attracted. Kant's demarcation of the differences between the representations of the objects in each of the faculties should avoid this confusion, by ensuring that the representation of an object by the faculty of feeling pleasure or displeasure is always different from a desired end, on the basis of his notion of 'interest'. The Kantian framework offers a firm distinction between feeling and desiring, because relation to an object is different. Feelings are, in Kant's view, always affects and the inclinations always desires. In Dilthey's time, however, there was much discussion on this issue, and

8. Ibid.
9. Ibid.
10. Ibid.

examining Brentano as a key proponent of an alternative view will provide a vital backdrop for understanding some of the intricacies of Dilthey's own position.

10.1.2 Brentano on feeling and willing

Franz von Brentano set out to reorientate philosophy after the speculative excesses of German intellectualism in the first half of the nineteenth century and was explicitly critical of Kant on various fronts. His *Psychology from an Empirical Standpoint* (1874) was immensely influential and provided Dilthey with certain important points of orientation.[11] The key point of influence for us concerns the relation between feeling and willing. On this point, Brentano challenges Kant's three faculties of mind. He cites the third *Critique* and states, 'Kant considers the classification of mental activities into cognition, feeling and will to be fundamental because he believes that none of these three classes is capable of being derived from the others or of being reduced with any other class to a third class which is their common route.'[12] He then goes on to offer a very different tripartite division of what he terms 'mental phenomena'.[13]

Brentano's understanding of 'mental phenomena' is distinctive, and a full discussion of it would divert us from our focus, but here we need only bear in mind that he does not differentiate feeling and willing as pertaining to separate classes of 'phenomena', but considers them facets of our relatedness to one phenomenon, which he terms 'emotion' [*Gemüt*]. He claims that although this term is 'usually understood to mean only affects', it can also include 'passionate desire', and thus questions Kant's view that feeling and desiring are irreducibly separate. For Brentano, some 'emotions' seek to cause their objects, and so his class of 'emotion' includes what we might term feelings *of* desire, like yearning or longing, which for Kant would be 'inclinations'. He states, 'If we compare our trichotomy with that which has been dominant ... since Kant' then the key difference is that 'it combines the phenomena of the last two classes [feeling and desiring] into one.'[14] He appeals 'to the testimony of immediate experience' in making his case, claiming that in such experience it is impossible to differentiate 'what counts as a feeling and what as a desire, a volition, or a striving'.[15]

Brentano thus states, 'I ... do not know where the boundary between the two classes [of feeling and willing] is really supposed to be.' He presents a continuous spectrum of feeling and willing, with the example of a feeling (as affect) of sadness

---

11. Examples would include Dilthey's general 'empirical standpoint' and his pursuit of a 'descriptive psychology'.

12. Franz von Brentano, *Psychology From an Empirical Standpoint*, London: Routledge, 1995, 182.

13. These phenomena are very different to Kantian phenomena ('presentation', 'judgment' and 'emotion', 'interest', or 'love'), ibid., 198.

14. Ibid., 200.

15. Ibid.

at one end of the spectrum, which moves into a 'yearning for the absent good', then a 'hope that it will be ours', then 'the decision to bring it about', followed by 'the courage to bring it about', 'the desire to act', and finally 'an act of will' to do so. If one compares the initial feeling of sadness with the ultimate act of will, the 'distance between these two extremes may appear great', but, he claims, if one describes these 'intermediate states' and 'always compare' the stages 'adjacent to one another, there is no gap to be found in the entire sequence'. He admits that 'no one would say' that 'he feels a decision', but at the same time he is unwilling to draw a boundary between feeling and willing with the juncture of decision, saying we should not let 'ordinary language settle the matter for us', because a decision itself is the 'ripening' of 'a germ of striving' which lay 'unnoticed in' an initial 'yearning' at the other end of a continuous spectrum of emotion.[16] With these two contrasting approaches to feeling and willing in Kant and Brentano, we have two key points of orientation for understanding Dilthey's practical philosophy.

10.1.3 Dilthey on feeling and willing

Kant differentiates feeling and willing by the way objects are represented by each faculty in terms of 'interest', and Brentano sees feeling and willing as stretching across a continuous spectrum of 'emotion'. Wilhelm Dilthey occupies a position between Kant and Brentano, agreeing with Kant that feeling and willing are irreducibly differentiated from each other, and yet maintaining an element of Brentano's thinking, insofar as he considers feeling and willing often to be continuously intertwined in human experience. That is, Dilthey acknowledges some overlap between feelings as affects and feelings as desires, yet resists conflating the two tout court. The progression of his thinking on this issue can be seen in terms of a move from a loosely Brentanian to a more Kantian position, and it is necessary to outline this development in Dilthey's thinking here to understand his view of unreflective and reflective agency in terms of how the act–content unity of the unreflective, and the 'moving apart' of act and content in reflection, pertain to feeling and willing.

Chapter 8 discussed Dilthey's intention to avoid *explaining* phenomena through grounding them on hypotheses, and this point is instructive as he invokes the distinction between explanation and description with regard to Kant's faculties. In Dilthey's view, to posit a *faculty* of mind is to posit an explanatory ground which rests 'outside' the nexus of lived-experience, for Kant's 'doctrine of faculties' can 'be ascertained' only 'by means of an explanative theory'.[17] For Dilthey, in the nexus of lived-experience itself, we do not demarcate Kant's modes of object representation, for in the 'flow of life' human beings are thinking, feeling and willing in complexly interrelated ways. He demonstrates this with the example of someone dodging being struck by a knife, saying that in this moment the perception of the knife (cognition), the reaction of fear (feeling), and the urge to

---

16. Ibid., 236–7.
17. SWI, 297.

recoil (desire) are equally intertwined in a complex web, or 'unit of *Erlebnis*'.[18] In the *Einleitung* (1883), published nine years after Brentano's *Psychology*, Dilthey adopts a roughly Brentanian position in holding that the tripartite division of faculties is not irreducible, for the doctrine of the faculties itself is explanatory and not descriptive of *Erlebnis*.[19]

Although Dilthey does not accept the tripartite division of the faculties as irreducible at this stage of his development, for the purpose of description he finds the division useful and uses it throughout the *Einleitung*. In the *Ideen* (1894), his position is unchanged, for he claims that 'every feeling has the tendency to go over into desire or aversion',[20] while acknowledging that it is 'extraordinarily difficult ... to establish exactly how feeling passes into desire', because 'what establishes the connection ... is precisely the most obscure part of all psychology'.[21] This admission leads Hodges to suggest that Dilthey is expressing a 'doubt' about whether feeling *always* passes over into willing, noting that Dilthey 'says that all feeling *tends* to pass over into volition' but not that it '*does* so pass over'.[22] Nonetheless, Dilthey's position on the interrelation of feeling and willing is still loosely Brentanian, for he sees a continuous spectrum between the two. He states, 'Feelings activate certain drives, desires, and processes of the will', for in 'life' the 'representations are interwoven' with the 'feelings' which then issue in 'expressions of the will'.[23]

Dilthey's final position, outlined in a fragment contemporary with the *Aufbau* from 1905, is different. Here, he carefully and explicitly delineates feeling from willing and also argues that cognition, feeling (*Gefühle*), and willing (*Wollen*) are irreducible, albeit not on the allegedly explanatory ground of the Kantian faculties, but in terms of what he calls 'pure description'.[24] Hodges claims that Dilthey 'came to recognise ... feelings which do not even tend to pass into volition, and volitions whose motive is not feeling'.[25] In this way, he comes closer to Kant,[26] but at the same time he also states that feelings often *do* pass over into volition, and so he is still

---

18. Ibid., 299.

19. Dilthey says Brentano's alternative is 'particularly instructive', but does differentiate himself from it in a way not strictly relevant to our concerns, considering Brentano's 'different kinds of intentional inexistence' also to be an 'abstraction'. Ibid., 297–300.

20. SWII, 154.

21. Ibid., 175.

22. Hodges, *Philosophy*, 42 (my emphasis).

23. SWV, 72.

24. SWIII, 77.

25. Hodges, *Philosophy*, 42.

26. The question as to why Dilthey changes his views between 1894 and 1905 cannot be answered here, but it is instructive that Dilthey was involved in the rediscovery of the manuscript of Kant's first introduction to the third *Critique* at the University of Rostock *c.* 1889, which Makkreel argues was instrumental on Dilthey's philosophy during this period and led him to instigate the Prussian Academy critical edition of Kant's works in 1900. Makkreel, *Philosopher*, 224.

influenced by Brentano's continuous spectrum of 'emotion'. Dilthey begins this fragment by restating his earlier position that 'there is an inner link that proceeds from feeling through impulse to desire and will'. But he denies that one should therefore decide that 'feeling is merely the first form of those attitudes that achieve their final form in a voluntary decision and in purposive action',[27] thus finally parting company with Brentano. Dilthey elucidates this volte-face in terms which seem loosely reminiscent of Kant's division in terms of 'interest', claiming the 'compelling' reason for separating feeling and willing is that there 'is a broad range of feelings that release no incentives toward action', namely, 'the feelings by which artistic enjoyment is produced', because this enjoyment 'derives from the fact that the object of these feelings are removed from the context of reality in which our will intervenes'.[28]

Moreover, Dilthey also illustrates the separation of feeling from willing from the perspective of volition. He claims action can 'be the result of an obligation of the will', such as when one has 'made a promise' and resolves 'I must act',[29] even if one *feels* attracted to doing otherwise. Dilthey acknowledges that along with the various feelings attracting the agent *not* to keep the promise, it could be that there are other feelings attracting the agent *to* keep it. That is, the agent could have drives working against each other in opposite directions; on the one hand attracting the agent to break the promise, and on the other attracting the agent to 'loyalty, reliability, etc'.[30] Nonetheless, he maintains that the volitional is still irreducibly differentiated from feeling, because the felt attraction to loyalty and reliability in this scenario only makes sense *if* the initial attraction of the feelings *against* the keeping of the promise has been overridden by a purely volitional intention to honour it. In his own words, this attraction could 'only be defined by the inner relationship in which the will finds itself obliged and recognises the obligation as compelling'.[31]

We have now set out the basic material required to determine Dilthey's understanding of both an act–content 'unity' and 'split' in feeling and/or willing, which will allow us to locate precisely how he understands unreflective and reflective agency. We shall focus firstly on unreflective agency specifically and outline how the act–content unity of 'direct consciousness' can be mapped onto feeling and/or willing in Dilthey's mature work.

10.2 Unreflective agency in Dilthey

10.2.1 Act–content unity in Gefühle

Dilthey differentiates feeling from willing with the example of artistic enjoyment. This suggests that one instance of the act–content unity of direct consciousness, or

27. SWIII, 77.
28. Ibid.
29. Ibid., 88.
30. Ibid.
31. Ibid.

Erlebnis, pertains to the sphere of feeling. It should be clear from the foregoing that we are not dealing with agency here, but it is important to outline this unity, because it provides some preliminary orientation for the important continuities between Dilthey's aesthetics and agency focused on in the following chapter. In *Gefühle*, the 'content' is the material being perceived (such as the images of a painting or musical sounds), and the 'act' is the motion of feeling which accompanies this, be it sorrow or happiness and so on. Here, feeling is *affective*, in the sense of being a response to an object/s, and only reactive, not at all outwardly directed. This affective relation is close to Kant's understanding of the relation to the object in the faculty of feeling pleasure or displeasure, and as limited to the sphere of feeling, it is also disinterested in the Kantian sense, meaning it is 'indifferent with regard to the existence of an object' and 'merely contemplative'. The subject in the sphere of feeling is not causing the object, there is nothing at stake in it, it is merely beheld contemplatively and stimulates affective responses.[32] This unity is the direct consciousness of an object/content in aesthetic appreciation in which one only 'sees' the content, and the appreciating 'I' is not thematized as a discrete element of *Erlebnis*, but is implicit within it. That is, one is not explicitly aware of oneself as feeling the affective responses, but 'sees' only the content itself.

10.2.2 An act–content unity involving both Gefühle and Wollen

In this subsection we encounter unreflective *agency*, for Dilthey describes an act–content unity which involves both *Gefühle* and *Wollen*, which enables us to discern Brentano's enduring influence. Dilthey's understanding of feelings is not restricted to only affects or responses, but includes outwardly directed feelings: emotive strivings, like yearning or longing, which he considers often to stimulate actions. In his mature work, he continues to maintain that 'there is an inner link that proceeds from the feeling through impulse and desire to will',[33] which involves an end being willed on the basis of the agent feeling attracted towards its fulfilment. The object itself here is construed in the sense of Kant's faculty of desire, whereby one is 'considered as ... the cause of [its] reality'.[34] Feelings like yearning, or other examples that Brentano classes as 'passionate desire', are seen as driving an agent to bring something about. The underlying drive in this case is an outwardly focused, non-affective feeling. For this reason, I will refer to this element of Dilthey's philosophy as *'felt* volition', meaning a desire to will which is driven by feeling. This act–content unity involves an agent being 'caught up' in seeking to fulfil a desired end (which is driven by feeling), where one does not 'move apart' from one's desired ends, but the (felt) drive and the end itself are

---

32. Dilthey often refers to 'attitudes' as an alternative to 'act' in the sphere of feeling, because he is dealing with emotive *responses*, it is awkward to think of, say, an 'act of feeling sad'.
33. SWIII, 77.
34. CpJ, 11.

'caught up' in the 'unified knowing' of *Erlebnis*. As Dilthey states, phrases 'such as "I have a desire to do something", express an inner state without reflecting on it' for it coheres in '*Erlebnis* without reflection; and no other origin and ground can be found than precisely in the *Erlebnis*'.[35] He speaks elsewhere of the act–content unity of felt volition in terms of 'striving', when 'objects simply offer themselves' in 'a state of unreflected naiveté'.[36] This demonstrates that we are dealing with a mode of unreflective agency, feeling a desire to perform an action and simply being absorbed in bringing something about, not assessing options or weighing alternatives, but attending unreflectively to the matter at hand.

10.2.3 Act–content unity in Wollen

Dilthey also outlines modes of unreflective agency (act–content unity) in the sphere of willing. These involve a unity between an act of willing, or a volitional drive, and a content, which is an intended action or end. Here, we will refer to this act–content unity as 'pure' volition, placing the word 'pure' in inverted commas to differentiate it from its Kantian usage. For Dilthey, no element of consciousness in lived-experience can be fully 'purified', or abstracted out conceptually, for this would undermine the 'original togetherness' of life. 'Pure' in this context, then, means only that both act and content are conceived of by Dilthey as involving only *Wollen*. As 'pure volition' involves no elements of *Gefühle*, it refers to the unreflective performance of a deed with no emotional attraction attached to it, or no drive from the inclinations. Dilthey describes unreflective agency of this type ('pure' volition) as occurring in circumstances in which 'the will finds itself obliged and recognises the obligation as compelling'.[37] However, importantly for our purposes, he demarcates two different forms of obligation, which will now be examined in turn. Although Dilthey considers that obligations of the will in 'pure' volition can take two different forms, he only gives one example, which we met above with the example of someone keeping a promise, even though they feel attracted to the possibility of breaking it. In order to demarcate the two forms of Diltheyan obligation clearly from each other, we will elucidate how each could pertain to Dilthey's example of keeping a promise in turn; that is, keeping a promise out of obligation to an 'other', or keeping a promise out of obligation to what Dilthey terms an 'ought'.

10.2.3.1 'Pure volition' in obligation to an 'other'
Dilthey acknowledges the First form of obligation only in passing, and he describes it rather obliquely, but it will prove important for us and so is worth examining here. Dilthey holds that an act–content unity of 'pure' *Wollen* occurs in situations where one feels compelled to act in accordance with the will of an 'other'. He makes this acknowledgement in an unfinished fragment, and perhaps this is why it is not clear what his purposes are

35. SWIII, 38.
36. Ibid., 89.
37. Ibid., 88.

in doing so. Nonetheless it is safe to suggest that he intended his discussion to offer some resources to his sociological concerns, as he mentions how 'the cooperation of individuals' in which 'a contract or a promise gives rise to an obligation of the will'[38] contributes to social organization and corporate, collective systems and so on.[39] As we learned in Chapter 8, a human science like sociology must, for Dilthey, be grounded 'in' or 'on' *Erlebnis*, and so he seems to be exploring how 'obligation[s] of the will' in human interrelatedness are a feature of lived-experience.

In order to demarcate what is distinctive about this instance of unreflective agency, we will demonstrate how Dilthey's example of keeping a promise could be interpreted firstly as obligation to an other.[40] He gives this example of someone keeping a promise to describe 'pure' volition, as he seeks to articulate a situation in which an agent has no attraction to keep the promise from the inclinations, but nonetheless experiences a drive to honour his or her word. He makes his point by arguing that, even if the person in question is conflicted – feeling attracted both to breaking the promise *and* keeping it – this internal conflict makes no sense unless there has been an initial moment of 'pure' volition, a moment where a drive to override one's inclinations occurs, which only afterwards feels like an attractive option.[41] This example enables him to demarcate volition as irreducibly differentiated from feeling, for he uncovers an *Erlebnis* he considers to involve a moment of *Wollen* only. Now, to interpret this situation of 'pure' volition in terms of an obligation to an 'other' would be to interpret the moment of pure willing as based on being obliged to fulfil an other's will. This can be seen as overriding any inclinations to break the promise simply because one is obliged to keep it, because one's own will subjects itself to the will of this 'other'.

As it stands, this is rather oblique, but we need only note that Dilthey considers circumstances such as these sometimes to involve unreflective agency: the straightforward performance of a deed, because the will is compelled to act, in which the 'I' as agent is not thematized or explicitly delineated as a discrete element of the experience, but is merely 'caught up' in the action in question. However, it should also be noted that it is somewhat questionable to include this in a discussion of practical reasoning as ethics, insofar as an obligation arising from an 'other' could be very morally dubious indeed. Yet, we shall see that this rather obscure element of Dilthey's discussion will prove fruitful for this book, but before we draw out why this is the case, we need to show first that Dilthey also understands unreflective agency as 'pure' volition in obligation to an 'ought'.

10.2.3.2 'Pure volition' as obligation to an 'ought' In discussing 'pure' volition, Dilthey is for the most part focused on obligation to what he calls an 'ought'.[42] In

---

38. Ibid., 83.
39. See SWIII, 273–94 for some of Dilthey's mature sociological writings.
40. SWIII, 90.
41. Ibid., 88.
42. Ibid., 90.

order to understand what he means by this, his example of someone resolving to keep a promise can be used again, but approached as involving such an 'ought' in his sense. In this example, as we have seen, he acknowledges that along with the various feelings attracting the agent *not* to keep the promise, it could be that there are also other feelings attracting the agent *to* keep it. Importantly for our purposes, however, if we interpret this scenario as involving an obligation to keep the promise as an 'ought' (and not in obligation to an 'other'), this points to the notion that to keep the promise is something 'good in itself', or 'good absolutely', something that arrives in consciousness as something one '*ought*' to do, and not to achieve some further end. That is, insofar as one *feels* attracted to keep the promise in order to be loyal or reliable, the keeping of the promise would not be something good in and of itself, but rather good on the basis of fulfilling the qualification or condition of being loyal or reliable.

Dilthey's obligation to an 'ought' is developed in dialogue with Kant's 'categorical imperative', and he goes on to demarcate his 'ought' from Kant's explicitly. First, he states that, in his understanding, the 'ought itself' is 'not contained in' the categorical imperative.[43] This abstruse and terse statement is intended to point to the fact that an absolute ought in *Erlebnis* can only involve a concrete demand to perform a *specific action* and not an alignment to a principle (like the formula of universal law). The 'ought itself', then, is a specific deed, which he considers to fall out of view if one construes the grounds for the deed as based on the higher-order apparatus of 'pure practical reason'. Secondly, Dilthey differentiates his 'ought' from the categorical imperative on the grounds that the latter 'contains only the logical relation under which a moral law is possible'.[44] For Dilthey, the categorical imperative provides a logical account for absolute oughts in terms of delineating necessary and universal laws at work in practical reason, but this logical relation, for him, is not given in *Erlebnis* itself. Therefore, he simply wants to articulate that certain deeds carry with them a compelling impression of impinging 'on' an agent, the impression that he or she ought to act.

Bearing in mind that for Dilthey this 'pure' volition can only ever inhere 'in' concrete and temporal *Erlebnis*, this offers us a concrete 'absoluteness', a sense of ethical demands arriving in life, which are 'good absolutely'. His 'pure' volition in obligation to an 'ought' thus seems promising for our purposes, because it shows his attempts to describe what we would term a concrete 'absoluteness' in the 'flow of life', which we would expect to investigate in order to examine how this might contribute to our search to understand how we can reflect on demands as 'absolute' without positing abstract criteria to qualify them as such. That is, as Dilthey denies the possibility of grounding the obligation to an 'ought' with abstract criteria, this form of concrete 'absoluteness' seems promising for us. However, his discussion frustrates our expectation of proceeding in this direction, for he explicitly states that instances of 'pure' volition cannot be established as 'good absolutely' through

---

43. Ibid., 88.
44. Ibid.

reflection *without* breaking down the 'original togetherness' of life. He writes that activities with a 'purely' volitional intention and no admixture of feeling 'can only be experienced' and 'cannot be presented in concepts'.[45] That is, even his own 'life-categories' seem unable to describe why an unqualified or unconditioned 'ought' must take place, without breaking down the 'original togetherness' of the experience itself, by grounding a motive for action on something not given in *Erlebnis*. As we saw in his description of the whole-part relation (from which his 'life-categories' are derived), he claims we would 'escape from this circle' if something 'unconditioned' were to 'set the standard for contemplating and apprehending history'.[46] Because an absolute 'ought' involves an unconditional good, it cannot be reflected on within Dilthey's descriptive limits.

In this section, we have delineated three forms of unreflective agency in Dilthey's practical philosophy, which each involve an act–content unity whereby an agent simply performs a deed without 'moving apart' from his or her options and evaluating how to proceed. First, there is unreflective agency as 'felt' volition, in which an agent feels attracted to the deed being performed. Secondly, there is unreflective agency as 'pure' volition in obligation to an 'other', in which an agent's will acts in subjection to the will of an 'other' without any subjective desire. Thirdly and finally, there is unreflective agency as 'pure' volition in obligation to an 'ought', in which the will is compelled by the impression that something 'ought' to take place. Bearing in mind our overall aim to coordinate unreflective and reflective agency, our next task is to discuss the reflective side to Dilthey's practical philosophy with a view to seeking to outline how the unreflective and reflective can be seen as continuous and harmonious. However, we have encountered obstacles with both forms of unreflective agency as 'pure' volition. Obligation to an 'other' does not seem in any way intrinsically related to ethical considerations; there is nothing in Dilthey's acknowledgement of it to suggest that it will issue in deeds which are good or principled. With obligation to an 'ought', however – although prima facie promising – Dilthey holds that it cannot be elucidated reflectively, 'it can only be experienced' [*erlebt*]. Nonetheless, Dilthey does present a reflective counterpart to unreflective agency as felt volition, and so we shall examine this in order to ascertain how it can contribute to this endeavour: understanding a mode of reflective discernment which does not involve autonomous criteria.

10.3 *Reflective agency in Dilthey*

Reflective consciousness, for Dilthey, is a 'moving apart' of the act–content unity of *Erlebnis* in which the reflecting subject is no longer straightforwardly absorbed in cognizing, feeling or willing an object, but explicitly and directly aware of him or herself *as* cognizing, feeling or willing. Dilthey applies this understanding of

---

45. Ibid., 82.
46. Ibid., 281.

reflection to his practical philosophy, specifically in terms of the 'moving apart' of the act–content unity of felt volition, which, as we have seen, involves actions driven by felt desire or outwardly directed feelings. Dilthey expounds this 'moving apart' in terms of an agent evaluating a desired end or ends, or more exactly, reflecting on one's grounding inclination, examining one's motives. This involves his life-category of value (*Wert*).[47] Calling to mind that his approach to reflective understanding as *Verstehen*, with categories which are not 'applied to life *a priori*' but 'lie in the very nature of life',[48] proved fruitful in the previous chapter, it could be promising now to ascertain how reflective understanding as *Verstehen* is put to work in his practical philosophy. With the life-category of value, Dilthey is again challenging aspects of Baden neo-Kantianism, where the notion of value is supremely important, but very different.

The importance of the concept of value to Heinrich and Rickert, is again indicative of what Heidegger calls the 'radical one-sidedness'[49] of the neo-Kantian privileging of *Verstand* over *Anschauung*. The neo-Kantian approach involves the conviction that a value has 'no actual existence' (*Wirklichkeit*), yet possesses 'validity' (*Geltung*).[50] This means values are not dependent on contingent circumstances or conditions, and promise to provide the abstract, universal and a priori norms which the Baden philosophers see as being the very business of philosophy to establish. That is, a value having no 'actual existence' is a 'purified' conceptual content, pertaining only to *Verstand* and not conditioned by *Anschauung*. Kant's second *Critique* is the background for this, for there Kant argues there that the moral law (arrived at through pure practical reason) provides a necessary and universal norm on all human action regardless of circumstantial conditions, a point where they see pure intellection as having complete precedence. Neo-Kantianism thus seeks to raise the notion of value to something which applies not only in the practical sphere but also to the cognitive and aesthetic spheres, with respect to the values of 'truth' and 'beauty', respectively. Philosophy in toto is then understood as essentially a study of *values*, and the fact the neo-Kantians made the 'one-sidedness' of pure practical reason in the second *Critique* so central gives us another indication of why they have been termed 'neo-Fichteans', for Fichte also centralized the same aspect of Kant's work.[51]

In looking specifically at the issue of value, we see another instance of Dilthey's concern to articulate a primordial unity of *Verstand* and *Anschauung*, through

---

47. Ibid., 258–63.
48. Ibid., 252.
49. Piché, 'Heidegger', 179–80.
50. Fisher, *Positivism?*, 57.
51. It is symptomatic of Hodge's misconstrual of Dilthey's relation to Kant that he argues that the term neo-Fichteanism indicates that the neo-Kantians 'grew' out of Kant like Fichte did. The term is actually is much more substantive and based on the centrality of the alleged 'one-sidedness' of the second *Critique* for Fichte and Baden respectively, Hodges, *Philosophy*, p. 72f.

outlining categories of *Verstehen*, which only inhere 'in' *Erlebnis* and cannot be 'abstracted out' from it. He seeks to challenge the centralizing of the one-sidedness of pure practical reason in the second *Critique* and thus to question those he sees 'truncating' the reality of 'life', or the primordial unity of *Erlebnis*, 'behind which thought cannot go'.[52] Dilthey insists that values cannot be separated from their emergence in consciousness, which takes the shape of *felt* attraction, and therefore considers values only as conceptual representations of our felt relations to objects.[53] By tying value specifically to only one of the tripartite classes of mental phenomena, namely feeling, Dilthey is challenging the Baden philosophers' presentation of value as *the* central notion of philosophy itself.

Moreover, Dilthey maintains that values cannot be completely purified from their original givenness in the conditionality of lived-experience, where they cohere in consciousness *prior to* any division of intuition and understanding. In this way, values are kept strictly within the purview of lived consciousness, and they only 'hold good' or are 'valid', for Dilthey, in concrete experience itself. He states that values can 'become conceptual' by being raised to consciousness abstractly *as* concepts, but this is permitted only if the resulting concept 'represents an attitudinal position' and 'enters into objective relations'. Representing 'an attitudinal position' means presenting the felt disposition of a human being as it pertains in lived-experience, or as he states, 'the abstract expression' for a 'designated attitude' (a felt desire).[54] This is where reflection comes into play; the act–content unity of *Erlebnis* is analysed into discrete elements, and a value is arrived at by codifying the felt desire of the person involved. For example, someone inclined towards giving money to a friend in need may reflect on his or her motives, which is a process of *evaluation*, distilling a value by representing the felt desire and assessing it. The value in this example could be 'generosity', a conceptual representation of the inclination of wanting to help the friend. The agent reflecting on this situation would be seen as examining his or motives and asking whether the value of generosity 'holds good' or is 'valid' under the conditions of the specific content, or desired end: helping a friend in need.

Situations like this are understood by Dilthey to arise particularly when an agent is faced with a dilemma and the stream of attractions in direct consciousness is halted. Then an agent delineates the elements of the dilemma, a choice between two or more possible ends, and engages in conscious deliberation of the motives driving those ends. In this scenario, one is not simply attracted to something and seeking its enactment, but rather reflecting on the nature *of* that attraction itself and conceptualizing the value or values involved. Reflection thus delineates conceptually the values rooted in the sphere of feeling in order to make a judgement prior to embarking on a certain course of action. Dilthey claims that when 'several possibilities' of bringing about changes 'present themselves' and 'these possibilities

---

52. SW1, 49; GSV, 5.
53. Hodges, *Philosophy*, 79.
54. SWIII, 261.

are raised to consciousness, then a choice arises'. In this situation, 'processes of deliberation' occur involving an 'estimation of values' prior to moving from a reflective 'act of estimating values and a choice'.[55]

This approach to reflective agency certainly offers a more contextualized and life-centred (concrete) notion of value than neo-Kantianism. Dilthey's resistance to abstraction here is instructive for us, in pointing to how practical reflection can be approached as deeply embedded in concrete life and not as inherently tending to abstraction. However, notwithstanding the instructive nature of his position, we are faced with a significant problem for our specific task of seeking to understand how reflective agency can proceed without involving autonomous criteria. That is, his construal of reflective agency as reflecting on values still involves criteria which are autonomously centred on the deliberations of the agent, and the description given above makes clear that this mode of reflective agency unavoidably involves a measure of self-validation and self-legitimization.

10.4 Summing up

The discussion of Dilthey's practical philosophy in this chapter has presented some apparently promising material for our objective of extending the Kantian insight that ethical demands arrive as 'absolute' in the concrete 'flow of life', with a view to exploring subsequently how reflective discernment can proceed without being based on autonomous criteria for action. This examination of his practical work offers three modes of unreflective agency; an act–content unity of 'felt' volition, and two variants of act–content unity in 'pure' volition, as either an obligation to an 'other', or an obligation to an 'ought'. This discussion found problems with both forms of unreflective agency in 'pure' volition in that Dilthey himself argues that his 'ought' cannot be reflected on without 'splitting' or 'interrupting' the 'original togetherness' of life and is thus intrinsically incommensurable with the reflective. Moreover, being under an obligation to an 'other' presents problems in that simply aligning one's will to an 'other' seems to involve no explicitly ethical content; there is nothing in Dilthey's description to suggest why or how being obliged to another can or should result in actions which are 'good'. Thus, our enquiry is frustrated somewhat as regards unreflective agency as 'pure' volition, which is presented as either inherently exclusive of the reflective or ethically neutral. With unreflective agency as felt volition, however, Dilthey does present a corresponding form of reflection in the assessment of value. But, this will not suffice for our purposes, for it presents practical discernment as centred on the deliberations of the agent and thus as autonomous, albeit in a more concretely situated way than we have encountered hitherto.

Therefore, we stand at a difficult juncture. Unreflective agency as 'pure' volition in obligation to an 'ought' is seen by Dilthey as exclusive of reflection,

---

55. SWIII, 85; see Makkreel, *Philosopher*, 100–1.

and unreflective agency in 'felt' volition, when reflected upon, offers a view of practical discernment as agent-centred. For this reason, the following chapter will turn to unreflective agency in obligation to an 'other' – notwithstanding its ethical neutrality – and ask how we might reflect in such situations, to discern how to proceed. That is, we shall ask how reflecting on how best to enact the will of an 'other' can contribute to our enquiry. Although Dilthey does not raise this question in his practical writings, he does write at length about reflectively understanding others in his literary aesthetics, so this will now require some attention.

Chapter 11

GESTALT: AESTHETICS AND AGENCY IN WILHELM DILTHEY

The previous chapter made only modest gains, and presented the task of seeking to explore how unreflective agency in obligation to the will of an 'other' might be commensurable with the reflective. This variant of reflection can be gestured towards as reflecting on how best to enact the will of an 'other', or rather, reflectively understanding an other's will. Although in his practical writings Dilthey does not explore how obligation to the will of an 'other' could be reflected on, he does write at length about reflectively understanding others in his aesthetics, and as shall be seen below, this is closely linked with elements of his practical philosophy.

11.1 Reflection and aesthetics

11.1.1 From agency to aesthetics

A sound rationale for moving from agency to aesthetics can be given first by showing how Dilthey seeks to understand aesthetics as worldly in the sense of being based resolutely in concrete *Erlebnis*, secondly by highlighting how he argues that the poetic imagination, particularly, is closely linked to practical activity, and thirdly by pointing to his drawing of an analogy between what Kant calls 'intellectual contentment' or *Selbstzufriedenheit*[1] in the *Critique of Practical Reason* with his understanding of aesthetic creativity.

It is symptomatic of Dilthey's approach to the *Geisteswissenschaften* that he understands art to work from a foundational bed of lived-experience, saying that the 'human-historical world' is 'the central subject' of the arts, 'specifically of sculpture, painting, narrative, and dramatic poetry'.[2] Thus he binds his understanding of art to the concrete, and he is not sympathetic with understanding artistic representation as giving form to metaphysical realities or anything similarly otherworldly. He states, 'The arts are rooted in the expressions of life and derive their material from it' and art therefore 'obviously has its basis in life-experience'.[3]

---

1. CprR, 234.
2. SWII, 242.
3. Ibid.

But this relationship between lived-experience and art is not only one-way, for he also argues that art *affects* life too. Although Dilthey delineates aesthetic concerns in a way which differentiates them quite clearly from the practical concerns of disciplines like economics or jurisprudence, he is firmly convinced that art extends, deepens and enriches experience. He writes, 'Through art' we 'are more intensely made conscious of the human world that we possess in life-experience'.[4]

These preliminary observations are broad and basic, so it is helpful to look now at a specific instance of Dilthey's concern for what we might term a worldly aesthetics. In *Insanity and the Poetic Imagination* (*Dichterische Einbildungskraft und Wahnsinn*)[5] and the *Bausteine* essay we discussed in Chapter 8 (both written in 1887), Dilthey argues that the poetic imagination is found in all human consciousness, but raised to a particular level of sophistication in poetic composition. His primary motive here is to take issue with Arthur Schopenhauer (1788–1860), who sees artistic genius as akin in some respects to insanity. For Schopenhauer, a poet exhibits a 'superfluity of intellect' involving 'a withdrawal from mundane concerns', so poets 'resemble madmen insofar as they are often so engrossed in perceiving the essential' that they 'are generally terrible in practical affairs'.[6] For Schopenhauer, then, the practical preoccupations of life are deeply antithetical to the work of the poetic imagination, which inhibits the poet from functioning effectively in life, by which standards it is pathological.[7]

Dilthey's concern for a worldly aesthetics entails that he wants to challenge Schopenhauer, and his reasoning leads him to focus on *Gestalt*, in relation to both agency and aesthetics. We shall focus closely on *Gestalt* below, but for now it must be pointed out that, for Dilthey, *Gestalt* is the developed and stable form of the acquired psychic nexus which met in Chapter 9. He argues that poetic composition is a specialized outworking of *Gestalt*, and *Gestalt* is something which all mature human beings have. Makkreel states that Dilthey first introduces the acquired psychic nexus into his writing, precisely 'in an effort to separate the poetic imagination from insanity'.[8] Dilthey's understanding of this nexus challenges the view of poetic creativity as pathological, insofar as it intrinsically links the facility of poetic composition to the nexus accrued by lived-experience in the world, rather than being as a facility that circumvents effective worldly participation and discloses some other reality. His point is that 'the poet' and 'ordinary practical men' are working from their acquired nexus, or *Gestalt*, which in both cases is coloured by, and directed to, earthly life in cultural, socio-historical complexity. This is not to

---

4. Ibid., 243.
5. GSVI, SWV.
6. Arthur Schopenhauer, *The World as Will and Representation Volume 1*, Cambridge: Cambridge University Press, 2010, 211–15.
7. Although this seems odd, Dilthey considers Schopenhauer's link between madness and poetry to have a long lineage and connects it with Democritus, Plato, Horace and Aristotle. SWII, 67.
8. Makkreel, *Philosopher*, 153.

say Dilthey thinks all people are poets, but that he sees the distinction of the poetic temperament to be one of *emphasis*. The 'ordinary practical person' is seen as more focused on the concerns of the volitional sphere, to fulfilling purposes, enacting changes and performing tasks in the world, for their *Gestalten* are 'confined to the function of having to adapt to reality'.[9] By contrast, the poet exhibits a 'relative lack of concern for adapting his creative activities' and moulding his 'directly given reality'.[10] Dilthey therefore sees the poetic imagination flourishing in those who are not involved in achieving specific ends in practical reasoning, because the concerns of life are directed elsewhere. But this is not a rarefied gift separating the poet from fellow human beings, it is just that the imagination is developed in a certain direction.[11]

Dilthey considers poetic composition to occur when the volitional is relatively out of view and the poet is working with acts and contents solely within the sphere of feeling. In this way, the objects or contents are of the sort Kant says are 'related merely to the subject' and not desired ends; the subject is 'disinterested' towards them. Desired ends, it will be recalled, are described by Kant as representations to which the subject is 'the cause of the reality of [an] object'.[12] Importantly, Dilthey sees the representation of both types of objects, items of aesthetic creativity and desired ends, as both dependent on the creative imagination; this imagination is employed in different purposes in each sphere. That is, there is *one* basic and fundamental stratum of imagination, which is developed either through predominately practical *or* aesthetic (poetic) endeavours. This is partly why Dilthey holds that ethical attentiveness and poetic creativity are activities which bear marked similarities. He therefore groups them together as examples of activities he sees as crucial for understanding the *Geisteswissenschaften*. In the *Bausteine*, for example, he mentions 'the moral ideal' and 'the poetic technique' together as at the summit of human achievement.[13]

There is a final link between ethics and aesthetics in Dilthey to be noted here, which arises from an analogy he makes with Kantian 'intellectual contentment' (*Selbstzufriedenheit*). He discusses 'reflective circumspection about life' and links this to art, saying that 'art ... moves life into a distance from the context of our own acting through which we, in relation to it, reach a free state'.[14] Being distanced from the humdrum of volitional impulses through aesthetic encounters thus constitutes for Dilthey a liberation of sorts, from the pressure to act to fulfil purposes. He goes on to draw a link between the 'enhancement and expansion of one's existence in aesthetic creation' as something 'akin to the delight that arises from the mode of

---

9. GSV, 168f, trans. Makkreel, in *Philosopher*, 154.
10. Makkreel, *Philosopher*, 154.
11. Ibid.
12. CpJ, 11.
13. SWII, 227.
14. Ibid., 244.

volitional activity involved' in 'courageous actions'.[15] He is referring here to the view that moments of ethical significance are deeply indicative of human freedom, in that 'courageous actions' follow from the 'psyche' assuming 'superiority over the crude satisfaction of impulses'.[16]

This point is best understood by linking Dilthey's aesthetics to his Kantian background. We should recall here that Kant's 'pure practical reason' is developed precisely to account for the possibility of self-legislation in practical action, that is, the capacity to be free from circumstantial demands as drives for action. He defines the rational will as free because 'it can act causally *without* being caused to do so by something other than itself'.[17] There is a link here between the freedom from the inclinations in Kant's 'pure practical reason' and Dilthey's freedom 'from the context of our own acting' in aesthetic creativity. Moreover, when Dilthey says that in this engagement the psyche delights '*in the inner form of its own activity*',[18] we see a parallel with Kant's *Selbstzufriedenheit*.[19] For Kant, 'consciousness' of the ability of 'pure practical reason' to obtain 'mastery over one's inclinations' can produce its own contentment; an intelligible, non-empirical form of satisfaction.[20] This is an alternative form of the 'happiness' towards which the inclinations are ultimately directed, which pertains only to the intellect, or in Dilthey's words a 'delight' found 'in the inner form of [the intellect's] own activity'. In this link, we seem close to the juncture of the *Critique of Judgement*, where a 'pure moral judgement' can, in Kant's view, share a characteristic with an aesthetic judgement, insofar as it is subjectively 'disinterested'. This subsection has thus shown that aesthetics and agency are closely linked in Dilthey's thinking, and so there is some justification for drawing on his aesthetic writings in our search for a mode of reflection commensurable with unreflective agency.

11.1.2 Poetics as reflection in Gefühle

Dilthey understands aesthetic reflection in his poetics as a mode of reflection occurring only in the domain of *Gefühle*. We are now familiar with the fact that Dilthey considers reflection to engender a 'moving apart' of the act–content unity of *Erlebnis*. In his poetics, Hodges describes Dilthey's work as including a 'contemplative' mode of reflection, in which the poet discerns the most appropriate imagery for creative expression and develops it into verse, and thus the act–content unity between feelings and the images of the creative imagination 'move apart'. These images are objects like those Kant describes as the representations of the faculty of feeling pleasure or displeasure, related 'merely to the subject' and to

---

15. SWV, 206.
16. Ibid.
17. Paton, in GMMb, 39 (original emphasis).
18. SWV, 206 (original emphasis).
19. CprR, 234.
20. Ibid., 235.

which the subject is 'disinterested'. The objection could be raised here that Kant's discussion is focused on aesthetic *appreciation* and not creativity itself. But, Dilthey is clear that the processes involved in both poetic appreciation and creation differ only in degree, and not in kind. He says that the elements of 'disinterestedness' in Kant's aesthetics 'can be extended' to aesthetic creativity because 'the same complex process is involved in aesthetic receptivity' and creativity, 'though the former is less strong'.[21] Therefore, the beholding of objects and contemplating the felt responses to them in artistic appreciation is seen as inhabiting a continuous spectrum with the process of selecting and constructing objects in an artist's imagination. Dilthey's reasoning is that both receptivity and creativity exhibit Kantian 'disinterestedness'. The imagination is at work in both reader and poet, constructing images 'without any relation to the faculty of desire',[22] images which are simply beheld on their aesthetic merits. The poet uses his or her own imaginary images, whereas the reader has his or her images guided by the words of the poet.

The reflective 'split' between act and content here involves focusing on the feelings which accompany the formation of aesthetic objects. To focus our discussion on poetry, which Dilthey considers to be the most significant mode of aesthetic expression, we can consider the poet constructing and manipulating imagery in the imagination to find the most appropriate and effective forms. Dilthey presents the poet as on the one hand 'caught up' in direct consciousness in the writing of poetry, but on the other hand as engaging in a 'calculation of the aesthetic impression' that the imagery will produce. Thus, 'poetic technique has two sides to it', and the calculating side employs reflective consciousness, with a 'moving apart' between act and content in the conscious beholding of one's feelings ('acts') in relation to poetic imagery (contents).[23] The poetic imagination works on the images, in a way whereby their selection, concentration and development are processes of *evaluation*. The poet reflects on and analyses the feelings which accompany the contemplation of these images and makes judgements as to their appropriateness and effectiveness. This evinces precisely the split between 'observer and observed'[24] in which the attitude–content unity of *Erlebnis* 'moves apart': the poet is explicitly aware of himself. Recalling Dilthey's view that the difference between creativity and appreciation is only one of degree, this move can be applied to, say, a literary critic, as one who consciously and deliberately beholds his or her felt responses to a poem and is thus explicitly aware of him or herself in the process. Again, this involves the reflective act–content 'split', in which the 'I' is explicitly thematized as a discrete element of the experience. A key point of interest of this will be seen below in the relatedness of this reflective consciousness to *Gestalt*.

21. SWV, 46.
22. Ibid.
23. Ibid., 125.
24. See Michael Ermarth, *Wilhelm Dilthey*, Chicago: University of Chicago Press, 1978, 117.

11.2 Gestalt: *Aesthetics and agency*

11.2.1 Dilthey on Gestalt

In Chapter 6 the etymological background to *Gestalt* was discussed, mentioning that it derives from the past participle of *stellen*, meaning 'to be stood' or 'placed', and has been used commonly in German philosophy to translate the Latin *forma*, referring to the 'intuitable' appearance of a thing. Crucially, a *Gestalt* is also whole, meaning a 'characteristic unity'[25] which is not merely a sum of parts. A *Gestalt* cannot be divided into components and then represented or understood by being broken down and reconstructed from constituent elements. For this reason the *Gestalt* is understood in philosophical discourse as something that can 'only be represented as a lived-whole [*Erlebnisganzes*]'.[26]

These significations of *Gestalt* also apply to Dilthey's usage, but he extends them into a wider semantic range which is related to the use of the term in literary criticism and psychology to mean 'personality' or 'character'.[27] For Dilthey, the *Gestalt* is the developed 'acquired psychic nexus', which comes to the fore in his *Ideen*, where he attempts a 'descriptive psychology' intended 'to bring out the *structural nexus* of mature psychic life'.[28] He argues there is a 'law of development operating longitudinally' which shows that 'the course of life' is 'characterised by development' in which 'all the process of psychic life cooperate in us to produce' a 'shape' (*Gestalt*).[29] He thus sees psychic development leading to an 'increasing articulation', for 'as life advances, psychic life assumes a more articulated *Gestalt*'.[30] But although this nexus assumes shape over time, it is not explicitly thematized or pondered on in *Erlebnis* itself; it is a background framework for direct consciousness which is '*lived-through*' (*erlebt*).[31] Dilthey therefore claims *Gestalt* unreflectively configures *Erlebnis*, conditioning 'every single act of consciousness'.[32] With maturation, the *Gestalt* becomes increasingly developed and fixed, exhibiting firmly established tendencies, habits of will, viewpoints, and conclusions which are deeply embedded and coordinated in consciousness, and thus provide an overall sense of a person's character: the '*Gestalt* of psychic life' created by the interplay between the psychic structure of an individual and the 'conditions under which

---

25. Regenbogen and Meyer, *Wörterbuch*, 260–1.
26. Ibid.
27. It is widely acknowledged in the secondary literature that Dilthey is a key figure in the genesis of what was to become known later in the twentieth century as *Gestalt* psychology.
28. SWII, 150 (original emphasis).
29. Ibid.
30. Ibid., 188, 190.
31. Hodges, *Philosophy*, 38.
32. SWII, 150–1.

we live'.³³ Makkreel thus describes it as 'a final articulation of the acquired psychic nexus by which we can define a person's character'.³⁴

Dilthey's linking of *Gestalt* with psychological maturity is elucidated by the fact that he understands human character to tend over time to equilibrium and harmonious internal interrelatedness. So, whereas each individual is initially primarily 'a structural configuration of certain dominant qualities in tension with a base of subordinate qualities', with temporal development this 'tension' can be resolved when 'finally a functional unity or *Gestalt* is achieved'.³⁵ His use of *Gestalt* has been described as embodying someone's 'overall response or attitude to reality';³⁶ it can be seen in anyone with a stable and mature nexus, he claims, but is seen 'most clearly in great men who have a historical destiny'. Nonetheless, says Dilthey, 'No life is so meagre that its course lacks all *Gestalt*.'³⁷ Although *Gestalt* functions unreflectively in *Erlebnis*, by understanding one's own *Gestalt*, or another's, in reflection, Dilthey considers that we gain a unique insight into human subjectivity. Because each *Gestalt* is defined by the complex interaction of self and milieu over time, it is considered to be unique and therefore a key focus for understanding the human. We can now discern how the broad references of the word *Gestalt* touched on above apply to Dilthey. It gives insight into where someone 'is stood' (*gestellt*), their place in the world, characterized by the intertwining of exterior and interior factors. Moreover, we behold a person's *Gestalt* through their expressions, and as we shall see shortly, this occurs particularly with artistic expressions and deeds. It is therefore the 'intuitable' (as in 'expressed') appearance of character or individual personhood.

Most importantly, *Gestalt* is seen by Dilthey as a whole which is more than the sum of its parts. No *Gestalt*, for Dilthey, can be fully grasped or captured by analysing someone's ingrained tendencies and elements of his or her context. This point is apparent in Dilthey's writing on biography, which is for him a highly instructive vehicle for apprehending a person's *Gestalt*, because the life of a biographical subject has ended and their life-trajectory is relatively complete.³⁸ But, even here, Dilthey goes to considerable lengths to ensure that the *Gestalt* cannot be broken down into constituent elements and evades being fully captured by the biographer.³⁹ In this discussion, we encounter an important difference between his use of the word 'totality' (*Totalität*) and 'whole' (*Ganz*). He maintains that we can glimpse the *Gestalt* as a whole, but not as something composed of parts, and a mass of composed parts is what Dilthey calls a 'totality'; he states that *Gestalt*

---

33. Ibid., 190.
34. Makkreel, *Philosopher*, 140 citing GSV, 225f.
35. Ibid., 140.
36. Makkreel and Rodi, in SWV, 8.
37. SWIII, 252–3; see 191.
38. Obviously, there is always some measure of openness in understanding a subject of history, of which Dilthey was highly sensitive.
39. SWIII, 265ff.

'never appears' as 'totality'.⁴⁰ *Gestalt* is highly valuable for Dilthey, therefore, as it brings an impression of a person's whole character to consciousness, but evades understanding if broken down into constituents. In this way it mirrors his concern for *Erlebnis* over *Erfahrung* and his aim to articulate concrete lived-experience in its unitary givenness.

11.2.2 Aesthetic reflection and Gestalt

11.2.2.1 Aesthetics as involving reflection on Gestalt Dilthey's aesthetic reflection is approached as reflection on *Gestalt* itself, a mode of reflection which he sees as brought to its fullest instance in poetics. The first point to bear in mind is that this is reflection in *Gefühle*, where the 'acts' are felt, emotional responses and the contents are objects beheld without 'interest' in the Kantian sense. In Dilthey's poetics, particularly, we see the 'split' between attitude and content in *Gefühle* in a way which is basically a conscious reflection on the *Gestalt* of the poet. Poetic reflection, for Dilthey, is a discerning of the appropriateness of contents (poetic images) against the background of the 'sense' the reader has of the poet's *Gestalt*. Thinking in terms of poetic composition, this evaluation of appropriateness takes place against the background of the poet's *own Gestalt*; the poet assesses the 'fittingness' of images, and this 'fittingness' is intrinsically configured and conditioned by his or her own structural nexus. The depth of the link between *Gestalt* and poetic creativity is shown in a discussion of what Dilthey terms in the *Bausteine*, 'the making whole' [*Ergänzung*] of poetic images.⁴¹ This is an attempt to discern the process which enables particular poetic images to become whole, in the sense of bringing a poem to completion. He considers that this occurs when images become embodiments of the poet's *Gestalt*, giving an impression of the whole person and not merely being discrete items of imagery. Makkreel states that the notion of 'making whole' is emblematic of the 'special link' between the poetic imagination and *Gestalt*.⁴² Dilthey sees an effective poetic image to exhibit a process of development in the course of a poem, which mirrors the unique response to reality of the poet himself, accrued over the poet's life-course. A poetic image is therefore understood by Dilthey as developing and growing on a specific path, which in the impression transposed into the understanding of the reader, gives a glimpse of reality *through* the subjectivity of the poet himself. Because Dilthey maintains that these images derive originally from particular lived experiences, he goes so far as to hold that transposing a powerful image into the mind of a reader can bring the reader into the dynamic 're-experiencing' (*nacherleben*) of

---

40. SWII, 154.
41. This is one of a series of Dilthey's 'laws of imaginative metamorphosis', discussed by Makkreel (*Philosopher*, 95–108), who translates *Ergänzung* as 'completion', but it is altered here because it is not a 'finality' at stake in this, and a sense of 'openness' should be preserved as an intrinsic consequence of its connectedness to the *Gestalt*.
42. Ibid., 101.

the original *Erlebnis* in which an image was first imprinted on the imagination of the poet.

It may well be asked why poetry is seen by Dilthey to have this ability to bring the reader into the subjectivity of another, over against, say, first-person prose. The answer lies in that he sees the reading of poetry to instigate and cultivate manifold resonances and interconnections in human consciousness, many of which structure the overall impression of a poem without being brought fully into explicit conscious awareness. In this way, poetry brings a marked depth of aesthetic impression, which mirrors the depth and inscrutability of human subjectivity itself. This inscrutability is partly a matter of *Gestalt*. For Dilthey, although the *Gestalt* has a reciprocal relation to the socio-historical context of the 'I', it has its own trajectory and does not simply reflect exterior conditions. At its core is a sense of a human being's character, which can be intuited but never fully grasped, and is insurmountably unique. The manifold subsurface resonances instigated by the reading of poetry bring the *Gestalt* of the poet into the mind of the reader with a depth unparalleled in other forms of expression.

Moreover, Dilthey sees the poetic expression of *Gestalt* as constituting a rare case in which the *Gestalt* is brought into consciousness by reflection and is no longer functioning only as an 'apperceptive framework'. The normally unreflective functioning of *Gestalt* is raised to consciousness by the poet through analysing felt responses to images. Therefore, the 'fund of past experience which usually decays into a blind conditioning factor for future behaviour' is 'made conscious' through poetic creativity.[43] As Makkreel states, when Dilthey speaks 'of the entire psychic nexus' as 'active in the process of making-whole' he means that 'this constitutes that rare case where local conditions or special requirements do not obscure the way the acquired psychic nexus itself regulates the imagination'.[44] The reflection involved in creating and developing poetic imagery is a form of aesthetic reflection, meaning the 'act'–content unity of direct consciousness 'moves apart' in *Gefühle*. That is, the content (poetic images) 'move apart' from their grounding 'acts', and these 'acts' are explicitly and deliberately contemplated. The framework of this evaluation is the poet's *Gestalt*, and in this sense, poetic contemplation is a discernment of the *Gestalt*.

It is important to recall that poetic creation and appreciation inhabit a continuous spectrum for Dilthey, so the *Gestalt* of the poet is also discerned by the reader of his or her poetry. That is, in assessing and evaluating a poetic form, the background framework by which the 'fittingness' or appropriateness of poetic images are evaluated is the 'sense' the reader has of the poet's *Gestalt*. Reading poetry is therefore, for Dilthey, a form of reflective contemplation of another's *Gestalt*, which will prove important later in this chapter. Before outlining why this is the case, a further dimension of Dilthey's poetics needs to be outlined here: his category of 'having-to-be-thus'.

---

43. Ibid., 154–5.
44. Ibid., 104.

11.2.2.2 Gestalt and 'having-to-be-thus' For Dilthey, great poems impress a unified sense of meaning on the mind of a reader, in which every item of component imagery, and each linguistic syllable, stands in a relationship of complex interdependence with every other element. The complete poem exhibits an internal sense of order, and one could not make any alterations without severely negating the impact of the whole. It is this type of complex interrelationship which, in Dilthey's view, is supremely indicative of the work of *Gestalt*. The unfolding of images is unique in each poet's work, as it is so intimately related to the subjectivity of the poet him or herself.

In his poetics, Dilthey furthers his attempts to formulate an epistemology for the humanities by presenting an alternative mode of necessity to the lawful necessity of natural science, and this, he argues, can be classed as such due to its dependence on the human *Gestalt*. He introduces it with a musical example, stating that on hearing the first notes of, say, Beethoven's Fifth, an audience member could not predict the rest of the composition, and 'yet we have a feeling once it has ended that this is the way it should have ended'.[45] This experience is the feeling that something 'has-to-be-thus', that precisely *this* is the trajectory something should have taken. Dilthey considers that 'having-to-be-thus' arises most perceptibly in poetry. He maintains that the impression of reading an effective poem is such that one feels it could not have been written any other way, without undermining the effectiveness of the whole, which feels as if it 'has-to-be-thus': that every image, syllable, pentameter or item of punctuation is intrinsically bound up with the unified impression of the poem. This sense of 'having-to-be-thus' cannot be conceptually distilled apart from the phenomena which instantiate it, unique in each case, for – as we have seen – his 'categories are not applied to life *a priori*' but 'lie in the very nature of life'. That is, there is no separable criterion for discerning that an element of a poem 'has-to-be-thus', but the sense of 'having-to-be-thus' belongs inalienably to the impression one gets from reading it.

Dilthey claims that his category of 'having-to-be-thus' arises in phenomena which are most deeply intertwined and intermingled with the human *Gestalt*. That is, phenomena which allow us to sense the fullness of someone's personhood, something belonging uniquely to him or her. With poetics, the key issue is that, as an artistic medium, Dilthey maintains that poetry gives an unparalleled depth of aesthetic impression, bringing someone into the *Gestalt* of the poet in an unsurpassable way. The depth of poetry mirrors the depth and inscrutability of human consciousness itself, and this inscrutability points to the *Gestalt*, for just as one cannot claim to have grasped another person in their fullness through listing their attributes and experiences, an effective poem offers a fullness of impression which similarly evades being captured through reductive analysis.

The category of 'having-to-be-thus' is closely related to Dilthey's view that a poem can be almost like a microcosm, or avatar, of the poet's self. When the *Gestalt* is active in this way, 'images transform themselves on the basis of it: innumerable,

---

45. Ibid., 392.

immeasurable, almost imperceptible changes occur' in the development of its images,[46] mirroring the dynamics inherent in the intricately interrelated facets of the poet's subjectivity. The key element of *Gestalt* at work in this is that *Gestalt* is by definition a whole which is more than the sum of its parts. With the characteristic unity of a poem, then, the complex interweaving of 'innumerable, immeasurable, almost imperceptible' interrelated elements and resonances between images, words and sounds combines to offer an overall impression which is more than the sum of its parts. This quality of *Gestalt* is given in poetry by the aforementioned depth of the poetic medium, its working on levels the reader is not explicitly aware of. In this depth there is unified effect which cannot be captured only by studying the constituent elements. A poem is thus seen to mirror the wholeness of *Gestalt*, in the sense of something only capable of representation as a 'lived-whole'.

The discussions of this section would seem to have taken this chapter a long way indeed from unreflective and reflective agency. To bring this book's aims back into view, the next section will show how this mode of aesthetic reflection (on *Gestalt*) offers a certain commensurability with unreflective agency in obligation to the will of an 'other'.

11.3 Gestalt *as locus of continuity*

Taking unreflective agency as 'pure' volition in obligation to the will of an 'other', the first task is to show how this could be reflected on, without involving autonomous criteria of the good like Dilthey's reflection on values. Let us approach this here with unreflective agency as obligation to the will of an 'other' and envisage reflecting on how best to proceed in terms of the discernment of another's *Gestalt*. This possibility presents a mode of reflection in which there are no determined criteria wielded by the agent, but instead a contemplation of another's subjectivity. That is, to reflect on an obligation, we can envisage the agent reflectively discerning the best course of action through evaluating its appropriateness according to another's *Gestalt*: the *Gestalt* of the one to whom one is obliged. This possibility depends in part on Dilthey's comment that aesthetic receptivity and aesthetic creation inhabit a continuous spectrum, that to behold poetic images in reading poetry is a difference in degree to the process involved in its composition.[47] Aesthetic receptivity is then a question of evaluating the appropriateness of poetic imagery in reading, according to the sense of the poet's *Gestalt*. Insofar as aesthetic expression only differs in degree from aesthetic receptivity, we can suggest that his philosophy enables us to demarcate a 'purely' volitional receptivity in obligation to another, a receptivity with no drive from the inclinations, in which we discern a course of action through evaluating its appropriateness with the sense one has of another's *Gestalt*.

---

46. Ibid., 103 citing GSVI, 175.
47. SWV, 46.

The reflective discernment of another's *Gestalt* in aesthetic receptivity, and the possibility of expressing another's *Gestalt* in unreflective agency, presents us with a form of continuity between unreflective and reflective agency. Under circumstances of obligation to an 'other', an agent can undergo the 'moving apart' of act and content by reflecting on the best course of action, without losing the singleness of purpose of the original unreflective content through bearing criteria of the good within himself. In reflecting on the best course of action as discerning the best way to express the *Gestalt* of another, the 'centre of gravity' remains with that other, and in the performance of the deed one is still absorbed in fulfilling the demands of that other without breaking continuity. Indeed, we can envisage the consciousness of an agent moving from one to the other continuously and harmoniously, discerning the best course of action through contemplating the *Gestalt* of the person to whom one is obliged.

11.4 Summing up

This chapter has located a form of subjectively disinterested reflection in Dilthey's aesthetics, as the discernment of another's *Gestalt*, and shown how this reflection presents a form of continuity with unreflective agency in the specific circumstance of being under an obligation to the will of an 'other'. In the following chapter, we shall apply this finding to the practical side of our problematic arising from the discussions of the previous chapters, namely, seeking to retain the volitional oneness of unreflective agency, and its non-autonomous (non-criteriological) nature, in a reflective discernment of how to proceed. Here, of course, we will find the semantic convergence between Bonhoeffer and Dilthey around the term *Gestalt* greatly advantageous, for, as we have seen, Bonhoeffer implies in *Ethics* that practical discernment can take the form of discerning how to enact the *Gestalt* of Christ. Indeed, insofar as this discernment 'within' *Gestaltung* was found in the earlier chapters to constitute a form of 'wisdom', and unreflective agency in obedience to Christ obviously pertains to simplicity, we are now at a suitable juncture to work towards fulfilling our practical objective of this book, and, with Dilthey's cognitively orientated continuities from Chapter 9, it remains only to integrate simplicity and wisdom.

Chapter 12

INTEGRATING SIMPLICITY AND WISDOM

This final chapter applies the analysis of the foregoing discussions to respond to the challenge of the unreflective in *Discipleship* by integrating simplicity and wisdom, building on Dilthey's philosophy to present an understanding of human subjectivity which accommodates both the unreflective centre of the human response to Christ and the unavoidable necessity of reflection in human life. Moreover, the unreflective and reflective will be set out here not merely as harmonious, but as integrated. The Dilthey-informed framework presented by the previous chapters will show how self-reflective wisdom can actually foster integral aspects of simplicity, deepening one's acknowledgement of Christ's centrality and grounding one's deeds on 'Christ alone'. Equally, we shall see how simplicity can foster wisdom, insofar as orientating self-reflective activity to the unreflective cultivates integral aspects of wisdom, such as sagacity, prudence and circumspection. The book will then close by drawing out certain broader implications of this integration of simplicity and wisdom, leading finally to certain implications for fundamental and perennial theological problems in the consideration of the human relation to God.

12.1 Integrating the unreflective and reflective in the cognitive

12.1.1 Explicative continuity

Chapter 9 ascertained how Dilthey considers that self-reflection explicates unreflective moments of direct consciousness. Dilthey considers the determination of the 'meaning' of the 'parts' of life to occur through bringing two 'poles' into relation (unreflective and reflective). First, he maintains that an indeterminate sense of the significance of what is occurring is spontaneously given 'to' an unreflective *Erlebnis* in direct consciousness, but this is not thematized or objectified in momentary awareness itself; the subject is merely caught up in the intertwined elements which present themselves as a unified impression. He then shows how, in reflecting on 'parts' of life (such as particular events, places, or relationships), we can determine their meaning as partial explications of the unified whole of a certain unreflective *Erlebnis*. So on the one hand, there is a discrete part (such as particular relationship, or a place, for example) beheld self-reflectively. On the other, there is the memory of a whole *Erlebnis*, a happening of direct consciousness which imparted an indeterminate sense (*Sinn*) of its significance during its original occurrence. To determine the meaning of the discrete part, Dilthey holds that we understand it as a partial unfolding of the 'sense' which was spontaneously 'present' in the original *Erlebnis* but not objectified or thematized in process.

Before applying this to Bonhoeffer's theology, it is necessary first to recall how this explicative continuity maintains the hiddenness of the subject qua subject in self-reflection. The 'I' is brought into reflection in this explicative determination of meaning, but – crucially – it is preserved as hidden, because in the imparting of the original sense in direct consciousness the 'I' is not delineated as a discrete element of the experience; the sense itself is inextricably bound up with the memory of a moment in which the 'I' is present but not thematized as a segregated component; it does not 'see' itself, but is merely caught up in the multifaceted impression of the original *Erlebnis*. If we were to focus in on the 'I' of that memory as a discrete element, the sense itself would be lost, because that sense is imparted precisely 'in' the dynamics of the original occurrence; the sense depends on the unique interpenetration of the diverse elements at play in those circumstances. To gaze on the 'myself' of the original *Erlebnis* would cause the focus of that *Erlebnis* – and the manifold elements enmeshed in that moment – to be displaced. By displacing the originally integral interplay of the elements involved, the sense would therefore be lost. By self-reflectively determining the meaning of a 'part' of life as an explication of this original occurrence, then, the 'I' is present 'in' this self-reflective process – but precisely as embedded ('hidden') in the 'sense' of the original whole.

The next task is to explore how Dilthey's explicative continuity can function within the purview of Bonhoeffer's theology. The most effective way to do this is to describe a theologically orientated example of explicative continuity, drawing on elements from Bonhoeffer's writing for demonstrative purposes. To this end, we will use as the unreflective 'pole' – or whole *Erlebnis* – a moment of beholding Christ in hearing the preached word. This mode of encountering Christ is vitally important to Bonhoeffer, as seen in the Christology lectures, or in *Act and Being*'s description of being 'assailed' (*Angegriffen*) by Christ in hearing preaching.[1] Let us consider the example of someone hearing a sermon on Jesus' command, 'take up your cross and follow me' (Mt. 16.24; Mk. 8.34; Lk. 9.23). We can envisage the kind of 'hearing' appropriate to our concerns as involving a moment like that Bonhoeffer describes as being 'taken hold of' in terms of carrying a strong sense of significance or 'impact' ('truth breaking in to the concrete moment'[2]) for the addressee. However, insofar as the hearer is caught up in the unreflective moment and has not determined exactly how this might apply to his or her own life, we can consider this sense of significance to be vague or undefined at the point of its actual occurrence; it is something unreflectively imparted to the hearer without

---

1. DBWE12, 315ff.; DBWE2, 126.
2. DBWE12, 317.

any reflective iteration or amplification as to why or how this verse carries such a sense of significance.

Turning to the other (reflective) pole in this example, we might first be reminded of Bonhoeffer's singling out of this verse in *Discipleship* as having personal importance for individual followers of Christ. He states that 'each has *his* own cross ready, assigned by God and measured to fit'.[3] In keeping with these comments, we can picture the individual in question engaging in a process of discerning how and why this verse applies personally to him or herself. Let us therefore envisage the hearer, subsequent to the event, reflecting on a deeply testing relationship with an elderly and dying parent which demands ongoing acts of tolerance and patience that far exceed the level of responsibility and compassion that same parent displayed to his or her own children during their upbringing. We can thus consider this person self-reflectively seeking to understand what the challenging and disorientating relationship with their dying parent *means*, that is, how to understand it and situate it within a greater whole. This relationship is a 'part' of life, which means a discrete element or an identifiably particular aspect. In isolating this 'part' by reflecting on it, the subject views him or herself as 'object', perhaps in reflecting on his or her upbringing, or evaluating his or her reactions to the challenges of this relationship in adulthood. In activities like these, the self-reflecting subject 'sees' itself as a discrete and thematized element and 'beholds' itself reflectively in the pursuit of self-understanding.

In reflectively determining the meaning of the 'parts' of life in this fashion, Dilthey maintains that a 'part' needs to be situated in reference to a 'whole', which – in his explicative continuity – is a whole *Erlebnis*. The whole in the example outlined above is the lived-experience of hearing 'take up your cross and follow me' in the preached word, and the 'part' is the testing relationship with an elderly, dying parent. We can now envisage the meaning of this 'part' being determined as an explication or outworking of that 'whole'. That is, how, for the reflecting subject, this relationship, which threatens to appear arbitrary, senseless and unintelligible, can be given meaning as explicating a sense of the suffering involved in following Christ which was impressed on the mind of this subject as a hearer of the preached word. We might thereby discern how this relationship could appear to be the outworking of a commission by Christ ('follow me'), resonating with numerous other scriptural passages and enabling an otherwise baffling set of circumstances to have concrete, determined meaning. We will now outline how application of Dilthey's explicative continuity to Bonhoeffer's theology fulfils the requirements of 'wisdom': 'seeing only Christ' and preserving the 'hiddenness of the disciple' in self-reflection.

Beginning with the 'hiddenness of the disciple', it is necessary to remember that, in *Discipleship*, self-reflection is presented as inherently suspect since it is seen as naturally linked with a desire for self-possession. The issue for us, then, is whether the hiddenness Dilthey connotes by preserving the 'I' as intractably

---

3. DBWE4, 87 (translation altered, original emphasis).

embedded in a manifold impression giving rise to a 'sense' is able to elude the desire for self-possession of which Bonhoeffer is suspicious; or more pointedly, whether this preservation of hiddenness in Dilthey will help us to preserve the belonging to 'Christ alone' of unreflective simplicity. The answer to this question is affirmative, not only because in the Diltheyan hiddenness the 'I' is not beheld as 'object', but more specifically because the sense imparted to the 'I' in the whole *Erlebnis* is not a *possession* of the 'I'. That is, the sense of the *Erlebnis* is imposed on the 'I' in the original happening and not composed or formed by the subject; it is imparted 'from outside' and thus does not come under the possessive jurisdiction of the 'I'. For this reason, reflectively determining the meaning of 'parts' of life as explications of the sense given by a 'whole' *Erlebnis* – transposed into a theological purview – offers us an instance of self-reflection which preserves what Bonhoeffer terms the 'hiddenness of the disciple', because this sense does not arise from, or satisfy, the desire for self-possession. We can thus conclude that this application of Dilthey's explicative continuity constitutes an effective example of, or better, opens the door to, the permissible entry of 'wisdom', a mode of self-reflection reconcilable with unreflective simplicity because the 'I' is not 'possessed' by the reflective gaze.

This preserving of hiddenness will be revisited in the final section, but before advancing in that direction, it is necessary first to examine how Dilthey's explicative continuity maintains the subject–'object' singularity of the unreflective, or 'seeing only Christ'. Returning to the example given above, subject–'object' singularity needs to be located first in the unreflective pole, the moment of being struck by the preached word. Here, given Bonhoeffer's Christological understanding of preaching, the person hearing the proclamation can be considered to be apprehending Christ, and so the 'object' of the *Erlebnis* is Christ. There is therefore a unity between the apprehending subject and the 'object' being apprehended, in that the apprehender 'sees' only the 'object' and is not aware of him or herself as a discrete element of the experience, being unreflectively caught up in the proclamation, 'take up your cross and follow me'. Now we must assess whether, in the directing of the subject's attention to him or herself to determine the meaning of the testing relationship with an elderly parent, the unified singularity of being directed at Christ is maintained. Here, something interesting comes to light. Although the self as object is self-reflectively delineated, Dilthey's analysis suggests that the centre of meaning lies with the object of the original *Erlebnis*. In the foregoing example, this stipulates that the meaning of the 'part' of life is reflectively understood *through its directedness to Christ*. We can suggest therefore that, in looking on him or herself in a self-examination of the testing relationship, this person is beholding Christ as the one who has called him or her into circumstances demanding self-sacrificial and unmerited compassionate action. This maintains 'seeing only Christ' insofar as meaning is only determined here as the unfolding of an original moment where Christ is at the centre, where someone was not explicitly aware of him or herself at all. Because the testing relationship would otherwise evade the determination of meaning, in understanding what the relationship means, the person in question is 'seeing only Christ'.

It is evident from the foregoing discussion that the application of Dilthey's explicative continuity offers us a robust continuity, which advances on Bonhoeffer's attempt to attain cognitive continuity in *Act and Being*'s 'self-understanding in remembrance'.[4] Insofar as determining the meaning of a 'part' of life as an explication of a 'whole' *Erlebnis* involves self-reflection which does not arise from, or satisfy, the desire for self-possession, this Dilthey-informed framework for approaching the continuity between the unreflective and reflective offers us a mode of self-reflection from which we need not be 'entirely wrenched away', because in the unpossessed mode of reflecting on oneself as explicating a moment of beholding Christ, one is still 'possessed' by Christ as the centre of meaning.

12.1.2 Implicative continuity

Recalling Dilthey's implicative continuity, this offers a way to see how the 'fruits' or 'effects' of self-reflection partially configure direct consciousness, insofar as reflective self-understanding alters or reconfigures the 'acquired psychic nexus', which is an 'apperceptive framework' carried through life, but of which we are not explicitly aware *in* experience; being merely 'lived-*through*' ('*erlebt*'). Before applying this to Bonhoeffer's theology, it is necessary first to show how this implicative continuity preserves the hiddenness of the subject qua subject. It should be recalled that Dilthey's concrete and temporal unreflective 'I' is delineated through the unity he discerns in 'reproductive processes' between momentary acts of awareness. That this unity pertains in his 'apperceptive framework' is illustrated by the fact that he is arguing that one's past is at work 'in' unreflective experience, configuring and changing the way we experience things. This constitutes a form of hiddenness, in that the unity of the 'I' is not apprehended itself, but considered to be present as unperceived.

In transposing this mode of continuity to the purview of Bonhoeffer's theology, it is best to use a theologically orientated example, again, which draws on elements from Bonhoeffer's writing for demonstrative purposes. As an example of self-reflection, let us consider someone's ruminations on him or herself as baptized and therefore 'forgiven' or 'pardoned'. This obviously resonates with Bonhoeffer's discussion of the 'Christian conscience' (seeing oneself as 'pardoned') and also calls to mind the genealogy of the terminology of *actus directus* and *reflectus* from discussions surrounding the practice of infant baptism. The issues with infant baptism in early Protestant dogmatics centre on how an experience undergone unreflectively (infant baptism as *actus directus*) relates to one's reflective self-understanding,[5] focusing on the warrants for initiating someone who has not

---

4. See Chapter 5 for a full discussion of 'self-understanding in remembrance'.

5. See DBWE2, 28, n17; 158–9, n29, n30; DBWE8, 489. The *actus* distinction taken from Frank Delitzsche's *A System of Biblical Psychology*, but related back to the discussions around infant baptism in Protestant dogmatics centred on the distinction between *fides directa* and *fides reflecta*.

reached the age of responsibility and consent. In exploring this, we can envisage a self-reflecting subject considering him- or herself as initiated into receiving the promise of redemption and – by the gracious action of God – under a pledge of exemption from the consequences of original sin. Thinking on oneself in this way involves seeing oneself as 'object', perhaps to evaluate the degree to which one is conducting oneself in accordance with one's status as a baptized Christian. To show how this self-reflection could then be *implicated in* direct consciousness, we need to envisage how self-reflection on oneself as baptized might restructure or reconfigure the way experiences are undergone unreflectively. That is, how the texture of lived-experience can be seen as formed, to some extent, by the awareness of oneself as pardoned being assimilated into what Dilthey terms the 'acquired psychic nexus'.

To imagine one who has assimilated the theological implications of baptism into the 'acquired psychic nexus', we can picture someone 'carrying' through life a sense of having been promised an unmerited participation in eternal life. We can suppose this to impact on someone's dealings with others with ramifications stemming from the recognition that he or she has received the entirely gracious gift of forgiveness, including those often mentioned in Scripture,[6] dealing graciously with others, to mirror the God's mercy and generosity. The important point here is that, for one who has thoroughly assimilated the awareness of oneself as baptized, the explicit recognition of oneself *as* baptized would not be present as a clearly delineated element of consciousness in every gracious dealing he or she has with others, although it is still effective. Rather, this recognition should be considered as deeply embedded 'in' consciousness implicitly, as partially configuring one's engagement with the challenges of human interrelatedness, without being perspicuously brought before consciousness in each instance where its effects are felt. We can therefore envisage the assimilative incorporation of the knowledge of oneself as baptized, 'feeding into' or being 'implicated in' unreflective experience, most basically issuing in acts of mercy, forgiveness and graciousness towards others. In this way, reflective self-understanding (of oneself as baptized) is present 'in' unreflective experience without an explicit awareness of that effective past in the unreflective moments themselves. With this, we can now appreciate how this involves continuity, from within a Bonhoefferian purview. The 'fruits' or 'effects' of self-reflection are envisaged here as cohering 'in' unreflective experience, so there is no 'split' or 'rupture' between reflective and unreflective, but rather an interrelatedness between them.

The question now arises of how Dilthey's implicative continuity involves an approach to self-reflection which preserves the 'hiddenness of the disciple'. This can be shown by focusing on a ramification of this implicative continuity: the reciprocal interrelatedness of the reflective and unreflective therein. Dilthey enables us to consider not only that self-reflection impacts on the unreflective unidirectionally, but also that unreflective experience instigates further processes

---

6. See Col. 3.13; Matt. 5.43–48; 1 Pet. 2.1–3.

of self-reflection. Most basically, changing circumstances of life, encountered unreflectively, necessitate further reflective consideration of oneself. To return to the foregoing example, we can envisage someone who considers him or herself to have assimilated the knowledge of oneself as pardoned, reacting to an experience of unfairness in a merciless fashion and being led therefore to self-reflectively examine that unforgiving reaction, and resolving to mirror God's mercy more effectively in future. This presents self-reflection as dynamically orientated to the unreflective, the ever-changing realities of life. By approaching self-reflection as orientated receptively to lived-experience, a certain hiddenness of the subject must pertain 'in' that self-reflection, because self-reflection which is open to disruption by unreflective experience offers only understandings of oneself that are provisional, circumspect and tentative. To gaze reflectively on oneself under the proviso that any understanding of oneself can be disrupted by lived-experience, and with a correspondingly cautious tentativeness, means that oneself as 'object' is not entirely given over to the reflective gaze as a self-possession; one does not fully grasp oneself.

This application of Dilthey's implicative continuity to Bonhoeffer's theology enables an effective response to the discontinuity in *Act and Being* between the 'Christian conscience' and 'the child'. There, Bonhoeffer contrasts the permitted self-reflective activity of the 'Christian conscience' (beholding oneself as pardoned) with a 'being determined by the future alone' in 'the child', which is described as 'beyond' any self-reflection.[7] But the question arises of how 'the child' does not constitute another surreptitiously incommensurable 'heavenly double'. If, however, we build on Dilthey's implicative continuity to argue that self-reflective activity is 'implicated' even in moments of 'pure *actus directus*' and, moreover, that – as receptively orientated to the unreflective and therefore as provisional – this activity is reciprocally interrelated with the unreflective, then the subjectivity of direct consciousness is continuous with reflective self-understanding.

12.2 Integrating the unreflective and reflective in the practical

12.2.1 Continuity between Dilthey's aesthetic reflection and unreflective agency as obligation to another

To outline the continuity between Dilthey's aesthetically 'disinterested' reflection and unreflective agency in obligation to another, we can begin with the reflective. Dilthey holds that, particularly in the reading of poetry, a reflecting subject consciously beholds and evaluates images as expressions of the poet's *Gestalt*. That is, the reader of poetry discerns how far the images presented to his or her imagination are appropriate expressions of the sense of the 'unified whole'[8] of the

---

7. DBWE2, 157.
8. SWV, 72.

poet's *Gestalt*, which is itself unconsciously imparted by the unified impression of the whole poem. In this process, the reflective evaluation of aesthetic 'objects' (as poetic images) is 'disinterested', insofar as the subject is not concerned with his or her own desires or inclinations, but focused on an other's subjectivity. Because Dilthey maintains that expressions (*Ausdrücken*[9]) of the human *Gestalt* include other instantiations of human activity, including embodied actions, we concluded that actions could be reflectively evaluated as expressions of someone's *Gestalt*, a discernment of the appropriateness of someone's deeds in respect of the fullness of his or her personhood. On the unreflective side, we brought this aesthetic reflection into relation with unreflective agency in obligation to an other, envisaging someone discerning how best to enact *an other's will* by reflectively evaluating how possible actions might appropriately express that other's *Gestalt*. This was thus seen to offer continuity between unreflective and reflective agency.

To give more detail on this, in circumstances of obligation to an other, we can envisage an agent undergoing this reflective split in a way which is not autonomously centred on the deliberations of the agent him or herself. That is, a reflection on intended actions ('objects'), which discerns how to proceed by evaluating possible actions as expressions of an other's *Gestalt*, is centred on that other, and – as aesthetically 'disinterested' – the subjective desires or inclinations of the person doing the reflecting are withdrawn. On the unreflective side, Dilthey's understanding of unreflective agency in situations of obligation to the will of an 'other' involves a singleness of purpose between an obedient agent and the one to whom that agent is obedient. In spontaneously acting on an other's demand, one's own will is withdrawn, and there is thus a volitional oneness between an agent and the 'other'. The commensurability we are presented with here, then, sustains the unreflective unity of subject–object (the singularity of purpose involved in obedience to another) 'in' the subject–object 'split' of the reflective (between an agent and his or her options). This commensurability can be aptly described by using some of Dilthey's terminology from his cognitively orientated discussions, as offering a practical 'explicative' continuity: a reflective discernment of how to proceed as an *explication* of an other's *Gestalt*.

Our task now is to show how this practical 'explicative' continuity functions within the purview of Bonhoeffer's theology. This seems, prima facie at least, to be more straightforward than the cognitive applications of the previous section, because of the semantic convergence between Bonhoeffer and Dilthey on their respective uses of the term *Gestalt*. To proceed without using a hypothetical example, we should call to mind Dilthey's use of *Gestalt*, which was shown to be based on its meaning a 'unified whole' which cannot be understood by being 'broken down' into constituent elements and reconstructed, and also that it refers to the 'intuitable' appearance of something. This converges with the background to Bonhoeffer's use of *Gestalt* in his 1933 Christology lectures, and *Gestalt* also proves important in *Ethics*, through its practical application in the noun *Gestaltung* and

9. SWII, 154.

the verb *sich gestalten*. As *Gestalt* refers to the intuitably concrete, the 'taking form' of Christ has a pressing sense of referring to the lived world of human beings in the 'here and now', and so *Gestaltung* implies that Christ is given form through present human action.

To undertake the transposition into Bonhoefferian theology: first, as regards unreflective agency in obligation to the will of another, this clearly aligns with Bonhoefferian obedience if the 'other' is approached as Jesus Christ. The volitional oneness of acting spontaneously in alignment to Christ's commands involves a singleness of purpose between the disciple and Christ himself. If we, following Bonhoeffer, approach the person of Christ as *Gestalt*, then enacting Christ's will in this fashion can be considered Christ's *Gestaltung* of the world through human action, Christ 'forming' or 'shaping' the world according to his own *Gestalt*. As Bonhoeffer's *Gestaltung* can be seen to include 'unreflective doing', the 'unity' between agent and intended action can be Christologically conceived as a unity between the agent and Christ, for the intended action is understood to be the real 'taking form' (*Gestaltgewinnen*)[10] of Christ himself in the world.

On the reflective side, Bonhoeffer writes in *Ethics* of 'legitimate and necessary' reflective discernment.[11] This must involve the 'moving apart' of an 'I' (as agent) from its 'objects' (intended actions), as can be seen, for example, in Bonhoeffer's statement that one must discern how to proceed when 'the will of God' lies 'deeply hidden among many competing possibilities'.[12] Insofar as this is permitted and endorsed, we can consider Bonhoeffer gesturing towards what he understands as 'wisdom', and moreover, in *Ethics* we encounter the 'simplicity and wisdom' passage which functions as this book's hermeneutical key. Bonhoeffer's descriptions of practical reflection can now be approached through the lens of Dilthey's aesthetic reflection. That is, envisaging an agent 'moving apart' from his or her intended actions, to discern what aligns to Christ's will, or rather, which course of action would enact Christ's *Gestaltung* of the world. In this, an agent decides how best to appropriate Christ's person 'in the given situation'. But, crucially, Bonhoeffer approaches Christ's personhood as *Gestalt*, and therefore, we can envisage this agent discerning how to proceed (in an aesthetically 'disinterested' fashion) against the background of the sense he or she has of Christ's *Gestalt*: an undefined impression of the fullness of Christ's person as a 'lived-whole' and 'characteristic unity', which serves as a background evaluative structure for practical discernment. Having shown how the unreflective and reflective sides to Bonhoeffer's ethics can be approached through Diltheyan obedience and aesthetically 'disinterested' reflection respectively, we can now put this to work in responding to the specific problems of the *Ethics* manuscripts outlined above.

The question now arises of how approaching reflective agency in this way preserves 'simple obedience' and 'purity of heart'. Beginning with 'simple obedience',

---

10. DBWE6, 96; DBW6, 84.
11. DBWE6, 320, 283.
12. Ibid., 321.

there are good grounds to affirm that approaching reflective discernment with Dilthey's aesthetic 'disinterestedness' (the withdrawal of subjective desires and inclinations) allows us to understand how deeds reflectively arrived at in this fashion would not be grounded on the disciple as agent. This is because such deeds would not be courses of action an agent has chosen or decided upon as his or her own desired way to proceed. Dilthey claims that through the aesthetic withdrawal of self-orientated desire, we effectively 'inhabit' the *Gestalt* of another, evaluating 'objects' of our attention exclusively through that unique and singular *Gestalt*, and so applied practically, reflection would issue in deeds grounded on that *Gestalt*, expressions of that person. Approaching this *Gestalt* as Christ's is to see an agent 'order' or 'formulate' his or her options according to Christ's 'form'. The resulting deeds would therefore be grounded on Christ, and we can thus envisage how the reflective discernment of how to proceed in this case involves the volitional unity of 'simple obedience', in that subjective desires of the agent are withdrawn and Christ's *Gestalt* is the only evaluative framework in that discernment. This therefore involves a 'moving apart' of agent and intended actions in 'simple obedience'.

Moving onto 'purity of heart', to reflect in this 'purity' would mean reflecting on how to proceed while being focused 'purely' on Christ's commands to such a degree that one's deliberations are not 'adulterated' by concerns rooted in the desire for self-legitimization. This undertaking will proceed in three interrelated steps. First, we shall point to the fact that we have already progressed some way towards showing how 'purity of heart' can be sustained in reflection in that a 'disinterested' withdrawal of subjective desires and inclinations itself precludes 'adulteration' by the desire for autonomous validation, which is further indicated in that Bonhoeffer's *Ethics* acknowledges the possibility that one can act obediently to Christ against one's own judgement of the good. Secondly, we shall see that the semantic background of the terms *Gestalt, Gestaltung,* and *sich gestalten* entails that a distillation of Christ's *Gestalt* into a framework of 'criteria' (or a sense of ethical security) cannot apply in this context, for *Gestalt* always and only means an 'intuitable' whole which cannot be analytically broken down into components and conditions. Finally, we shall build on the foregoing steps to tackle the question of Bonhoefferian necessity using Dilthey's category of 'having-to-be-thus'.

Beginning with the first step, approaching the reflective discernment of a course of action (seeking after the will of God) via Dilthey's 'disinterested' aesthetic reflection, entails that this discernment of God's will is not stimulated, orchestrated, or coordinated by subjective (autonomous) inclinations, and cannot therefore be motivated by the desire for self-validation. This is because the desire for self-legitimization is by definition rooted in the self, and Dilthey's aesthetic reflection – as we have seen – involves the withdrawal of self-orientated desires. This presents a mode of reflection which coheres with what Bonhoeffer describes as when an agent is not 'pulled back and forth by wishes and intentions of his own' and has been called to 'die' with his or her 'desires' (*Begierden*).[13] We

---

13. DBWE4, 108, 88.

can also amplify this, by pointing out that a withdrawal of autonomously centred concerns can lead to deeds which might even *challenge* one's own judgement of the good. In effectively circumventing the possibility of attaining ethical security through aesthetic 'disinterestedness', some of Bonhoeffer's more challenging assertions in *Ethics* can be elucidated, such as his statement that the redeemed can 'relinquish any effectual self-justification',[14] which leads him to claim the redeemed can even undergo a 'taking on of guilt' ('*Schuldübernahmung*'[15]). By considering that a circumvention of the desire for autonomous validation is aptly articulated through Dilthey's aesthetic reflection, we can now appreciate more deeply how Bonhoeffer can maintain that the heart of one 'shrouded in the twilight that the historical situation casts upon good and evil' can still be 'pure'; for even in the midst of ethical ambiguity, we can discern how that heart is fixed on Christ alone, 'disinterestedly' contemplating how to enact his *Gestaltung* of the world.

With the second step, we turn directly to the key problem of differentiating between the reflectively discerned knowledge of God's will and knowledge of an 'absolute good'. It should be recalled that *Gestalt*, by definition, refers to the 'spatial' and 'intuitable' appearance of something. Therefore, we cannot confuse *Gestalt* with anything other than the concrete, and so the 'objects' of reflecting on Christ's *Gestaltung* of the world must be courses of action which can bear on concrete life, genuine possibilities of action in the lived world of human beings, and therefore not abstract 'objects' like the principles involved in knowing an 'absolute good'. Although possibilities themselves are not fully concrete (as unrealized), the semantic background of *Gestalt* dictates that for these possibilities to qualify as ways to enact the *Gestaltung* of Christ, they must be actions within reach of an agent, actions which can be concretely realized. The question then arises as to how the evaluative framework of Christ's *Gestalt* does not offer another point of self-legitimizing ethical security to rival knowledge of an absolute good. To respond to this, we need to ask if Christ's *Gestalt* threatens to become a set of criteria, which, in being autonomously borne, could serve as a self-centred means to maximize one's goodness. It could be claimed, for example, that the Beatitudes, or the Pauline lists of virtues, determine criteria showing us what Christ's person is like and therefore provide transparent means of validation; their meaning can be ascertained and then *applied* to the concrete. Again, however, approaching Christ's personhood as *Gestalt* closes off the possibility. This is because Dilthey shows us that a *Gestalt* can only be glimpsed as a 'lived-whole' and not distilled into components or constructed from a set of conditions. If the 'how' of Christ's *Gestalt* cannot be broken down and reconstructed from its constituents, as Bonhoeffer claims, then neither can the 'how' of Christ's *Gestaltung* (the question of how I should act) be analytically broken down and reconstructed on the basis of a set of criteria.

14. DBWE6, 284.
15. Ibid.

Now this section can close by addressing the problem of Bonhoeffer's use of the term necessity to describe the knowledge of God's will. We have seen that Bonhoeffer's description of God's will as involving what 'is necessary in the given situation' intensifies the problem of distinguishing the knowledge of God's will from knowledge of an absolute good insofar as Bonhoeffer exemplifies an absolute good in Kant, and Kant's 'categorical imperative' involves by definition necessary conditions. It should be recalled that Dilthey's aesthetics include the category of 'having-to-be-thus' (*Sosein-Müssen*), which is an attempt to offer an alternative to the 'necessity' (*Notwendigkeit*) of the natural sciences for the *Geisteswissenschaften*. With *Sosein-Müssen*, Dilthey tries to classify a sense of 'appropriateness' which is particularly discernible in poetry, when every component of a poem 'has-to-be-thus' in order for the impression of that work to hold. It should also be recalled that 'having-to-be-thus' is seen by Dilthey as intrinsically based on the inextricable interrelatedness of works of art with the artist's *Gestalt*. He holds that the impression of a work of art transposes the unique, structuring 'singular response to reality' of the artist into an artistic form, so his or her work functions as a microcosm of the artist him or herself. If we take this form of necessity as 'having-to-be-thus' and apply it to Bonhoeffer's doing the 'necessary in a given situation', we can envisage a situation whereby discerning what deed best enacts Christ's *Gestaltung* of the world can be seen as presenting a deed which is necessary. That is, a certain deed might 'have-to-be-thus' as only in the performance of that deed can we glimpse Christ's *Gestalt* and to act differently would undermine the sense that that specific action instantiates Christ's person in the here and now. Dilthey has shown us how, when a *Gestalt* is instantiated in a specific context, this involves a framework of appropriateness carrying a sense of necessity without any abstractable criteria to qualify it as such; that is, a concrete necessity. On this basis, we can respond to the problem of necessity in distinguishing knowledge of an 'absolute good' from knowledge of God's will; for the latter only pertains to possibilities which can genuinely bear on concrete life (and for which a level of abstraction entirely removed from life is precluded), and – as based on the *Gestalt* – involves an evaluative framework which carries a sense of appropriateness which cannot be grounded through transparent criteria, meaning a certain deed may 'have-to-be-thus' as the only possible expression of the *Gestalt* of Christ.

12.3 Integrating simplicity and wisdom

Having shown how the prior examination of Dilthey enables the establishing of continuity or harmoniousness between unreflective simplicity and reflective wisdom, this can be extended to enquire into how the interrelation of simplicity and wisdom can be strengthened so they are integrated. Bonhoeffer himself presents simplicity and wisdom as inalienably interconnected, such that neither can be authentic without the other. This is most perceptible in his claim that it is the combination of simplicity and wisdom he is looking for: 'Only the one who *combines* simplicity and wisdom can endure.'[16] Moreover, Bonhoeffer asserts the as yet vague and challenging claim that 'there is no true simplicity without wisdom, and no wisdom without simplicity'.[17] In what follows, the task is to explore how the modes of continuity outlined above can be developed so that simplicity and wisdom are mutually integral. In each case, disclosing the mutual integrity shall enable us to read afresh some of the problematic assertions from *Discipleship* with which this book began.

12.3.1 Explicative continuity as integrating simplicity and wisdom

Examining Dilthey's explicative continuity, the mutually integral interrelation of simplicity and wisdom requires that integral and *sine qua non* aspects of unreflective simplicity are actually more clearly disclosed, or more firmly established, for our understanding of human subjectivity 'in Christ' through reflective wisdom, when approached in this Dilthey-informed way. The key *sine qua non* aspect of unreflective simplicity, particularly in the cognitive domain, is Christ's centrality. Bonhoeffer claims those in simplicity 'no longer cast even a single glance on [their] own life', for Christ 'is in the centre' (*Mitte*).[18] Under the proviso that self-reflection – as wisdom – is conducted within the requirements of 'seeing only Christ' and the 'hiddenness of the disciple', we can now discern how reflective wisdom extends the centrality of Christ which is integral to simplicity. First, Christ's centrality is more clearly disclosed through being reflected on, in that 'parts' of life which otherwise do not exhibit a Christ-centred orientation – through having their meaning determined as an explication of a moment where Christ is unreflectively 'in the centre' – disclose Christ-centred dimensions of life which would otherwise go unheeded or unacknowledged. With the example of someone reflecting on a 'part' of life as a relationship with an elderly, dying parent, it is precisely through reflection that this relationship is seen to have Christ at the centre. Reflective wisdom therefore enforces the centrality of Christ which is integral to simplicity. In this sense, Bonhoeffer's claim that 'there is no true simplicity without wisdom' can be properly understood. That is, 'true simplicity' (Christ in the centre) is thus integrally bound up with wisdom (where this centrality is disclosed in the 'fullness of life'[19]).

Moreover, wisdom can also be considered to disclose Christ's centrality more firmly in human self-understanding. For example, an unreflective moment of apprehending Christ (like hearing the preached word), if not brought into a communicative interrelationship with reflective facets to human subjectivity (while fulfilling the requirements which make that situating possible), would, in a sense, fail to carry out or execute the full 'impact' which is integral to its very

---

16. Ibid., 86 (my emphasis).
17. DBWE6, 82.
18. DBWE4, 287, 93; DBWE12, 324; DBWE8, 406–7.
19. See DBWE6, 369; DBWE8, 45, 405.

nature. The centrality of Christ is thereby firmly established as genuine centrality only if it impacts beyond transient moments of unreflective apprehension and impinges on other aspects of life, so these aspects can also be acknowledged as centred on Christ. Again, this enables us to discern how 'there is not true simplicity without wisdom', for if moments of unreflective simplicity do not unfold into or explicate other aspects of life, Christ is not established as the centre of those other aspects and not therefore 'the centre of our existence'. We are thus led to affirm that reflectively determining the meaning of 'parts' of life as explications of a 'whole' *Erlebnis* of unreflectively apprehending Christ presents an understanding of human subjectivity in which the centrality of Christ is actually more clearly disclosed and more firmly established across a much broader range of human experience, precisely through being related to wisdom. This is a significant gain, not least because this centrality is described so forcefully in *Discipleship* as pertaining to simplicity exclusively.

Working from wisdom to simplicity, our task is to show how this explicative continuity can be extended to show how wisdom is inalienably bound up with simplicity, such that there is no true wisdom 'without simplicity'. Of course, some progress has been made towards this, by establishing how self-reflection can be approached *as* wisdom in line with the requirements of 'seeing only Christ' and the 'hiddenness of the disciple'. Nonetheless, these gains can be added to, by examining whether or not an integral and *sine qua non* aspect of wisdom is more clearly disclosed or more firmly established through simplicity. To do so, let us take an integral aspect of wisdom from Bonhoeffer's assertion that the 'wise person sees reality as it is'.[20] This of course chimes with one of the most basic meanings of the word wisdom: 'sound judgement' or 'sagacity'. To judge something soundly means to judge it correctly or accurately, and seen in this light, our question is then whether, to judge things soundly and see 'reality as it is', wisdom needs to be integrally bound up with simplicity. Within a theological purview, this is the case for Bonhoefferian simplicity and wisdom, on the basis of the basic and fundamental conviction of Christian theology that reality has God at its centre, as its source and its summit. Ascertaining the most accurate or correct understanding of oneself in reflection, then, must on the basis of this conviction involve reflection on oneself with God at the centre. This can be seen in that reflectively determining the meaning of the parts of life as explications of moments of unreflectively beholding Christ, we can discern how someone undergoes what we can term a 'perspectival shift', so he or she 'views' or 'sees' reality in a God-centred fashion – as someone who is 'captivated by the gaze of Jesus Christ'.[21] By not seeing oneself at the centre of reality (remaining hidden) and being 'captivated by the gaze of Jesus Christ' (seeing only Christ), wisdom (approached theologically) can be seen as involving sound judgement (seeing reality as it is) precisely and only in its integral interrelatedness to simplicity. Therefore, were self-reflection to become untethered

20. DBWE6, 81.
21. Ibid., 147.

from simplicity and lapse into self-centredness and self-orientatedness, sound judgement would be undermined.

On this basis, *Discipleship*'s challenging assertions can be read afresh, as integrally bound up with wisdom. Discipleship, says Bonhoeffer, means 'we see only' Christ, and the disciples are those who are 'fully absorbed in seeing God', so much so that a disciple must ask 'How can I protect myself … [f]rom my own reflection?'[22] The foregoing analysis provides two means by which this 'dangerous' statement can be interpreted afresh. First, a disciple need not protect him or herself from all reflection *tout court*, but rather only from reflection that is untethered from simplicity and which would thus 'interrupt' intentionality to Christ and tend towards possessive self-centredness. But secondly, and more importantly, we can now acknowledge that to truly 'see only Christ' and to genuinely be 'fully absorbed in seeing God' in 'the fullness of life', the disciple *must* engage in self-reflective activity – such as that in the explicative continuity above – for without self-reflection, the centrality of Christ in simplicity would not be fully disclosed or established, and, moreover, it is only by being tethered to unreflective simplicity that wisdom will involve the sound judgement of seeing 'reality as it is'.

12.3.2 Implicative continuity as integrating simplicity and wisdom

In exploring how the implicative continuity of simplicity and wisdom enables integral and *sine qua non* facets of each to be more fully realized, it should be pointed out that Christ's centrality can be seen as more fully disclosed or established by reflective wisdom in this case, because the Christ-centredness of certain aspects of life is, again, not always given to unreflective consciousness otherwise. The example above of infant baptism demonstrates this. This ritual conducted on an infant is not something that is remembered, but only accepted and acknowledged *reflectively* as pertaining to oneself. Experiences like this do not *im*-mediately seem to apply to oneself, but – through reflective mediation – can bear on one's life. In this way, the centrality of Christ is more clearly disclosed and more firmly established by reflective wisdom (always assuming that the requirements of 'seeing only Christ' and remaining 'hidden' are met). This can be amplified further, by highlighting the mutual reciprocity between simplicity and wisdom in implicative continuity. This continuity suggests that unreflective experience instigates further processes of self-reflection, most basically through envisaging that changing circumstances encountered unreflectively necessitate further reflective consideration of oneself. Using the example of infant baptism, we envisaged someone thinking he or she had assimilated the self-understanding of being 'pardoned' and then self-reflectively resolving to mirror the gift of baptismal redemption more effectively in future. In this reciprocal interaction between reflective self-understanding and unreflective lived-experience, unreflective experiences themselves should become increasingly Christ-centred, and crucially, were ongoing self-reflection not to occur, knowledge

---

22. DBWE4, 154.

of oneself as baptized would not impact 'on' unreflective experience as deeply. We can therefore see that wisdom fosters simplicity, cultivating and 'feeding into' Christ-centredness in the unreflective, so 'there is no true simplicity without wisdom'.

Working from the other direction, the means by which integral and *sine qua non* aspects of wisdom might betoken an integral interrelatedness with simplicity are the focus. Here, let us consider two basic associations of the word wisdom: first, wisdom as practical knowledge, and secondly, highlighting semantic undertones associated with the synonym prudence, in the sense that being 'wise' or 'prudential' tends to denote a careful, circumspect and measured consideration of things. To consider wisdom as integrally involving practical knowledge is to highlight that knowledge which arises 'from' and is effective 'in' worldly experience, in contrast to, say, purely noetic or conceptual knowing. Returning to someone reflecting on him or herself as baptized, this integral aspect of wisdom (practical knowledge) is actually gained through the interrelation of the reflective and lived-experience, much of which is unavoidably unreflective, so that wisdom as such as enabled to be genuine (practical) wisdom precisely through the unreflective. That is, were the reflective acknowledgement knowledge of oneself as 'baptized' not to 'feed into' or be 'implicated in' unreflective experience, it would – in a sense – not qualify as genuinely experiential or practical knowledge, and moreover, were there not an ongoing reciprocity between acknowledging oneself as baptized and experiencing the 'forging' or 'sharpening' of that knowledge in life itself, this knowledge would be disconnected from life, and thus would not be the sort of knowledge we would associate with wisdom. We can also apply the same line of reasoning with some of the semantic undertones of the synonym prudence. In the reciprocal interrelationship of simplicity and wisdom in implicative continuity, we saw that the reflective self-awareness which 'feeds into' lived-experience must be considered perpetually 'open' to further disruption in life. This provisional self-reflection – qualified as such by its relatedness to the unreflective – suggests precisely the qualities associated with wisdom as prudence: being careful, circumspect and measured. Were wisdom to become untethered from the unreflective, this prudent carefulness and moderation would be undermined, and it can thus now be established again how, there is no true 'wisdom without simplicity'. Reflectively gleaned knowledge of oneself can only be 'wise' in the sense of prudential or circumspect, if properly orientated to the ever-changing circumstances of life.

To apply this integration of simplicity and wisdom to some of the challenging assertions from *Discipleship*, an appropriate example is Bonhoeffer's claim that one's life as a disciple must be hidden from oneself, because 'in the same moment I would desire to see it, I would lose it'.[23] By showing that wisdom depends on its interrelatedness to lived-experience, on its being 'forged' and 'sharpened' in life, we can now discern that this 'seeing' of oneself which Bonhoeffer forbids, forbids a 'seeing' of oneself which is disconnected from life, untethered from

---

23. Ibid., 207–8.

ongoing unreflective encounter with Christ, and thus not genuinely 'wise' in the sense of being practical and experiential knowledge. Similarly, Bonhoeffer admonishes followers of Christ to turn Peter's denial ('I do not know the man')[24] onto themselves, and now we can interpret this – not merely as referring to momentary unreflective encounters – but as suggestive of a broader disposition whereby self-knowledge is approached prudentially and with considerable reserve across the 'fullness of life'. That is, we can envisage that self-reflection as wisdom actually *fosters* a disposition whereby one can say of oneself: 'I do not know the man', and stand with Bonhoeffer in acknowledging that 'lack of understanding *is* real understanding'.[25]

12.3.3 Practical explicative continuity as integrating simplicity and wisdom

For the practical domain, let us take as an integral facet of simplicity – unreflective obedience – as belonging to Christ alone. Deeds enacted in unreflective simplicity belong to Christ alone in their being grounded on Christ's commands, and the disciple belongs to Christ alone insofar as his or her deeds are not driven by agent-centred desires. First, we can contend that simplicity must be brought into play with wisdom, for otherwise God's will is only encountered when given to, or apprehended by, direct consciousness spontaneously. One's belonging to 'Christ *alone*' therefore depends in part on reflectively discerning God's will at times when there is no spontaneous apprehension of it, for if belonging to Christ is a genuinely singular 'being possessed', then this 'belongingness' must penetrate the 'fullness of life'. We can thus acknowledge that 'there is no true simplicity [belonging to Christ *alone*] without wisdom'.

Working from the other direction, let us return to the basic aspect of wisdom discussed above: 'sound judgement', or seeing 'reality as it is'. Within Bonhoeffer's Christological-theological purview, the approach to wisdom as 'disinterestedly' reflecting on how best to enact Christ's *Gestaltung* of the world brings something interesting to light. As we have seen, a basic tenet of Christian theology is that to see 'reality as it is' is to 'see reality in God', and, in the more specialized context of his *Ethics*, Bonhoeffer argues that 'seeing reality as it is' is to see the unity of the world and God in Jesus Christ. He states that the wise person 'sees reality in God', and 'because there is one place where God and the reality of the world ... have become one, is it possible ... there alone to fix one's eyes on God and the world together at the same time'. As it stands, these assertions seem somewhat vague and impenetrable. However, by approaching wisdom as an aesthetically 'disinterested' discernment of how to enact Christ's *Gestaltung* of the world, we uncover some valuable pointers for a more detailed understanding. Because, as we have seen, a *Gestalt* is always concrete, spatial and intuitable; this mode of reflective discernment will not lapse into transparent abstractions and thus remains

---

24. Ibid., 86.
25. Ibid., 91 (Bonhoeffer is quoting Luther, my emphasis).

thoroughgoingly 'worldly'. Moreover, insofar as this mode of reflective discernment is predicated on the conviction that 'simple obedience' involves the genuine 'incarnating' (*Gestaltung*) of Christ in the here and now, Bonhoeffer considers such deeds to be – in a sense – those of God himself. Therefore, this combination of simplicity and wisdom enables us to see 'God and the world together at the same time' through being singularly directed at Christ, while contemplating genuinely earthly deeds. As seeing 'God and the world' in simultaneity, we see reality wisely ('as it is'), and therefore, there is no 'wisdom without simplicity'.

Revisiting some 'dangerous' assertions of *Discipleship* in light of this, some of Bonhoeffer's best-known assertions are apposite; such as 'the call goes out, and without any further ado the obedient deed of the one called follows', or that 'nothing precedes' an encounter with Christ 'and nothing follows except the obedience of the called'.[26] On the basis of the integration of simplicity and wisdom via the practical explicative continuity presented here, such statements can now be best interpreted, not as pointing only to exceptional moments of life, but serving a much broader disposition across the 'fullness of life'. First, we can see how our 'belonging to Christ alone' takes possession of dimensions of life which would otherwise be ensnared in self-possession because Christ's commands are not explicitly perceptible. Secondly, we can discern that 'the proximity of call and deed' in such assertions, rather than being limited to exceptional circumstances, can actually pertain across the 'fullness of life', precisely through the binding together of the world and God discerned in wisdom, and thus applying to any deed contemplated according to the *Gestalt* of Christ.

12.4 Broader implications of integrating simplicity and wisdom

This book can now be brought to close by pointing to three broader implications of the integration of simplicity and wisdom set out in the foregoing section. First, implications for our interpretation of *Discipleship*; secondly, for 'simplicity and wisdom' as a hermeneutical key the Bonhoeffer corpus; and finally, for perennial questions surrounding the human relation to God.

Beginning with *Discipleship*'s interpretation, a juxtaposition of the book's reception (highlighted in Chapter 3) should be recalled. On the one hand, *Discipleship* is acknowledged as central for historical–biographical understandings of Bonhoeffer's life and work. He worked over it more thoroughly and painstakingly than his earlier publications, it is the first book he personally chose to publish after undergoing the significant personal changes which he later described famously as 'becoming a Christian', and it is inseparable from his time at Finkenwalde, which he called 'the fullest time of my life'.[27] On the other hand, this historical–biographical centrality is juxtaposed with *Discipleship*'s more precarious academic reception.

---

26. DBWE4, 57.
27. Bethge, *Bonhoeffer*, 341.

We saw that it was interpreted early on as the product of a 'detour' in Bonhoeffer's intellectual development, and although scholars in recent decades have interpreted *Discipleship* as more integral to the wider corpus, there are good grounds to state that its apparently 'dangerous' character means it tends to be 'stood by' with some difficulty, as an outlier on the more radical fringes of Bonhoeffer's thinking.

One means of holding together the two sides to this juxtaposition is provided by applying an image suggested by Andreas Pangritz, who argues that Bonhoeffer's development should not be seen as linear, but as a 'helix' or 'spiral'.[28] Insofar as surprising changes of direction or emphasis can be seen as contributing towards the directionality of an overall *oeuvre* in the image of a 'helix', Pangritz offers us a way to 'stand by' *Discipleship*, by locating the moments of apparent contradiction with other points in the corpus, as pertaining to a radical edge or peripheral point on the fringes of this 'helix'. The location of *Discipleship* on the 'helix', perhaps, can then be approached as offering a perspective from which other points or junctures are not in view; as Plant states, *Discipleship* is 'disturbing' because of its exclusivity, for 'it gives the impression there can be no other way of understanding Christian faith'.[29] However, applying his 'helix' to the juxtaposition outlined above still leaves the two different sides of *Discipleship*'s reception in an uneasy relationship, for – at least biographically and historically – *Discipleship* was clearly not a book standing at the peripheral edges of Bonhoeffer's life and work, but at its very centre. However, the integration of simplicity and wisdom offered in this book seems to offer a valuable alternative approach. Insofar as simplicity and wisdom are mutually integral, the implication arises that, by concentrating so resolutely, uncompromisingly and forcefully on unreflective simplicity in *Discipleship*, Bonhoeffer was enabled to discover and unearth further dimensions of reflective wisdom, which, rather than recanting his uncompromising simplicity, further foster and perpetuate it. Indeed, a motif of 'concentration' can be found in writings surrounding the Finkenwalde period, for example in Bethge, who argued that *Discipleship* was not a forsaking of the world, but 'a concentration' intended to issue in deeper worldliness and committed responsible action.[30]

Integrating simplicity and wisdom thus implies an interpretation of *Discipleship* which places the book at the centre of Bonhoeffer's work, showing how other elements of the corpus (the reflective) can be integrally located in relation to it. This integrating of hitherto uneasily related elements of the corpus implies that this hermeneutical key promises to offer a means of integrating other spheres of concern in Bonhoeffer scholarship beyond our focus on human subjectivity. As discussed in Chapter 1, that Bonhoeffer's thinking is characterized by 'oppositional pairs' is well known, and high-profile examples of such pairs include the *actus directus–reflectus* distinction, 'ultimate' and 'penultimate things', 'church'

---

28. Discussed by Ann L. Nickson, *Bonhoeffer on Freedom*, Aldershot, Hampshire: Ashgate, 2002, 6; cf. n27.
29. Plant, *Bonhoeffer*, 98.
30. Bethge, 'Challenge', 48–50; see DBWE14, 89.

and 'world', 'act' and 'being', 'resistance' and 'submission', and so on. Different commentators have presented different pairs as offering modes of interrelation enabling cohesive, integrated and homogenous readings of the broader corpus, beyond the specific set of concerns with which these individual dualities originate.

Bethge holds that Bonhoeffer's theology involves a Christological mode of oneness which is neither 'diastasis' or 'synthesis'.[31] Bringing this into dialogue with the integration of the duality of 'simplicity' and 'wisdom' in this book, we can suggest that the integration offered here of simplicity and wisdom promises to have broader implications beyond the unreflective–reflective tension. The foregoing analysis of this book suggests that the *actus* distinction tends towards diastasis in that the differentiation between each side of the duality is stark (direct and reflective consciousness are, at bottom, mutually exclusive), and this is borne out in the residual fragmentation of Bonhoeffer's attempts at establishing continuity in *Act and Being*. Yet, our investigation has also made clear that DeJonge's centralizing of the tensions between 'act' and 'being' as 'solved'[32] in the concept of person veers towards synthesis and threatens to undermine the perennial tension between the two. The integration of simplicity and wisdom offered here, however, avoids synthesis, while presenting a genuine 'oneness' through an integral interrelationship. Moreover, it avoids diastasis by accommodating the unavoidable differentiation between the two, and so we suggest that 'simplicity and wisdom' offers an exemplary instance of what Bethge describes as Bonhoeffer's underlying pattern of thinking. This promises therefore to integrate and cohere different facets of Bonhoeffer's thinking beyond the unreflective and reflective, and deserves further exploration as one of what Bethge calls elsewhere Bonhoeffer's 'creative formulas'.

Bonhoeffer's creative formulas attempt to hold together and interrelate two prima facie conflicting components. This holding together of two apparently conflicting sets of concerns, which, even when interrelated, can exhibit an ongoing, perpetually challenging dissimilarity, resonates with what we might term the 'perennial tensions' which frequently reoccur in theology, for they are fundamentally grounded on abidingly perplexing aspects of the human relation to God. This book can now be brought to a close by gesturing towards a way this discussion can extend beyond Bonhoeffer scholarship and into a basic tension of theological enquiry. This tension is rooted in what is frequently considered an issue of interrelating transcendence and immanence. The issue here is how God transcendent (by definition beyond capacities of human knowing) can be revealed (communicated or disclosed) to human beings, for human capabilities of understanding are by definition 'immanent' to what is within their capabilities. Our unreflective–reflective tension is a particular anthropological outplaying of this basic issue, for in the human–divine encounter, the human 'subject' is understood as 'renewed', 'transformed' or 'reborn' by the gracious action of God

---

31. Bethge, 'Challenge', 74.
32. DeJonge, *Formation*, 96.

transcendent, but by reflecting on that encounter, this 'transformation' threatens to be ensnared by (and therefore limited to) 'immanent' capacities of understanding. Put differently, to reduce God's action to what can be reflected upon veers towards an apparent 'synthesis' of God's action with human capacities of understanding, which threatens to undermine the purely God initiated or enacted nature of that transformation itself. Yet, if this transformation is not reflected on, and does not become bound up with the identity of the transformed, then, in veering towards diastasis, the genuineness of an actual encounter in relatedness between human and divine is undermined, in that the fruits of this encounter are not fully recognized.

The integration of simplicity and wisdom presented in this book bears certain implications for this abidingly perplexing tension. In the first place, insofar as simplicity cannot be authentic without an integral link to wisdom, we can state that integral and *sine qua non* aspects of a transformative encounter with God *as* transcendent – in being reflected upon – actually foster our reverence for God (which is necessitated precisely on account of his transcendence) by situating that encounter at the heart of the 'fullness of life'. That is, God is 'wholly other', and this God should therefore stand in the centre of our existence, and we should belong to him entirely. The three modes of interrelation discussed above have shown that it is precisely God's *centrality*, and our 'being possessed' *singularly* by him, which are fostered by the reflective, for otherwise this centrality and 'belonging' cannot wholly pertain in the 'fullness of life'. In this sense, for an encounter with God to be maintained as an encounter with God *transcendent*, the framework offered here implies that the impact of this encounter on human 'immanence' fosters an appropriate response by disclosing God's centrality and our belonging to him alone. Working from the other direction, of course we need to ensure that, in binding God's transcendence to our immanence, this transcendence is not reduced and undermined thereby. The three means of integrating simplicity and wisdom discussed above, from the perspective of wisdom, imply that our 'immanent' reflections will be appropriately and suitably qualified and measured to ensure just this, in that seeing 'reality as it is' in wisdom was seen to involve a 'perspectival shift' to God-centredness, the openness of self-reflection to disruption in life renders it always only careful and circumspect, and we attain a perception of God and the world in unity through the *Gestaltung* of Christ. In short, wisdom as presented here offers 'dispossessed' modes of reflection, which – enabling us to reflect on our own life as 'hidden with Christ' in the God who stands at 'the centre of our existence' – deepen and intensify the very transformation itself, which Bonhoeffer describes compellingly as issuing only from the 'immediate, unconditional, and inscrutable' call of Jesus: 'follow me'.

BIBLIOGRAPHY

Abromeit, Hans-Jürgen, *Das Geheimnis Christi: Dietrich Bonhoeffers erfahrungsbezogene Christologie*, Neukirchen-Vluyn: Neukirchener Verlag, 1991.
Barth, Karl, *Die Christliche Dogmatik Im Entwurf*, München: Chr. Kaiser Verlag, 1927.
Barth, Karl, *The Epistle to the Romans*, trans. from the 6th edn by Edwyn C. Hoskyns, Oxford: Oxford University Press, 1968.
Barth, Karl, *Der Römerbrief 1922*, Zürich: Theologischer Verlag, 2010.
Barth, Karl, 'Schicksal und Idee in der Theologie', *Zwischen den Zeiten* 7 (1929): 309–48.
Beck, Lewis White and Hoke Robinson, *Selected Essays on Kant*, Rochester, NY: University of Rochester Press, 2002.
Bethge, Eberhard, 'The Challenge of Dietrich Bonhoeffer's Life and Theology', in Ronald Gregor Smith (ed.), *The World Comes of Age: A Symposium on Dietrich Bonhoeffer*, London: Collins, 1967, 24–88.
Bethge, Eberhard, *Dietrich Bonhoeffer: Theologian, Christian, Man for His Times*, trans. Eric Mosbacher et al., ed. Edwin Robertson, revised and ed. Victoria J. Barnett, Minneapolis: Fortress Press, 2000.
Bonhoeffer, Dietrich, *Dietrich Bonhoeffers Hegel-Seminar 1933*, ed. Ferenc Lehel and Ilse Tödt, München: Chr. sKaiser, 1988.
Bonhoeffer, Dietrich, Dietrich Bonhoeffer Werke 2 Band: *Akt und Sein: Transzendentalphilosophie und Ontologie in der systematischen Theologie*, ed. Hans-Richard Reuter, München: Chr. Kaiser, 1988.
Bonhoeffer, Dietrich, Dietrich Bonhoeffer Werke 3 Band: *Schöpfung und Fall*, ed. Martin Rüter and Ilse Tödt, München: Chr. Kaiser, 1989.
Bonhoeffer, Dietrich, Dietrich Bonhoeffer Werke 4 Band: *Nachfolge*, ed. Martin Kuske and Ilse Tödt, München: Chr. Kaiser, 1989.
Bonhoeffer, Dietrich, Dietrich Bonhoeffer Werke 5 Band: *Gemeinsames Leben und Das Gebetbuch der Bibel*, ed. Gerhard Ludwig Müller and Albrecht Schönherr, München: Chr. Kaiser, 1987.
Bonhoeffer, Dietrich, Dietrich Bonhoeffer Werke 6 Band: *Ethik*, ed. Ilse Tödt, Heinz Eduard Tödt, Ernst Feil and Clifford Green, München: Chr. Kaiser, 1992.
Bonhoeffer, Dietrich, Dietrich Bonhoeffer Werke 8 Band: *Widerstand und Ergebung: Briefe und Aufzeichnungen aus der Haft*, ed. Christian Gremmels, Eberhard Bethge and Renate Bethge, in Zusammenarbeit mit Ilse Tödt, München: Chr. Kaiser, 1998.
Bonhoeffer, Dietrich, Dietrich Bonhoeffer Werke 12 Band: *Berlin, 1932–1933*, ed. Carsten Nicolaisen and Ernst-Albert Scharffenorth, München: Chr. Kaiser, 1997.
Bonhoeffer, Dietrich, Dietrich Bonhoeffer Works in English Volume 1: *Sanctorum Communio: A Theological Study of the Sociology of the Church*, ed. Clifford J. Green; trans. Reinhard Krauss and Nancy Lukens, Minneapolis: Fortress, 1998.
Bonhoeffer, Dietrich, Dietrich Bonhoeffer Works in English Volume 2: *Act and Being: Transcendental Philosophy and Ontology in Systematic Theology*, ed. Wayne Whitson Floyd, Jr; trans. H. Martin Rumscheidt, Minneapolis: Fortress, 1996.

Bonhoeffer, Dietrich, Dietrich Bonhoeffer Works in English Volume 3: *Creation and Fall: A Theological Exposition of Genesis 1-3*, ed. John W. de Gruchy; trans. Douglas Stephen Bax, Minneapolis: Fortress, 2004.

Bonhoeffer, Dietrich, Dietrich Bonhoeffer Works in English Volume 4: *Discipleship*, translated from the German edition, ed. Martin Kuske and Ilse Tödt; English edition, ed. Geffrey B. Kelly and John D. Godsey; trans. Barbara Green and Reinhard Krauss. Minneapolis: Fortress, 2003.

Bonhoeffer, Dietrich, Dietrich Bonhoeffer Works in English Volume 5: *Life Together; Prayerbook of the Bible*, ed. Geffrey B. Kelly; trans. Daniel W. Bloesch and James H. Burtness, Minneapolis: Fortress, 2005.

Bonhoeffer, Dietrich, Dietrich Bonhoeffer Works in English Volume 6: *Ethics*, ed. Clifford J. Green; trans. Reinhard Krauss, Charles C. West and Douglas W. Stott, Minneapolis: Fortress, 2005.

Bonhoeffer, Dietrich, Dietrich Bonhoeffer Works in English Volume 8: *Letters and Papers from Prison*, ed. John W. de Gruchy; trans. Isabel Best [et al.], Minneapolis: Fortress, 2010.

Bonhoeffer, Dietrich, Dietrich Bonhoeffer Works in English Volume 9: *The Young Bonhoeffer: 1918-1927*, ed. Paul Duane Matheny, Clifford J. Green and Marshall D. Johnson, trans. Mary C. Nebelsick with the assistance of Douglas W. Scott, Minneapolis: Fortress, 2001.

Bonhoeffer, Dietrich, Dietrich Bonhoeffer Works in English Volume 10: *Barcelona, Berlin, New York: 1928-1931*, ed. Clifford J. Green; trans. Douglas W. Stott, Minneapolis: Fortress, 2008.

Bonhoeffer, Dietrich, Dietrich Bonhoeffer Works in English Volume 12: *Berlin: 1932-1933*, ed. Larry R. Rasmussen; trans. Isabel Best and David Higgins, Minneapolis: Fortress, 2009.

Bonhoeffer, Dietrich, Dietrich Bonhoeffer Works in English Volume 13: *London: 1933-1935*, ed. Keith Clements; trans. Isabel Best; supplementary material trans. Douglas W. Stott, Minneapolis: Fortress Press, 2007.

Bonhoeffer, Dietrich, Dietrich Bonhoeffer Works in English Volume 14: *Theological Education at Finkenwalde: 1935-1937*, ed. H. Gaylon Barker and Mark S. Brocker; trans. Douglas W. Stott, Minneapolis: Fortress Press, 2013.

Bonhoeffer, Dietrich, Dietrich Bonhoeffer Works in English Volume 15: *Theological Education Underground: 1937-1940*, ed. Victoria J. Barnett; trans. Victoria J. Barnett [et al.]; supplementary material trans. Douglas W. Stott, Minneapolis: Fortress, 2012.

Bonhoeffer, Dietrich, Dietrich Bonhoeffer Works in English Volume 16: *Conspiracy and Imprisonment: 1940-1945*, ed. Mark S. Brocker; trans. Lisa E. Dahill; supplementary material trans. Douglas W. Stott, Minneapolis: Fortress, 2006.

Bonhoeffer, Dietrich [et al.], *Love Letters from Cell 92*, Nashville: Abingdon Press, 1995.

Boomgaarden, Jürgen, *Das Verständnis Der Wirklichkeit* Gütersloh: Kaiser, Gütersloher Verl.-Haus, 1999.

Boring, Edwin G., *A History of Experimental Psychology*, New York: Appleton-Century-Crofts, 1950.

Brentano, Franz von, *Psychology from an Empirical Standpoint*, introduced by Peter Simons, ed. Oskar Kraus; English edition, ed. Linda L. McAlister; trans. Antos C. Rancurello [et al.], London: Routledge, 1995.

Bulhof, Ilse Nina, *Wilhelm Dilthey: A Hermeneutic Approach to the Study of History and Culture*, The Hague: M. Nijhoff Publishers, 1980.

Buroker, Jill Vance, *Kant's Critique of Pure Reason*, Cambridge: Cambridge University Press, 2006.
Busch, Eberhard, *Karl Barth: His Life from Letters and Autobiographical Texts*, Philadelphia: Fortress Press, 1976.
Carter, Guy [et al.] (eds), *Bonhoeffer's Ethics: Old Europe and New Frontiers*, Kampen: Kok Pharos Publishing House, 1991.
Caygill, Howard, *A Kant Dictionary*, Malden, MA: Blackwell, 2004.
Clark, Adam C., Michael G. Mawson and Clifford J. Green (eds), *Ontology and Ethics: Bonhoeffer and Contemporary Scholarship*, Eugene, OR: Pickwick Publications, 2013.
Dahill, Lisa E., *Reading from the Underside of Selfhood*, Eugene, OR: Pickwick Publications, 2009.
De Gruchy, John (ed.), *Dietrich Bonhoeffer: Witness to Jesus Christ*, London: Collins, 1998.
DeJonge, Michael, *Bonhoeffer's Theological Formation*, Oxford: Oxford University Press, 2012.
Delitzsche, Frank, *A System of Biblical Psychology*, trans. Robert Ernest Wallis, Edinburgh: T&T Clark, 1890.
Dilthey, Wilhelm, *The Essence of Philosophy*, ed. Stephen A. Emery and William T. Emery, Chapel Hill: University of North Carolina Press, 1954.
Dilthey, Wilhelm, *Gesammelte Schriften. Bd. 1, Einleitung in die Geisteswissenschaften: Versuch einer Grundlegung für das Studium der Gesellschaft und der Geschichte*, Göttingen: Vandenhoeck & Ruprecht, 1959.
Dilthey, Wilhelm, *Gesammelte Schriften. Bd. 2, Weltanschauung und Analyse des Menschen seit Renaissance und Reformation*, Göttingen: Vandenhoeck & Ruprecht, 1957.
Dilthey, Wilhelm, *Gesammelte Schriften. Bd. 3, Studien zur Geschichte des deutschen Geistes: Leibniz und sein Zeitalter; Friedrich der Grosse und die deutsche Aufklärung; Das achtzehnte Jahrhundert und die geschichtliche Welt*, Göttingen: Vandenhoeck & Ruprecht, 1959.
Dilthey, Wilhelm, *Gesammelte Schriften. Bd. 5, Die geistige Welt: Einleitung in die Philosophie des Lebens. 1. Hälfte, Abhandlungen zur Grundlegung der Geisteswissenschaften*, Göttingen: Vandenhoeck & Ruprecht, 1957.
Dilthey, Wilhelm, *Gesammelte Schriften. Bd. 6, Die geistige Welt: Einleitung in die Philosophie des Lebens. 2. Hälfte, Abhandlungen zur Poetik, Ethik und Pädagogik*, Göttingen: Vandenhoeck & Ruprecht, 1958.
Dilthey, Wilhelm, *Gesammelte Schriften. Bd. 19, Grundlegung der Wissenschaften vom Menschen, der Gesellschaft und der Geschichte: Ausarbeitungen und Entwürfe zum zweiten Band der Einleitung in die Geisteswissenschaften (ca.1870–1895)*, Göttingen: Vandenhoeck & Ruprecht, 1982.
Dilthey, Wilhelm, Selected Works Volume 1: *Introduction to the Human Sciences*, ed. with an introduction by Rudolf A. Makkreel and Frithjof Rodi, Princeton, NJ: Princeton University Press, 1989.
Dilthey, Wilhelm, Selected Works Volume 2: *Understanding the Human World*, ed. Rudolf A. Makkreel and Frithjof Rodi, Princeton, NJ: Princeton University Press, 2010.
Dilthey, Wilhelm, Selected Works Volume 3: *The Formation of the Historical World in the Human Sciences*, ed. with an introduction by Rudolf A. Makkreel and Frithjof Rodi, Princeton, NJ: Princeton University Press, 2002.
Dilthey, Wilhelm, Selected Works Volume 4: *Hermeneutics and the Study of History*, ed. with an introduction by Rudolf A. Makkreel and Frithjof Rodi, Princeton, NJ: Princeton University Press, 1996.

Dilthey, Wilhelm, Selected Works Volume 5: *Poetry and Experience*, ed. Rudolf A. Makkreel and Frithjof Rodi, Princeton, NJ: Princeton University Press, 1985.
Dorrien, Gary J. *Theology without Weapons: The Barthian Revolt in Modern Theology*, Louisville, KY: Westminster John Knox Press, 2000.
Dramm, Sabine, *Dietrich Bonhoeffer and the Resistance*, Minneapolis: Fortress Press, 2009.
Dumas, André, *Dietrich Bonhoeffer: Theologian of Reality*, New York: Macmillan, 1971.
Ermarth, Michael, *Wilhelm Dilthey: The Critique of Historical Reason*, Chicago: University of Chicago Press, 1978.
Feil, Ernst, *Die Theologie Dietrich Bonhoeffers*, München: Kaiser, 1971.
Feil, Ernst, *The Theology of Dietrich Bonhoeffer*, Philadelphia: Fortress Press, 1985.
Fichte, Johann Gottlieb, *The Science of Knowledge*, trans. Peter Heath and John Lachs, Cambridge: Cambridge University Press, 1982.
Fisher, Simon, *Revelatory Positivism? Barth's Earliest Theology and the Marburg School*, Oxford: Oxford University Press, 1988.
Floyd, Wayne Whitson, Jr, *Theology and the Dialectics of Otherness: On Reading Bonhoeffer and Adorno*, Lanham, MD: University Press of America, c1988.
Floyd, Wayne W. and Charles Marsh, *Theology and the Practice of Responsibility*, Valley Forge, PA: Trinity Press International, 1994.
Frank, Manfred, *The Philosophical Foundations of Early German Romanticism*, Albany, NY: State University of New York Press, 2004.
Frick, Peter [et al.] (eds), *Bonhoeffer's Intellectual Formation: Theology and Philosophy in His Thought (Religion In Philosophy & Theology)*, Tübingen: Mohr Siebeck, 2008.
Gadamer, Hans-Georg, *Truth and Method*, New York: Seabury Press, 1975.
Godsey, John D., *The Theology of Dietrich Bonhoeffer*, London: SCM Press, 1960.
Green, Clifford J., *Bonhoeffer: A Theology of Sociality*, revised edn, Grand Rapids, MI: Eerdmans, 1999.
Green, Clifford J., *The Sociality of Christ and Humanity: Dietrich Bonhoeffer's Early Theology, 1927–1933*, Missoula, MT: Scholars Press for the American Academy of Religion, 1972.
Green, Clifford J. and Guy Christopher Carter (eds), *Interpreting Bonhoeffer*, Minneapolis: Fortress Press, 2013.
Greggs, Tom, *Theology against Religion: Constructive Dialogues with Bonhoeffer and Barth*, London: T&T Clark, 2011.
Gremmels, Christian, *Mündige Welt und Planung*, Marburg/Lahn: N.p., 1970.
Guyer, Paul (ed.), *The Cambridge Companion to Kant's Critique of Pure Reason*, Cambridge: Cambridge University Press, 2010.
Guyer, Paul (ed.), *Kant*, London: Routledge, 2006.
Guyer, Paul (ed.), *Kant and the Claims of Knowledge*, Cambridge: Cambridge University Press, 1987.
Harnack, Adolf von, *What Is Christianity? Lectures Delivered in the University of Berlin during the Winter Term 1899–1900*, trans. Thomas Bailey Saunders, London: Williams & Norgate, 1902.
Haynes, Stephen R., *The Bonhoeffer Phenomenon*, Minneapolis: Fortress Press, 2004.
Hodges, H. A., *The Philosophy of Wilhelm Dilthey*, London: Routledge & Paul, 1952.
Hume, David, *A Treatise of Human Nature*, ed. Mary J. Norton and David Fate Norton, Oxford: Clarendon Press, 2007.
Husserl, Edmund, *Logical Investigations Volume 1*, trans. J. N. Findlay, London; New York: Routledge, 2001.

Jacquette, Dale (ed.), *The Cambridge Companion to Brentano*, Cambridge: Cambridge University Press, 2004.
Janz, Paul D., *The Command of Grace: A New Theological Apologetics*, London: T&T Clark, 2009.
Janz, Paul D., *God the Mind's Desire: Reference, Reason and Christian Thinking*, Cambridge: Cambridge University Press, 2008.
Kant, Immanuel, *Critique of the Power of Judgment*, ed. Paul Guyer; trans. Paul Guyer and Eric Matthews, Cambridge: Cambridge University Press, 2000.
Kant, Immanuel, *The Critique of Pure Reason*, trans. and ed. Paul Guyer and Allen W. Wood, Cambridge: Cambridge University Press, 1999.
Kant, Immanuel, *The Moral Law: Kant's Groundwork of the Metaphysics of Morals*, trans. and analysed by H. J. Paton, London: Hutchinson University Press, 1948.
Kant, Immanuel, *Practical Philosophy*, trans. and ed. Mary J. Gregor, Cambridge: Cambridge University Press, 1999.
Kelly, Geffrey B. and F. Burton Nelson, *The Cost of Moral Leadership*, Grand Rapids, MI: Eerdmans, 2003.
Klemm, David E. and Günter Zöller, *Figuring the Self: Subject, Absolute and Others in Classical German Philosophy*, Albany: State University of New York Press, 1997. Print.
Klemme, Heiner F. 'The Origin and Aim of Kant's Critique of Practical Reason', in Andrews Reath and Jens Timmermann (eds), *A Critical Guide to Kant's Critique of Practical Reason*, Cambridge: Cambridge University Press, 2010.
Klubeck, William and Martin Weinbaum, *Dilthey's Philosophy of Existence*, New York: Bookman Associates, 1957.
Köhnke, Klaus Christian, *The Rise of Neo-Kantianism*, Cambridge: Cambridge University Press, 1991.
Korsgaard, Christine M., *Creating the Kingdom of Ends*, Cambridge: Cambridge University Press, 1996.
Lawrence, Joel, *Bonhoeffer: A Guide for the Perplexed*, London: T&T Clark, 2010.
Lockley, Harold, *Dietrich Bonhoeffer*, Swansea: Phoenix Press, 1993.
Lohmann, Johann Friedrich, *Karl Barth und Der Neukantianismus*, Berlin: De Gruyter, 1995.
Makkreel, Rudolf A., *Dilthey: Philosopher of the Human Studies*, Princeton, NJ: Princeton University Press, 1975.
Makkreel, Rudolf A. and Sebastian Luft, *Neo-Kantianism in Contemporary Philosophy*, Bloomington: Indiana University Press, 2010.
Marlé, René, *Bonhoeffer: The Man and His Work*, New York: Newman Press, 1968.
Marsh, Charles, *Reclaiming Dietrich Bonhoeffer: The Promise of His Theology*, Oxford: Oxford University Press, 1994.
Marty, Martin E., *The Place of Bonhoeffer*, New York: Association Press, 1962.
McAlister, Linda L., *The Philosophy of Brentano*, Atlantic Highlands, NJ: Humanities Press, 1977. Print.
McCarty, Richard, *Kant's Theory of Action*, Oxford: Oxford University Press, 2009.
McCormack, Bruce L., *Karl Barth's Critically Realistic Dialectical Theology*, Oxford: Clarendon, 1997.
McGarry, Joseph, 'Formed While Following: Dietrich Bonhoeffer's Asymmetrical View of Agency in Christian Formation', *Theology Today* 71, no. 1 (2014): 106–20.
Moran, Dermot, *Introduction to Phenomenology*, London: Routledge, 2000.
Moses, John A., *The Reluctant Revolutionary*, New York: Berghahn Books, 2009.
Müller, Hanfried, *Von der Kirche zur Welt*, Hamburg-Bergstedt: Reich, 1961.

Nickson, Ann L., *Bonhoeffer on Freedom: Courageously Grasping Reality*, Aldershot, Hampshire: Ashgate, 2002.
Nielsen, Kirsten Busch, *Die Gebrochene Macht der Sünder: Der Beitrag Dietrich Bonhoeffers Zur Harmartiologie*, Leipzig: Evangelische Verlagsanstalt, 2010.
Nielsen, Kirsten Busch, Ulrik Nissen and Christiane Tietz (eds), *Mysteries in the Theology of Dietrich Bonhoeffer*, Göttingen: Vandenhoeck & Ruprecht, 2007.
Ott, Heinrich, *Reality and Faith*, Philadelphia: Fortress Press, 1972.
Owensby, Jacob, *Dilthey and the Narrative of History*, Ithaca, NY: Cornell University Press, 1994.
Pangritz, Andreas, *Karl Barth in the Theology of Dietrich Bonhoeffer*, Grand Rapids, MI: Eerdmans, 2000.
Paton, H. J., *The Categorical Imperative: A Study in Kant's Moral Philosophy*, London: Hutchinson, 1947.
Phillips, John A., *The Form of Christ in the World: A Study of Bonhoeffer's Christology*, London: Collins, 1967.
Piché, Claude, 'Heidegger and the Neo-Kantian Reading of Kant', in Tom Rockmore (ed.), *Heidegger, German Idealism & Neo-Kantianism*, Amherst, NY: Humanity Books, 2000, 179–207.
Plant, Stephen, *Bonhoeffer: Outstanding Christian Thinkers*, London: Continuum, 2004.
Plantinga, Theodore, *Historical Understanding in the Thought of Wilhelm Dilthey*, Toronto: University of Toronto Press, 1980.
Reath, Andrews and Jens Timmermann (eds), *A Critical Guide to Kant's Critique of Practical Reason*, Cambridge: Cambridge University Press, 2010.
Regenbogen, Arnim and Uwe Meyer, *Wörterbuch Der Philosophischen Begriffe*, Hamburg: F. Meiner Verlag, 2013.
Rickman, H. P., *Dilthey Today*, New York: Greenwood Press, 1988.
Rickman, H. P., *Wilhelm Dilthey, Pioneer of the Human Studies*, Berkeley: University of California Press, 1979.
Rieger, Julius, *Bonhoeffer in England*, Berlin: Lettner-Verlag, 1966.
Ritschl, Albrecht, *Die Christliche Lehre Von Der Rechtfertigung Und Versöhnung Volume 1*, Bonn: Marcus, 1888.
Robinson, John, *Honest to God*, London: SCM Press, 1960.
Rockmore, Tom (ed.), *Heidegger, German Idealism & Neo-Kantianism*, Amherst, NY: Humanity Books, 2000.
Scharff, Robert Caesar, *'Erlebnis' and 'Existenz'*, PhD Thesis submitted to Northwestern University, Evanston, Illinois, 1970.
Schlingensiepen, Ferdinand, *Dietrich Bonhoeffer 1906–1945*, trans. Isabel Best, London: T&T Clark, 2010.
Schmitz, Florian, *'Nachfolge': Zur Theologie Dietrich Bonhoeffers*, Göttingen: Vandenhoeck & Ruprecht, 2013.
Schnädelbach, Herbert, *Philosophy in Germany, 1831–1933*, Cambridge: Cambridge University Press, 1984.
Schopenhauer, Arthur, *The World as Will and Representation Volume 1*, trans. and ed. Judith Norman, Alistair Welchman and Christopher Janaway, introduced by Christopher Janaway, Cambridge: Cambridge University Press, 2010.
Tietz, Christiane, *Dietrich Bonhoeffer: Theologe im Widerstand*, Munich: C.H. Beck Wissen, 2013.
Torrance, Thomas F., *Karl Barth: An Introduction to His Early Theology, 1910–1931*, London: SCM Press; New York: Harper & Row, 1962.

Werth, Julian, 'The Paralogisms of Pure Reason', in Paul Guyer (ed.), *The Cambridge Companion to Kant's Critique of Pure Reason*, Cambridge: Cambridge University Press, 2010, 210–44.
Willey, Thomas E., *Back to Kant*, Detroit: Wayne State University Press, 1978.
Wüstenberg, Ralf K., *Bonhoeffer and Beyond,* Frankfurt am Main: Peter Lang, 2008.
Wüstenberg, Ralf K., *Eine Theologie Des Lebens*, Leipzig: Evang. Verl.-Anst., 2006.
Wüstenberg, Ralf K., *A Theology of Life*, Grand Rapids, MI: Eerdmans, 1998.
Zimmerman, Wolf-Dieter and Gregor Ronald Smith (eds), *I Knew Dietrich Bonhoeffer*, trans. Käthe Gregor Smith, London: Fontana, 1973.

INDEX

Abromeit, Hans-Jürgen 131–2
Act and Being (Bonhoeffer) 7, 30–1, 49–51, 54–61, 68–84
actus directus/reflectus 46–8, 62–3, 74–9, 80–2

Barth, Karl 58, 67–75
Bethge, Eberhard ('The Challenge of Dietrich Bonhoeffer's Theology') 10, 39–42
Brentano, Franz von 158–9

conscience
  'Christian conscience' 79–80, 82
  as resolved in the person of Christ 96–9
  as truly calling to unity while falsely proposing 'absolute criteria' 94–5

DeJonge, Michael 10–11
  Theological Formation 48–51, 133
Dilthey, Wilhelm 15–17, 117–84
  aesthetic reflection 178–81, 189–90
  in Bonhoeffer's work 128–34
  continuity of unreflective and reflective consciousness 146–52, 183–7, 189–203
  Erlebnis, *Verstehen* and *Bedeutung* ('life-categories') 120–6
  feeling (*Gefühle*) and willing (*Wollen*) within unreflective agency 161–6
  Geisteswissenschaften 117–20
  Gestalt 171–4, 176–82, 191–2
  against neo-Kantianism 126–7, 144–6
  reflective agency 166–9
  'reflexive awareness' (*Innewerden*) of lived experience (*Erlebnis*) 135–9
  the 'unreflective I' (or 'acquired psychic nexus') 140–4 (*see also* Dilthey, *Gestalt*)

  value and feeling, against the neo-Kantians 167–8
Discipleship (Bonhoeffer) 2–6, 23–35, 200–1
  reception 37–39

Ethics (Bonhoeffer) 7–9, 85–99

Freil, Ernst (*The Theology of Dietrich Bonhoeffer*) 45–8, 129–30

Gestaltung ('formation') 19, 86–9
  Christ as *Gestalt* 88–91, 190–4
  reflective 91–2
Godsey, John D. (*The Theology of Dietrich Bonhoeffer*) 39–40
Green, Clifford J. (*The Theology of Sociality*) 42–5

hiddenness of the disciple 18, 29–31, 63–4, 185–6, 188–9, 198–9
Hume, David 105–6

Kant, Immanuel 57–60, 102–15
  categorical imperative 110–15
  faculties of cognition, feeling (taste) and desire (will) 156–8
  'flow of life' 108–9, 115–16
  'transcendental unity of apperception' ('the transcendental I') 103–9

obedience 31–3

post-Kantian idealism 40–1, 61

reflection
  'bedevilled' (Bethge) in Bonhoeffer's *Creation and Fall* 41–2
  neutral within limits of genuine transcendentalism 65
  in post-Kantian idealism 40–1
  'the theological way of knowing' 76–7

Schmitz, Florian D. 51
'self-understanding-in-
    remembrance' 76–9
  as wisdom 81–2
simplicity (*Einfalt*) 25–35
  mutually integral with
    reflective wisdom 8, 20,
    194–203

Tietz, Christiane 49
transcendental attempt ('genuine
    transcendentalism') 40–1, 56–60,
    63–4, 82

Whitson Floyd, Wayne, Jr 54
Wüstenberg, Ralf K. (*Theology of Life*)
  130–2

www.ingramcontent.com/pod-product-compliance
Lightning Source LLC
Chambersburg PA
CBHW052040300426
44117CB00012B/1905